LAW and AUTHORITY in COLONIAL AMERICA

Selected Essays

LAW AND AUTHORITY IN Colonial America

Edited by

George Athan Billias

Barre Publishers
Barre, Massachusetts

Composed and printed in the United States of America
Library of Congress Catalogue Card Number 65-16655

CONTENTS

FOREWORD

If the early American legal system did not diverge as widely from contemporary English practice as was once thought, it nevertheless possessed a distinctive style, and its incorporation of common-law elements varied from jurisdiction to jurisdiction. These perceptive essays illuminate both the style and variations in American law of the seventeenth and eighteenth centuries. The American colonists brought only so much English law as they knew, and a good deal of that was local custom and practice found in borough and county courts. There was little room for lawbooks in the baggage of departing emigrants who might well allot the precious space to a Bible. In some cases, as with the Puritans, the emigrants brought along a set of purposes and goals which shaped in no small measure the theory and practice of the law in those colonies they settled and controlled. In the case of New York an established Roman-Dutch legal system confronted the English conqueror. Finally, what Justice Holmes felicitously called "the felt necessities of the time" helped determine the rules by which men should be governed and the sources from which authority should be derived.

In all the colonies the authority of the home government seemed remote, certainly in the first generations. In the Puritan colonies authority was shared by the civil government with the church, and the arm of church discipline reached considerably beyond the narrow range of faith and morals. In turn, churches showed remarkable independence of central authority. This atomization of public authority is perhaps best demonstrated by that extraordinary grassroots invention, the town meeting. Finally, despite a considerable mobility, the social structure of colonial days was more rigid than in recent times, and the authority of the gentry was widely accepted, even with the coming of the Revolution, when an elite mobilized, directed, and controlled the movement of rebellion.

In a society where authority was so fragmented and where legal experimentation and innovation was so pervasive, one would not, perhaps, expect to find lawyers exercising the degree of power they had pre-empted by the eve of the Revolution or to find the English common law to be so widely received, despite variations from colony to colony, as was the case by 1776. Yet the increasing degree to which English law and practice were received and the phenomenal rise in prestige of lawyers in America can be attributed only in part to the tightened bonds of imperial control; in larger part the reception attests the growing affluence of the propertied and commercial groups. With the mounting political crisis many lawyers were, as Jefferson attests, "seduced by the honeyed Mansfieldism of Blackstone" and "began to slide into Toryism," but a respectable number joined the Revolutionary cause and directed its battle strategy. And this gave the American Revolution its distinguishing stamp. Since so much of the seventeenth-century common law, as Mark DeWolfe Howe sagaciously observes, dealt with issues of public law, it is understandable why the patriot lawyers, who looked back to the previous century for their precedents, should consider that they were fighting for the preservation of the rights of Englishmen, as they believed them to be guaranteed by the British constitution, and for the rights of man as they understood them to be guaranteed by Nature and Nature's God. Thus the lawyer-dominated American Revolution was to be distinguished by its concern for and emphasis upon legality. True, there was a seamier side to the administration of justice in the Revolutionary period, as Hiller B. Zobel points out, just as there was to the treatment of Tories, but what is significant is that the entire Revolutionary movement was encompassed within the framework of legality.

The student of American history as well as of legal institutions will be indebted to George Athan Billias and the learned contributors he has assembled herein for the many and suggestive insights they afford the reader on the subject of law and authority in early America. When Mr. Justice Story asserted that the common law of England was substantially in force in the colonies from the time of their settlement, at least so much of it as "was applicable to their situation," he was really begging the question; more accurately, he was describing what nineteenth-century jurists *thought* had happened to the law rather than offering a useful rule for gauging colonial legal experience. It is now recognized that no monolithic interpretation will suffice to explain the course and reception of the law in America — whether we are dealing with seventeenth-century seaboard colonies as disparate as Puritan Massachusetts and the plantation colonies of Maryland and Virginia, or the later western territories. Many strands were woven into the fabric of American law, as these contributors reveal, and the patterns vary from place to place.

So far as American law is concerned, we are still in the era of reconnaissance and discovery. Before its definitive history can be written, studies in depth like those found in this volume must be initiated over the far-ranging field of legal institutions and covering the entire area of settlement of the English colonies in North America.

RICHARD B. MORRIS

Columbia University

EDITOR'S INTRODUCTION

"A country which ignores its legal history," wrote Dean Alison Reppy of the New York Law School, "is like a captain of a vessel at sea who neglects periodically to take his latitudinal and longitudinal position in order to be sure that he is on his true course." Despite such words of warning, America has ignored its legal history to a disturbing degree. Both of the professional groups best equipped to work in the field — historians and lawyers — have shunned it. Historians have shied away from the subject because of its legal technicalities. Lawyers, on the other hand, have shown a lamentable lack of interest in historical developments that give rise to legal changes. Except for certain topics, such as the history of constitutional law and the Supreme Court, much of America's legal past remains unexplored.

Of all periods in American legal history, none has been neglected more than the colonial era. Undoubtedly this is due in part to its special difficulties. Scholars studying the seventeenth and eighteenth centuries must contend with problems posed by America's colonial status that have little relevance for legal historians working in the national period. One such problem is to determine the degree to which English common law was adopted within a given colony and to what extent English statutory law was applied within its borders. Another problem arises in attempting to identify how much colonial law was based upon English local law, i.e., the customary law administered by English local courts sitting in the county towns and in the boroughs and manors. Discovering the degree to which different kinds of English law were modified to meet American frontier conditions poses a third problem. A fourth involves a determination of how much law in early America was indigenous law. The complexity of these problems, coupled with the scarcity of contemporary printed law reports and published legislative records, has understandably discouraged scholars from doing research in American colonial law.

The purpose of these essays is to analyze certain aspects of law and authority in colonial America in the hope of arousing more interest in this much-neglected field. The project as a whole is admittedly a modest one. Exploratory in nature, the essays make no pretense at being definitive. Nor for that matter do they aim at any kind of comprehensive geographical coverage. The first group of essays, investigating various legal systems, covers only three colonies — Massachusetts, New York, and Maryland. The second group, concentrating more on the topic of authority, is confined solely to Massachusetts and Virginia. Despite the different topics and colonies being considered, all of the essays deal with a common theme: the impact of English law and English legal, political, and social institutions upon American society.

One of the major controversies in American colonial legal history revolves around a single question — to what extent was English common law adopted in the colonies? Few historians have stopped to ponder a related question — just what was the status of common law in the mother country at the time the first colonies were being settled? Mark DeWolfe Howe addresses himself to this question in the first essay. Tracing much of the law found in seventeenth-century Massachusetts back to its sources in the mother country, Howe suggests that far less common-law doctrine had been formulated in England in the early 1600's than we have generally assumed. If this is the case, then legal historians must re-examine much of the ground previously covered. To employ an inaccurate notion of the English common law as a measure with which to gauge colonial accomplishments in the legal field is, after all, to use a yardstick that is not quite three feet long.

Howe deals with another question, much broader in scope, which is even more crucial to the legal historian of the colonial period — what was the American colonists' conception of English law? After analyzing the famous Declaration of 1646 of the Massachusetts General Court, Howe argues that the Bay Colony Puritans were fully cognizant of the pluralistic nature of English law and recognized that the common law represented but one segment of the law of England. When Massachusetts leaders formulated their own legal system, they drew freely upon several of the fifteen separate categories of English law described by Sir Edward Coke.

The common law was, of course, one of those categories, but Howe suggests that the Bay colonists defined the term *common law* differently from the way that this segment of the English law actually operated in the mother country. They conceived of the common law as being a limited set of essentially constitutional principles — principles of public or constitutional law. The colonists chose, therefore, to adopt only that portion of the common law which concerned itself with the ordering of public matters; they tended to disregard the part dealing with the delineation of private affairs. Howe's analysis of the Bay colonists' attitude toward the common law leads him to advance two tentative conclusions. First, the reason the colonists did not trouble to answer English charges that they were building a body of private, non-constitutional law that conflicted with the contemporary law of England was that the variations between their own law and the law of England, as that law related to private matters, was, in their eyes, quite appropriate. Second, the colonists saw the common law as part of their constitution — as a charter of public law; hence, they looked upon the common law not as a delegation but a limitation of governmental power. This second hypothesis — that seventeenth-century colonists conceived of the common law as a set of rather specific limitations on public power — may help to explain why eighteenth-century colonists placed such a heavy emphasis upon the common law in their constitutional clashes with Great Britain in the period just prior to the American Revolution.

The extent to which English common law did influence the early colonists is strikingly illustrated in the second essay, George L. Haskins' case study of the Massachusetts Dower Act of 1647. By comparing the provisions of the Bay Colony statute with the common-law rules of the dower right, Haskins shows clearly that the Massachusetts act was modeled upon the common-law doctrine. This case study is an important one, for examples of such a wholesale importation of common-law doctrine into the colony are relatively rare. But, Haskins hastens to add, when it came to administering the Dower Act the situation was somewhat different. Massachusetts courts interpreted the law in such a way as to meet the needs of the colonists, and colonial judges frequently departed from common-law rules.

The colonists sometimes found themselves embroiled in a controversy over common-law practices which had had a history of long standing in the mother country. A case in point was that over the extent of jurisdiction of vice-admiralty courts. In England, there was a dispute between admiralty and the common law stretching as far back as the fourteenth century when two statutes were passed in the reign of Richard II limiting the jurisdiction of admiralty courts to things "done upon the sea" and not "within the bodies of the counties." In the eighteenth century, English common law courts, jealous of their jurisdiction, used these statutes to curb the powers of admiralty courts. The colonists, cognizant of this historic struggle between common law and admiralty, argued that the limiting acts of Richard II extended to America as well and that the colonial courts could exercise similar powers over the vice-admiralty courts.

What the actual practice of the colonial courts of common law was toward the vice-admiralty courts, however, has rarely been investigated. L. Kinvin Wroth, in his study of the available records of the Massachusetts Vice-Admiralty Court and courts of common law, concludes that in civil maritime cases admiralty jurisdiction was limited by the statutes of Richard II, and that observance of such restrictions was enforced by writs of prohibition from the Massachusetts Superior Court. Most litigants in cases of this kind, in fact, preferred the common-law courts because of the protection provided by cherished common-law safeguards. But in determining the jurisdiction of the Massachusetts Vice-Admiralty Court in customs and revenue cases, Wroth finds a difference of opinion arising from two opposing points of view of the constitution held by the British on the one hand, and the patriot faction in America on the other. The orthodox British view, reflected by the Massachusetts Superior Court, seems to have been that since the power of Parliament was absolute, the statutes of Richard II could not defeat later parliamentary grants of admiralty jurisdiction, even in cases arising within the body of a county. The opposite view, which had no standing in the courts but became the position of the Massachusetts patriot faction, was based on the theory that Parliament must yield to fundamental right. Although it is not clear that the statutes of Richard II were considered as embodying fundamental right, trial by jury in cases where the sovereign sought to deprive a man of his property certainly had this status. Thus, the grants of jurisdiction in customs cases which made it possible for the Massachusetts Vice-Admiralty Court to hear suits under the Acts of Trade without the use of a jury were considered by the patriots as being beyond the power of Parliament. The issue of Parliament's power in this and other matters, of course, was never settled in the courts; it was resolved ultimately by the break with Britain.

Turning from the legal history of the Massachusetts Bay Colony to that of colonial New York, one finds a much more complicated situation. Between the 1660's and 1690's there were at least three major legal systems to be found in the proprietary province of New York: Roman-Dutch law resulting from the original settlement of the region by the Dutch; the so-called "Bible Codes," indicating the presence of Puritan settlers from neighboring Connecticut who brought along their own law codes when they migrated into New York to establish communities in Westchester and Suffolk counties; and the English common law introduced in the Duke's Laws of 1665 after Britain had taken possession of the former Dutch colony. Herbert Alan Johnson's essay not only describes the clash among these three legal systems, but also gives the reasons why English common law was eventually accepted as the established mean within the colony after the judiciary was organized along English lines in 1691.

Maryland's legal history, although influenced less by alien law systems than that of New York, was just as complex. Joseph H. Smith, in his essay, analyzes nine important elements which constituted the foundation of Maryland's system of law from the mid-1630's to 1715. During this eighty-year period Maryland shifted from proprietary rule to royal government, and her legal institutions underwent certain changes that inevitably resulted from such a move. Smith's essay, like those on the Massachusetts system of law, demonstrates the pluralistic nature of the legal code in each of the colonies and underscores the degree to which Americans in some instances modified English law to accommodate local conditions.

The second group of essays focuses on the subject of authority. The term "authority" as used in this book means more than the capacity to exercise power through laws passed by the central and local governments or the rulings and mandates of the courts. It includes also the workings of other instrumentalities of social control — the family, the church, and the community — by which men's lives are ordered and regulated. The colonists, it should be realized were members of a number of social groupings which could exercise authority over them and to which they professed loyalty.

In Virginia during the first part of the seventeenth century, the most important bond of loyalty was the king. Colonial Virginia was a king-centered community whose major allegiance was to the sovereign who personified the largest political organism — the British empire — of which the colonists were a part. It was with justifiable pride that Charles II pointed to the colony's loyalty to him during the Puritan Revolution and proclaimed Virginia as his "Old Dominion." But in his essay, Wilcomb E. Washburn suggests that there was a pronounced shift in sentiment wthin the colony around the time of Bacon's Rebellion. There occurred a change of values in which the colonists came to view the state as existing to further the ends of the individual rather than the other way around. This shift from a king-centered society to one in which the greatest solicitude was shown for the interests of the individual resulted in a philosophical revolution that long antedated the American Revolution. Although the new individual-centered society did not acquire legal sanction until the era of the Revolution, Washburn claims that the Virginia colonists had ceased to look upon the king as the single most important source of political authority long before that time.

Clifford K. Shipton, writing about Massachusetts, notes a similar tendency toward decentralized authority. More often than not, the sources of both civil and religious authority in the Bay Colony were located on the local level. In the political sphere, authority tended to devolve upon the town governments rather than to remain at the provincial level. In the area of religion, the churches evolved along congregationalist lines, each church developing its own doctrine from a consensus of the religious views of the town inhabitants or congregation rather than by the creation of an established church with its own dogma to serve the entire colony. This tendency to locate the sources of authority at the local level, according to Shipton, was revolutionary in its implications. Development of a more decentralized machinery for the control of town and church affairs enabled the individual settlers in Massachusetts, almost from the start, to take into their own hands the management of all matters relating to property, civil government, and religion which could be handled at that level. The result was the growth of a society in colonial Massachusetts much more democratic than that found in England during this same period.

Shipton takes to task those scholars who depict early Massachusetts as a theocracy — a colony dominated by an undemocratic Puritan clergy who were dedicated to perpetuating their own political power and maintaining a rigid religious orthodoxy. If political power rested for the most part in the towns, and if the magistrates had to look to the local level for approval of their actions, how, Shipton asks, could an oligarchy of Puritan ministers control the government of Massachusetts as a theocracy? If each church developed its own doctrine on the basis of a consensus of the inhabitants of individual communities or congregations, how can historians speak of a "Puritan orthodoxy" and an "established church" when describing the religious situation in Massachusetts?

Darrett B. Rutman, in his essay, likewise attacks the stereotyped picture of Puritan Massachusetts as a strict authoritarian society during its early years. Most modern historians have depicted the typical Puritan town as a cohesive community with a highly structured social order in which authority intruded at every level of life — the authority of the father in the family, the minister in the church, and the magistrate in the town and province. Both the cohesiveness of society and authority, according to this view, were held by the Puritans to be God-ordained because man from the moment of Adam's fall was a degenerate being who required direction from his fellows to avoid committing sin. Thus, man had to submit himself to the dictates of his congregation and through it to his minister, in so far as religious authority was concerned. He was to submit also to the civil authority of the magistrate lest he live an ungodly life in a world of sin. Selflessness was required of the truly pious Puritan, these historians have argued, and he would sublimate his personal ambitions to the interests of the community as a whole.

This conceptualized version of Puritanism, says Rutman, does not square with the realities of life in seventeenth-century Massachusetts. There is considerable evidence of conflict in this supposedly stable society, and numerous instances show that men placed their personal ambitions above communitarian interests. Within the towns there occurred many disputes — disagreements among proprietors over land usage, religious quarrels in choosing a minister, and political struggles for local office. Between the towns themselves, sharp rivalries arose. Boundary controversies raged interminably between many communities; artisans of one town became intensely jealous of those in another; and the northern towns of Ipswich, Salem, and Newbury started a series of political maneuvers in the mid-seventeenth century to reduce Boston's pre-eminent position within the commonwealth. Moreover, there were clashes between the ministers and the magistrates when the latter declined to take ministerial advice on civil matters. With the removal of certain traditional functions such as education and community welfare from the religious to the civil sphere, the colonists came to view the church and state as separate entities and the elements of authority at work within the colony as being divided rather than united. In the end, Rutman finds in early Massachusetts — as Washburn does in Virginia — a tendency to move in the direction of an individual-centered society.

If authority as a whole had a weaker hold over the colony in the seventeenth century than is commonly supposed, it is obvious that by the eve of the American Revolution one aspect, political authority, had broken down completely. Nowhere was this breakdown in the orderly processes of government more evident than in the Massachusetts judiciary. John D. Cushing's essay describes one measure — the charge to the grand jury — which judges of the Superior Court of Judicature employed in their efforts to stem the rising tide of public sentiment against the mother country. Traditionally, the charge to the grand jury was intended to serve a juridical purpose. But Cushing finds in his survey of charges surviving from the Revolutionary era that some were more political than juridical in content. Prior to the Revolution, judges often seized upon such charges to lecture the people on the necessity of backing the provincial government and upholding the laws of Parliament. During and after the Revolution, judges resorted to this same device to gain support for the new regime and state constitution.

One way of gauging the degree to which justice had deteriorated in Massachusetts during the pre-Revolutionary years is to examine some of the trials that took place in that period. Hiller B.

Zobel discusses a number of more significant cases heard before the Massachusetts courts in two crucial years, 1769-1771. Although the Massachusetts bench and bar had competent men, a long legal tradition, and a suitable judicial apparatus for the disposition of such cases, Zobel finds that the political temper of the times made a fair trial well-nigh impossible. The jurors in most instances were controlled by the patriot faction and they often decided in favor of their friends without regard for the evidence presented or the charge made by the bench to the trial jury.

Taken together, these essays highlight the multiplicity and diversity of forces which, from the very beginning, shaped the course of law and authority in the colonies. Although most of the selections focus directly upon developments in the colonial period as such, the conclusions that stem from them adumbrate the American Revolution. If, as John Adams said, the Revolution antedated the War for Independence and took place "in the minds and hearts of the people" long before Lexington and Concord, then one of the powerful forces which helped to transform British colonists into Americans was the law. The revolutionary movement was, after all, based at bottom upon a rejection of conventional British constitutional theory.

The transit of British legal institutions to America set into motion two conflicting and contradictory trends. The first was an outright adoption of the great bulk of English law, causing the colonies to appear as replicas of the mother country in this regard. The second was the modification of English law on American soil in many instances, creating a gulf between the mother country and her colonies — a gulf which time and practice continued to widen. When Burke, in his famous speech on conciliation, catalogued the causes of the "disobedient spirit" found in the colonies, he placed American study and knowledge of the law high on his list. Thus, the variations that emerged between English law in the Old World and the New constituted a significant element in the cultural separation that developed between England and America.

The breakdown of authority in British America described in these essays did not always serve to democratize American society, but it did work to free that society from Old World strictures. The loosening of family ties, the weakening of the kingship bond, and the diminution of clerical influence all helped to decentralize authority and to make American civilization different from that of the mother country. At the same time, the fragmentation of authority made the colonists more receptive to ideas which challenged the British concept of an empire ruled by a single sovereign. Schooled by experience to recognize that they could modify the sources of civil and religious authority on the local level, Americans were quite ready by 1776 to go one step farther and contest with Britain the locus of sovereignty itself.

This book of essays is an outgrowth of the Fifteenth Conference on Early American History co-sponsored by the American Antiquarian Society and Clark University at Worcester, Massachusetts on April 3-4, 1964. Plans for the Conference program were made by Clifford K. Shipton, Director of the American Antiquarian Society, Professor George H. Merriam of Clark University, and the editor of this volume. Six of the ten essays in the pages that follow – those of Mark DeWolfe Howe, Herbert Alan Johnson, Wilcomb E. Washburn, Clifford K. Shipton, John D. Cushing, and Hiller B. Zobel – were read at the Conference in substantially the same form as they appear in this publication. The conferees benefited from constructive criticism offered by commentators on the same program who included Jack P. Greene of Western Reserve University, Irving Mark of Adelphi University, Bernard Bailyn of Harvard University, L. Kinvin Wroth of the University of Maine Law School, and Cecilia Kenyon of Smith College. The remaining four essays—those of George L. Haskins, L. Kinvin Wroth, Joseph H. Smith, and Darrett B. Rutman—were submitted by invitation of the editor. One of these four essays —that of Professor Haskins—has appeared in print elsewhere, but is reprinted in this volume because of its pertinence to the subject at hand.

My thanks go to a number of persons and organizations who made possible the publication of this volume. First and foremost to the contributors for their essays and for their patience in putting up with my editorial demands. Clifford K. Shipton is deserving of my deepest gratitude for his help; he read and commented upon each of the essays, gave me the benefit of his years of scholarship, and encouraged me every step of the way. Dean Milton M. Klein of Long Island University contributed a number of incisive insights to my introduction. Alden P. Johnson, President of the Barre Publishing Company, provided strong moral support for this project at the time it was first conceived and was most helpful in getting these papers through the press. The William Nelson Cromwell Foundation, an organization dedicated to the publication and dissemination of works devoted to research in American colonial legal history, gave a generous grant that covered, in part, the costs of publication. Two librarians, Miss Mary Terpo of the Worcester County Law Library Association and Miss Marion Henderson, Reference Librarian, Clark University, helped me considerably in my research. To my keen-eyed wife, Joyce, go my heartfelt thanks for her sound editorial suggestions and her assistance in the time-consuming chore of reading proof. But above and beyond the services she performed in getting this book ready for press, I am grateful to her for sustaining my spirit in those moments of discouragement and despair that inevitably arise in the course of an enterprise of this nature.

GEORGE ATHAN BILLIAS

Clark University
March 26, 1965

THE SOURCES AND NATURE OF LAW IN COLONIAL MASSACHUSETTS

MARK DEWOLFE HOWE

Harvard University Law School

WHAT LAW had force in the Massachusetts Bay Colony? There are two ways of approaching this complex question that has puzzled legal historians: one is to examine the substantive content of the law of colonial Massachusetts; another is to look at the institutions — the tribunals, that is — by which the law was enforced. This essay proposes to employ the second method on the premise that if we look upon the agencies through which the law was created and made effective, we may receive some useful intimations as to the nature and character of law in the Bay Colony. To follow this route towards understanding legal history calls for no boldness in imagination or inventiveness of mind. It has always been the way among historians of English law to seek for understanding of that law by study and comprehension of the courts which brought it into being. The most accurate definition that one can give of the common law of England is that which describes it as the non-statutory law administered in the King's Courts of Common Law. When the great Maitland, in the closing years of the nineteenth century, endeavored to tell his students what the word "equity" meant in its technical sense, he felt compelled to say that "it is that body of rules administered by our English courts of justice which, were it not for the operation of the Judicature Acts, would be administered only by those courts which would be known as Courts of Equity."[1] In a similar way if we are to ask ourselves what was the law in the Massachusetts Bay Colony we are forced to say that it was the body of law enforced by the courts sitting in the Colony.

A number of misconceptions as to the nature of law in the Bay Colony are traceable, one suspects, to a casual unawareness or forgetfulness of the vast complexity of the legal institutions of England at the beginning of the seventeenth century. It is a natural but most unfortunate habit among lawyers to assume that the institutional framework of the English law in 1900 was not significantly different from what it had been three hundred years before. This has led us too often to assume that at the time when the colonies were being settled the non-statutory law of England was to be found, almost wholly, in the decisions of the three great courts of common law — Queen's Bench, Common Pleas, and Exchequer — and in the decrees of the Chancellor. Common law and equity — these constituted the law of England. Historians are less likely than lawyers to stumble into such distorting illusions as these. They do not forget, as lawyers have been likely to, that there were many other courts in England than those of common law and of equity and that each of these other courts, whether it were that of the Admiral, that of the Bishop, that of the Mayor, that of the local lord, or one of those prerogative courts of the King — Star Chamber, perhaps, or High Commission, Court of Chivalry, Court of Requests — administered other systems of law than those known as "the common law of England" and as "equity". Doubtless it was the fact that men of vision and statesmen of imagination realized that in the centuries ahead good fortune and wise management in the affairs of state might bring to the courts of common law and to the Chancellor that supremacy over all competing systems of law which earlier prevailed, and over all the excesses of prerogative which were becoming increasingly painful for Englishmen to bear. Those who were concerned more with fact than with prophecy, with reality rather than with reform, would have been fully justified, however, in recognizing that the common law was but a part of the laws of England. After Sir Edward Coke announced in his Commentaries on Littleton that "there be divers lawes within the realme of England" he went on to list fifteen separate categories of law. Though he put the common law high in his list — fourth, to be exact — he did not hesitate to recognize that the other fourteen brands of English law were reputable products of history possessing their own dignity and entitled to receive the respect of scholars and statesmen.[2]

By emphasizing the multiplicity of the systems of law which prevailed in England at the birth of the first British empire, we do not mean to suggest that each of these systems was of equal importance in the life of every Englishman. That certainly was not the case. Yet the pluralistic character of England's legal order was a familiar reality to most members of that society. The borough resident not only knew the courts of the borough; he knew its customs and laws as well. The drunken sinner knew that the Church's law and its tribunals would have something to say of his misconduct. The legatee of property under the most simple of wills knew that his inheritance was governed by the Church's law and administered by its authority. The beneficiary of a trust in land realized that his rights were dependent upon laws created and rights defined in the Court of Chancery. The merchant trading overseas recognized that his obligations and his rights might find their definition in the maritime law and their enforcement in the Court of Admiralty. And all Englishmen knew that the King's courts of common law had many things to say to them which might deeply affect their destiny.

It is necessary to be reminded of these familiar facts of legal history in order to understand that if one had asked the average, informed Englishman in 1600 to say what law governed his affairs he would have given a somewhat complicated answer — an answer which would have referred to many courts, some the Queen's, some not the Queen's, and many laws, some derived from royal prerogative, and others rooted in traditions beyond that fertile mother of law. If the answer of a discerning Englishman would have been so elaborate, how would a perceptive Colonial, living in Boston in 1640, have answered the same question: — Under what law are you living?

One cannot say, of course, just what our bright Colonial would have said, but we can, with some confidence, assume one thing he would not have said — and in the not-saying he would have given us an important clue to understanding. In speaking of the legal institutions of the Colony he would say nothing of Courts of Law, Courts of Equity, Courts of Admiralty, Courts of the Borough, or Courts of the manor. If he were a covenanted member of one of the churches in the Colony he would, perhaps, speak of that Church's law and its authority. Save for that one possible exception, he would boast of the fact that in the Bay Colony all laws — from whatever source and out of whatever tradition they may have been derived — were made effective in a unified judicial system. If his tastes were antiquarian he might take pleasure in telling his interrogator that some of the law enforced in County Courts, Court of Assistants, and General Court was traceable to the decisions of the Courts of Common Law in England, some to the decisions of the Chancellor, while other portions were derived from *lex mercatoria* of the western world. With a shame-faced apology he might even admit that some important segments of the Bay Colony's law could be traced back to the canon law of Rome. But he would take vigorous pride in the knowledge that the legal system of the Colony was built upon revolutionary lines — a system which no longer knew anything of Courts of Equity, Courts of Law, Courts of Admiralty, Courts of the hundred, and Courts of the manor. He would have dismissed as somewhat academic and irrelevant to things that count, any questions concerning the substance of the law enforced in the courts of the Colony. Of course there would be some common law. Of course there would be some equity in the decisions of the colonial courts. Naturally local custom as it had been known at home would play its part in the adjudication of controversies between colonists. The fact of largest moment, however, would be that through the unification of process had been begun that movement towards unification of law which all law reformers recognized as indispensable to improvement in the laws of England.

If we would know what the Massachusetts colonials in 1640 saw as the critical problems with respect to law, it is clear that we should discover what the Englishmen of that day and age thought about the troubles and shortcomings in the English legal system. Among the historians of English law it is a well-known fact that the movement for law reform which produced so many bold plans and an occasional achievement in the period of the Commonwealth reflected something more respectable than the Puritan's radicalism. It bespoke that same desire which Bacon had recognized, which John Selden had supported, and which Lord Hale, in his turn was to support — the desire to effect radical changes in the structure and the procedures of the courts, — whether those were courts of common law, of equity, or of the Church. The disorder with which the English legal system sprawled across the British Isles at the beginning of the seventeenth century was, in truth, a national disgrace. One or two subtle masters of its mysteries — most notably, of course, Sir Edward Coke — were able to see virtue in the elaborate confusion in which the rights of Englishmen were concealed and by which their obligations were sustained. But surely it did take a subtle mind and an ingenious form of learning to find virtue in a legal system — all the King's — in which one court took pleasure in undoing the work of its rival, and that rival took remunerative satisfaction in duplicating the jurisdiction of another — and all found it virtuous to stand in the ancient ways, confident that if the processes available in courts of common law, equity, admiralty, or in ecclesiastical tribunals were inadequate, some court born of the King's prerogative — High Commission, Star Chamber, Privy Council — would somehow take care of public and private needs.

During the interregnum, the period, that is, of the English Commonwealth, the resentments against the legal disorder found their first possibility of effective recognition. The striking fact about the programs of law reform which were brought forward in the Puritan interlude, is that it showed far more concern for changing the form of law than for altering its substance. The persistent demand was that the system of courts should be organized upon a basis which would reflect the simple rationality of convenience rather than the complex rationality of history. Among the plans which received the closest and most serious attention of the responsible law reformers was one by which in each county of the realm there should be established a court of general jurisdiction competent to hear and dispose of cases of virtually all categories — civil, criminal, equitable, testamentary, and mercantile. From such local courts appeals could be had to a higher central court, speaking for the whole Commonwealth. Other important proposals for law reform, less directly related to the organization of courts, concerned the establishment of registries of deeds and registries of probate in each county — administrative offices through which a degree of certainty and order might be introduced into the management of testamentary and other rights in property.

Unhappily for England, few if any of these radical reforms of the legal disorder took effective hold during the interregnum. An English Puritan, in the interlude of the Commonwealth, would not have been able, unfortunately, to boast that his revolution had brought that institutional simplification which the reformers had promised. Improvements had, of course, been effected in the last desperate years of Charles I. Star Chamber, the High Commission, the Court of Requests, the Court of Chivalry, the Palatine courts — all these had gone. The Committee of Law Reform, in 1653, demanded more, however. It proposed that "all actions between subjects" should be kept "under that 'lock and key of the Common Law' — the Court of Common Pleas," and in the same year an act, which never went into effect, was adopted by which the Court of Chancery — a tribunal which, as the reformers saw it, "swarmed with 'a numberless armado of caterpillars' and 'Egyptian grasshoppers' " — was to be abolished.[3] These largely abortive efforts at reform reflected the conviction of many persons throughout the land that the greatest nuisance in the legal system of England was not the confusion of its laws but the multiplicity of courts through which the laws were made effective.

What effect did these efforts at legal reform in England have on America? In returning to the question posed at the outset— What laws were in force in the Bay Colony? — one realizes more than ever that it can only be answered by recognizing the full and revolutionary import of the judicial system which was set up in the Colony. It may well be that other considerations than those which moved the radicals at home to seek a drastic reorganization of the judicial system had predominant importance in Massachusetts — that the folly and impracticability of reproducing the clumsy confusion of England's disorder made the simplicities that were chosen quite natural. Yet it remains a fact that a theory of government buttressed the decision of the Bay colonists that they would create courts of general rather than specialized jurisdiction. When, at the end of the seventeenth century, imperial authority set their decision aside, what kind of judicial system did it impose? In the regime of Governor Dudley we see the beginnings of reaction. In addition to the Superior Court there were set up Courts of Pleas and Sessions of the Peace. Probate matters were in the hands of the Supreme Ordinary and Judges of Probate in the distant counties. In the brief interlude of Governor Andros, the restoration of confusion went forward. The legal structure found, at last, a place for the Justice of the Peace, for Quarterly Sessions, for Inferior Courts of Common Pleas, and in the Superior Court there was vested the jurisdiction of the King's Bench, Common Pleas, and Exchequer as they were exercised in England. And provision was also made for a Court of Chancery with as full and ample powers in all matters of equity as those of the High Court of Chancery in England.

One of the theses of this essay, in short, is to suggest that a significant element in the decisions made at the very beginning of the organization of the legal system in the 1630's and 1640's was the resolution to establish a structure of courts of the sort which Puritan reformers in England were favoring. When that resolution was made effective it brought in its wake, as it were, a modest degradation in the status of the common law. While England maintained her courts of common law (Exchequer, King's Bench, and Common Pleas) separate from the other courts within the realm, it was natural that Englishmen should think of "common law" as something separate and apart from other systems of law which were in force within the realm. It was natural also that men trained to practice before the Courts of Common Law should look upon its virtues as preeminent. When the jurisdiction of the courts of common law and the product of that jurisdiction — the common law itself — are merged in a single tribunal with the jurisdiction of all other courts and the products of their jurisdictions, it is hardly surprising that the officers of the new court — its judges and its practitioners — quickly forgot that the unity now in their charge was once a chaotic diversity scattered among innumerable agencies of government.

To say these things, is not, of course, to say that those at home who sought unity and those abroad who found it, forgot the political and moral overtones which color the Englishmen's feelings for that special something known as "common law". It is well to remember, however, that the charter of the Massachusetts Bay Colony made no explicit reference to that particular segment in the totality of English law. The charter conferred upon the General Court the power "to make, ordain, and establish all manner of wholesome orders, laws, statutes, and ordinances, directions, and instructions not contrary to the laws of this our realm of England . . . . " Of course the laws thus referred to included the common law. There is no reason, however, to assume that other laws of the realm, whether those enacted by Parliament, those developed in the court of Chancery, or those included within the law merchant, were not embraced by the inclusive language.

Lawyers and historians have often given their attention to the so-called Declaration of 1646 — the General Court's defensive effort to meet the accusation of Dr. Robert Child and other malcontents that the governors of the Bay Colony were not respecting the limitation on their legislative power imposed by the prohibition against laws contrary to those of England.[4] Almost invariably the attention of the scholars has been drawn to the right-hand column in the "parallels"—the column in which the customs, laws, and liberties of the Colony were summarized. That attention has been revealing and worth-while. A glance at the left-hand column of the "parallels", however, is equally suggestive. The structure of that column bears out the assurance of the prefatory statement that there the General Court has set down "the fundamental and common laws and customs of England, beginning with Magna Carta, and [then] go on to such others as we had occasion to make use of, or may at present suit with our small beginnings."

It should be noticed that this statement is built upon the assumption that there are at least three classes of law with which a questionable enactment of the Colony must be compared. The prefatory separation of categories is clarified in the contents of the left-hand column — that in which the relevant and comparable laws of England are set forth. First there are listed rules of law drawn, with some distortion, from the text of Magna Carta. Then follow twenty-two numbered propositions grounded in "the common laws of England." And finally there are separately listed seven additional rules of law — these evidently constituting in the eyes of the colonists selections from those other laws of England that are not to be considered either parts of Magna Carta or principles of the common law. The significant fact is that this Declaration of 1646 revealed the entirely natural assumption of the colonists that the laws to which their statutes and decisions should conform were to be found in separate compartments of tradition. The same assumption explains, of course, the General Court's recognition in 1650 that "this commonwealth is much defective for want of laws for maritime affairs" — a recognition which was accompanied, first, by the acknowledgment that "there are many good laws made and published by our own land and the French nation, and other kingdoms and commonwealths"; and, second, by the resolution to secure a copy of the book "called *Lex Mercatoria*" in order that the Court might model a code of mercantile law upon its wisdom.[5]

The Declaration of 1646 has an additional significance worth commenting upon. It casts a suggestive light upon the conception which the colonists had of those elements in the legal system of England to which they owed an appreciable degree of respect. It should be noted that almost all of the provisions of English law summarized in the Declaration came from what may fairly be called the public, rather than the private sector of that law. Whether the declarants were lifting provisions from Magna Carta or summarizing principles of the common and customary law of England their concern was, almost exclusively, with the English law's ordering of public affairs rather than its delineation of private relations. One would not be unfair in describing the factor of selectivity as one directed towards the specification of constitutional principles. "The Church shall enjoy her liberties." "No man shall be condemned but by lawful trial." "Courts of judicature shall be kept in a place certain." These restatements of provisions found in Magna Carta may not be wholly accurate, but they are sensibly selective, — they wisely exclude the specificities which encumber the original document itself. Similarly, when the declarants endeavor to summarize those principles of the common law which they consider of force in the Bay Colony they limit the list of applicable principles to the broadest of constitutional generalities: "The supreme authority is in the High Court of Parliament."; "In all criminal cases where no certain penalty is prescribed by law, the judges have power to impose arbitrary fines or penalties, according to the nature and merit of the offences."; "All public charges are born by the public revenue or treasury." Even when the colonists add a touch of bitter humor to their comparison of English and colonial law, they do so in connection with provisions relating to the "public" law. Describing the criminal law of England and its scandalous doctrine with respect to benefit of clergy, the Declaration thus restates that law: "Notorious and great felonies, as treason, murder, witchcraft, sodomy, &c, are punished capitally, but simple theft and some other felonies are not punished with death, if the offender can read in scripture." The equivalent law in the Bay Colony is stated thus: "Treason, murder, witchcraft, sodomy and other notorious crimes, are punished with death. But theft &c is not so punished, because we read otherwise in the scripture." In England, the reading of scripture may save the neck; in the Colony, it liberates the mind.

This emphasis upon the fact that it was public or constitutional law which was set forth in the Declaration underlines another aspect of the problem with which we are concerned. Is it not probable that the colonists of Massachusetts Bay in the early years of settlement — like their descendants one hundred and fifty years later — saw the common law as compared with the other systems of English law with which they were familiar, as made up essentially of the public law of the nation? To suggest that, is to suggest that they never assumed that the whole, or anything like the whole of what we have come to consider to be "the common law of England", was in force in the Colony. Rather they looked upon that something known as the common law as a limited set of essentially constitutional principles — principles of public order to which their own scheme of government whether shaped by the General Court or the judges of County Courts and the Court of Assistants, should conform. They knew a great deal of English law of a different sort and much of that other law they were willing to accept and treat as applicable to their own circumstances.

Yet, quite naturally, they saw the nonconstitutional and private segments of the laws of England as parts to which they owed no special deference or respect. When they were charged, from time to time, with building a body of private, nonconstitutional law of their own — a body of law that in many details was quite out of line with the contemporary law of England — the Bay colonists saw no reason to answer the accusation. Variations between their own law and the law of England, as that law might relate to purely private matters, was, in the eyes of the colonists quite appropriate. When, however, they were charged with disregarding the public or constitutional law of England, they resisted the charge with energy and ingenuity.

There were, of course, great distinctions between the private and the public law of England. But I am persuaded that the line between public law and private law had far more clarity in 1600 than it has today. To assert this position is to reiterate another of the major points of this essay — that in 1600 there were far fewer doctrines of the common law — in other words, far less common law — than came into being after that date. It should be remembered that common law principles of contract in 1600 were very few and painfully inadequate for the needs of a mercantile society. It should be remembered also that a theory of torts had yet to be conceived. Nor should it be forgotten that many of the most important rules with respect to interests in land were unknown to the common law and were protected nowhere but in the Court of Chancery. In such a structuring of things it was surely not surprising that the Englishman, whether residing in the realm or in a colony, should see the common law as that segment of the totality of laws which dealt with the public order. It might deal with that order through its rules of criminal law, or it might establish the rules of the public game. It might even fix some of the fundamental principles of private right and in doing so not quite realize that it was becoming, like its rivals, a governor of private relationships. Perhaps in modern eyes it would seem natural to classify rules of inheritance as rules of private law. Yet, when the draftsmen of the Declaration of 1646 included within their summary of the laws of England and the Bay Colony the conflicting doctrines of primogeniture and partible inheritance, they did not, by that inclusion, make our modern classification theirs. In their scheme of things it seemed quite natural to look upon a rule of inheritance which the King and his Courts of Common Law had, time out of mind, enforced upon the people of England as a rule of the public law.

This analysis of the attitude of the Bay colonists towards the common law not only suggests that they saw it as a part of their constitution — as a charter of public law. It suggests also that they saw that law and that constitution not as a source of their government's power but as a limitation on its authority. We should not forget that it took most of the eighteenth and nineteenth centuries and many perceptive minds of those later generations to discover the simple truth that the common law is an altering, almost a dynamic form of law. In the early decades of the seventeenth century the glory of the common law was conceived to be its immutability. Those radicals within the Bay Colony who found its government intolerable asked that more respect should be shown for the common law of England, not because they longed for its creativeness, but because they saw security in its stability. They built their indignation on the conviction that the "scale of justice [was] to[o] much bowed and unequally balanced"—to quote the language of Dr. Robert Child. The fears and jealousies which the learned doctor enumerated were "of illegal committments, unjust imprisonments, taxes, rates, customes, levyes on ungrounded and undoing assessments, unjustifiable presses, undue fynes, unmeasurable expenses and charges . . . in a word, of a non-certainty of all things we enjoy." He went on, of course, to ask that the prevailing powers should establish in the Colony "the fundamentall and wholesome laws of our native country"—an appeal which may seem to ask for few laws that we would not classify as "public."[6] The appeal, it seems to me, had limited significance because of the stubborn fact that in 1646 there were few "fundamental" laws in the native land that dealt with purely private matters.

Another legal action in the middle decades of the seventeenth century which bears out this thesis — that in colonial eyes the common law was not a pervasive system of order but a set of rather specific limitations on public power — was the opinion of Judge Samuel Symonds in Giddings v. Brown.[7] The Giddings case was one in which Judge Symonds, sitting on the County Court for Essex County, condemned for unconstitutionality an order of the Town of Ipswich that 100 pounds should be collected from all members of the community towards building or buying a house for Mr. Cobbet — the local minister. Judge Symonds searched the colonial records for precedent in the hope that he would find a decision in the General Court which would control the matter before him. Failing in that search, he turned to the pages of two handbooks of the common law — handbooks thoroughly familiar to the English bench and bar. They were Dalton's *Country Justice* and Henry Finch's *Description of the Common Laws of England*. There he found pronouncements indicative of a principle condemning public exactions for private benefit. Though Judge Symonds felt an obvious and a real reluctance to condemn as unconstitutional the legislative action of the town meeting, he felt obliged to do so as soon as he discovered in the common law of England — of which the law of nature was a part — a prohibition of such exactions.

Perhaps a parenthetical reflection about a neglected item in the legal history of Rhode Island might help to substantiate this point further. Judge Symonds at one stage made reference to the work of Michael Dalton — a compendious handbook for English Justices of the Peace, the *Country Justice*. For some time historians have commented on the surprising fact that Rhode Island, almost from the very first years of settlement, seems to have shown a higher degree of respect for the common law of England than did her New England neighbors. Local pride has sometimes concealed the extent of that respect and fidelity. In his *History of the State of Rhode Island*, Samuel Greene Arnold wrote of the splendor of Rhode Island's Code of 1647. "We hazard little," he announced, "in saying that the digest of 1647, for simplicity of diction, unencumbered as it is by the superfluous verbiage that clothes our modern statutes in learned obscurity; for breadth of comprehension, embracing as it does the foundation of the whole body of law, on every subject, which has since been adopted; and for vigor and originality of thought, and boldness of expression, as well as for the vast significance and the brilliant triumph of the principles it embodies, presents a model of legislation which has never been surpassed."[8] The enthusiasm of the native son might not evaporate, but surely it would appreciably dissipate if he recognized that most of the provisions in the Rhode Island Code of 1647 were lifted, verbatim from Dalton's *Country Justice*.

It would require a closer inspection of the details of this plagiarized enactment of the Code of 1647 to determine whether or not the Rhode Islanders' translation of a handbook of the common law into a code for an American colony bespoke a profoundly different attitude towards the common law than that which I have ascribed to the founders of the Bay Colony. Although Rhode Island is always credited with having shown a higher degree of respect for the common law of England, one wonders whether even the fidelity of her theft from Dalton shows an attitude significantly different from that which prevailed at the time in Massachusetts. The common law contained in Dalton is largely public law — in the sense in which I have already been using that phrase. Where common law was seen as constitution it could either be stolen from Dalton and put in the form of a Code or it could be restated by theologians and statesmen in the form of a Body of Liberties and adopted by the General Court. In either case the end product constituted the definition of the principles of public law to which the colony stood committed.

Where have these scattered reflections taken us? They have led through a series of related generalizations to a somewhat indefinite conclusion. My generalizations have been these. First, I have suggested that at the opening of the seventeenth century the complexity in the organization of England's courts had produced a chaotic confusion of laws — such a pluralism as to make almost meaningless a slack reference to the law of England and to require, instead, on analysis of her laws—common, ecclesiastical, maritime, statutory, and equitable. Secondly, I suggested that those Englishmen who were eager to effect law reform recognized that the first necessity was for a new and simplified structuring of England's courts. In the Bay Colony this reform was quickly effected, with the consequence that the old and familiar segregations became largely irrelevant. When common law, equity, admiralty, borough customs and ecclesiastical law were all administered in one tribunal, the old distinctions lost most of their operative significance. This suggestion that the colony's integration of law through its simplification of the judicial structure did not lead me to assert that the Bay colonists no longer recognized that "the common law" was an identifiable element in their law. They saw it, I believe, as contemporary Englishmen tended to see it — as a set of unchanging principles of public law, principles which our usage would decribe as "constitutional". This meant, of course, that for the colonists the chief significance of the common law of England was limiting, not creative.

Those have been my generalities. If they should be accepted, would we find it easier to answer the old familiar question: What law had force in the Massachusetts Bay Colony? While these generalities do not provide anything remotely resembling a definitive answer, I wonder if they might not usefully inform our search for an answer? They remind us that our frame of reference must not be the legal system and the laws as we know them, but the laws and the system that were known to Englishmen more than three hundred years ago. The common law was not corpus juris in seventeenth century New England. It was a fixed and limited body of rules, chiefly concerned with matters of public and royal moment. Even that colonist whose convictions were radically puritan and whose tastes were restlessly subversive could find life tolerable in a society bound to respect a few chapters of Magna Carta and a selected segment of the public law of England. His creativeness might not be wholly unbounded, but he enjoyed an adequate freedom in which a new legal order might be brought into being. When he devised a judicial system with courts of general jurisdiction at its base, he had performed the crucial act of reformation.

LAW AND AUTHORITY

FOOTNOTES

1. Frederick W. Maitland, *Equity, Also Forms of Action at Common Law*, ed., A. H. Chaytor and W. J. Whittaker (Cambridge, England, 1929), 1.
2. Coke on Littleton, 11b.
3. R. Robinson, "Anticipations under the Commonwealth of Changes in the Law," *Select Essays in Anglo-American Legal History* (Boston, 1907), I, 467, 470-471. See also Frederick A. Inderwick, *The Interregnum* (London, 1891), chapters III and IV.
4. See e.g., Richard B. Morris, "Massachusetts and the Common Law: The Declaration of 1646," *American Historical Review*, XXXI (1926), 443. The Declaration itself may be found in Thomas Hutchinson, *A Collection of Original Papers Relative to the History of the Colony of Massachusetts Bay* (Boston, 1769), 196; hereinafter *Hutchinson Papers.*
5. Nathaniel B. Shurtleff, ed. *Records of the Governor and Company of the Massachusetts Bay in New England* (Boston, 1854), III, 193.
6. *Hutchinson Papers*, 190.
7. *Ibid.*, 287.
8. Samuel G. Arnold, *History of the State of Rhode Island* (New York, 1894), 206.

RECEPTION OF THE COMMON LAW IN SEVENTEENTH-CENTURY MASSACHUSETTS: A CASE STUDY*

GEORGE L. HASKINS

University of Pennsylvania Law School

THE PROBLEM of the sources of the law in the American colonies has continued to attract attention of scholars because its solution is pertinent to an understanding of the history and social organization of the early settlers. Important as a chapter in American legal history, the background of colonial law is likewise significant from a sociological point of view as a study in survival and adaptation of patterns of thought and habits of life. Historians have pointed out that the colonists drew extensively upon their English experience in their political institutions, in their religious ideas, even in their methods of farming, patterning their ways of thinking and of acting upon what had been familiar to them at home. In the law, too, it is beginning to be seen that the settlers availed themselves of their cultural heritage, bringing with them the knowledge or recollection of English law which they shaped to meet the needs of a new civilization.

If the process of transplantation, adaptation, and innovation is to be described with accuracy, it is essential that the legal systems of the colonies be studied independently of one another. The background of the settlers differed widely from colony to colony, as did the social and economic conditions which affected the growth of the law; consequently, statements which are true for one colony are very often untrue for another. Accordingly, before a complete exposition of the sources and development of the law can be made, detailed accounts of the legal system in each are necessary in order to find the threads which will guide a sure path across the precarious territory of generalization. Such accounts have not, in general, been forthcoming,[1] but it is nevertheless possible to

*Reprinted with revisions from the *University of Pennsylvania Law Review*, Vol. XCVII (1949), 842-853.

make some advance by means of studies of particular branches of the law in particular colonies. The present study is concerned with aspects of the law of dower in seventeenth-century Massachusetts; its purpose is to suggest the sources of that law and to show how it was shaped to meet the needs of the colonists.

Especial interest attaches to the origins and growth of the law in Massachusetts Bay both because of the availability of published records and because of the early development of an indigenous legal system in that colony. At one time that development was not well understood, and it was possible for writers to say that the seventeenth century was "a period of rude, untechnical popular law"[2] and that "the Scriptures were an infallible guide for both judge and legislator."[3] Close study of the records has resulted in the abandonment of that view. It has become apparent that within fifty years of the settlement of the colony its courts were concerning themselves with difficult and complex questions of law to a degree which belies the assertion that during the seventeenth century Massachusetts possessed a "layman law, a popular, equitable system."[4] To say that the law was technical or complex is not, however, to say that by the third quarter of the seventeenth century the common law of England had been transplanted to New England shores. On the contrary, much of the law in early Massachusetts was noticeably different from the common law of England,[5] despite the injunction of the colony charter that no laws should be made contrary to the laws of England.[6]

Such departures from common law rules have attracted the attention of scholars interested in the processes of legal development. Some years ago Professor Goebel suggested that those departures were comprehensible if the background of the settlers were kept in mind.[7] His thesis, which grew out of an examination of the records of Plymouth Colony, was that the first settlers were recruited largely from the country districts in England from a class of society more familiar with the law and procedure in the local courts of the borough and the manor than with the common law which was administered in the king's courts, and that they brought with them many of the local customs which they had known at home. In the seventeenth century in England, the common law had not acquired complete ascendancy over the local courts which administered a customary law. Those courts loomed large in the eyes of the average Englishman, for it was to them that he would turn to replevy a cow or collect a bill. By way of proof of his thesis Professor Goebel pointed to some remarkable parallels between the laws of Plymouth and the local customs prevailing in those districts of England from which the settlers had come. Subsequent examination of the records of the colony of Massachusetts Bay provided support for his thesis with respect to the sources of the law in that colony, where the influence of borough and manorial customs appears almost as prominent as at Plymouth.[8]

The law administered in the English local courts does not account for all sources of the law in seventeenth-century Massachusetts. In developing their law, the colonists appear to have drawn also upon the Mosaic code[9] and perhaps even upon Dutch law.[10] Other portions, however, seem to have been direct adoptions of English common law rules. Although it has been urged that the common law remained an alien system until the mid-eighteenth century, when it was received into Massachusetts by trained lawyers and judges,[11] the publication of the Laws and Liberties of 1648 has made it plain that the settlers had a certain familiarity with the common law and drew upon their knowledge of it in framing their code of laws.[12] An illustration of their familiarity with the common law can be seen in the colonial law of dower.

Since the days of the Norman kings, English law had assured to a wife surviving her husband certain rights in his property after his death. Those rights had varied both in character and in extent, but typically they were rights in land.[13] Until relatively modern times, land has been the chief form of wealth, so that the practice of allowing the widow a share in her deceased husband's lands afforded her the protection and means of livelihood which she required after his death. The rule early became established in the courts of common law that a widow should receive after the death of her husband an estate for her life in one-third of all the lands of which he had been seised during the marriage and to which issue of the marriage might by a possibility succeed.[14] That interest was known as dower. Dower rights attached upon marriage, unless the husband had made an adequate settlement on his bride beforehand,[15] but she could not otherwise be deprived of her rights by will[16] or by any other act of the husband alone during the marriage. She was entitled to dower in addition to what land or other property he might leave her by will[17] or to what personal property she might be entitled if he died intestate. She might release her rights of her own volition, and she could be barred from them if she deserted her husband [18] or if he divorced her for her adultery.[19] After the death of her husband the widow's inchoate right became consummate, and she was entitled to have her third or thirds assigned to her by the husband's heir or other tenant of the land.[20] If no assignment were made, she was entitled to a writ of dower to realize her rights.[21]

In addition to dower, local custom and the practice of the ecclesiastical courts which administered the personal estates of decedents generally gave the widow a share of his personal effects, if he died intestate.[22] Of that portion her husband could not only in early days deprive her by will,,[23] but after the fourteenth century, except by local custom,[24] he acquired complete freedom of testation and might deprive her by will of any share in his personal effects.[25]

Such, generally, were the rights of a widow in the property of her deceased husband in seventeenth-century England. As to her rights in the colony of Massachusetts Bay, little is known before 1641. In that year it was provided in the Body of Liberties that

> If any man at his death shall not leave his wife a competent portion of his estaite, upon just complaint made to the Generall Court she shall be relieved.[26]

Evidently that provision was thought inadequate, for in 1647 the following enactment, prefaced by an italicized preamble, was made by the General Court:

> *Forasmuch as no provision hath yet been made for any certein maintainance for Wives after the death of their Husbands, be it ordered and enacted by this present Court and Authoritie thereof;*
>
> That every married Woman (living with her Husband in this Jurisdiction or other where absent from him with his consent or through his meer default, or inevitable providence, or in case of divorce where she is the innocent partie) that shal not before marriage be estated by way of joynture in some houses, lands, tenements or other hereditaments for term of her life, shall immediately after the

death of her Husband have right and interest by way of *dower*, in, and to one third part of all such houses, lands, tenements, rents and hereditaments as her said Husband was seized of, to his own use, either in *possession*, *reversion* or *remainder* in any estate of inheritance (or *franc-tenement* not then determined) at any time during the marriage to have and injoy for term of her natural life according to the estate of such Husband free, and freely discharged of and from all titles, debts, rents, charges, judgments, executions and to other incumbrances whatsoever had, made, or suffered by her said Husband during the said marriage between them; or by any other person claiming by, from, or under him otherwise then by any act or consent of such Wife, as the laws of this Court shall ratefie and allow: and if the Heir of the Husband or other person interrested, shall not within one month after lawfull demand made, assigne and set out to such widow, her just third part with conveniencie or to her satisfaction according to the intent of this Law, then upon a *writt of dower* in the court of that Shire where the said houses, lands, tenements or other hereditaments shall lye; or in the court of Assistants (if the same lye in several Shires) her *dower* or third part shal be assigned her to be set forth in severall by mets and bounds, by such persons as the same Court shall appoint for that purpose, with all costs and damages susteined. Provided alwayes that this Law shall not extend to any houses lands, tenements or other hereditaments solde or conveyed away, by any husband *bona fide* for valuable consideration, before the last of the ninth month now last past. And it is farther inacted that everie such Wife as is before expressed immediatly after the death of her Husband, shal have interest in, and unto one third part of all such monie, goods and chattels, real and personal of what kinde soever as her Husband shall dye possessed of (so much as shall be sufficient for the discharge of his Funerall and just debts being first deducted) to be allowed and set out to her as is heer before appointed for her Dowrie. Provided alwayes that every such widow so endowed as aforesaid shal not commit or suffer any strip or wast, but shal maintain all such houses, fences and inclosures as shall be assigned to her for her Dowrie, and shall leave the same in good and sufficient repairations in all points. [1647][27]

The enactment was included in the edition of the Laws and Liberties of 1648 under the title "Dowries."

The 1641 enactment continued in force after the 1647 Dower Act, and the courts interpreted it to mean that the widow was to have, in addition to dower, whatever might be necessary for her support.[28] A widow might presumably avail herself of the provisions of the Dower Act whether her husband died testate or intestate. In the event that he left a will which did not make adequate provision for her, she might complain to the General Court under the 1641 law and claim additional property. If the husband died intestate, she was entitled, by virtue of a law of 1649, to such part of his personal estate as the county court thought just and equal.[29] In the 1660 edition of the Massachusetts laws, the word "personall" was omitted.[30] The foregoing continued in force with but slight changes until 1692.[31]

Although the acts of 1641 and 1649 make certain provisions for the widow, we are not presently concerned with them, since they do not relate to dower. However, the principal provisions of the 1647 act must be carefully noted: (1) the benefits of the act extended to every woman in the colony who was either married and living with her husband, or married and not living with him as a result of his consent or inevitable providence, or divorced and she was the innocent party; (2) the rights conferred by the act accrued upon marriage;[32] (3) the widow's interest was an estate for her life, after the death of her husband, in one-third of all the realty of which her husband had been seised, in an estate of inheritance,[33] at any time during the marriage; (4) although the estate did not come into her possession until her husband was dead, she could not be deprived of her inchoate right during the marriage by any act of her husband, or by any one claiming under him, unless she consented thereto; (5) her interest might be barred only by a jointure before marriage, by desertion on her part, or by divorce when she was the guilty party; (6) her estate was free from the claims of the husband's creditors; (7) upon her husband's death, her estate was to be assigned to her by her husband's heir or other person interested; (8) if the lands were not assigned to her within a month after her demand, she was entitled to a writ of dower to enforce her rights. The provision for giving the widow one-third of the husband's personal property outright, in addition to one-third of the realty for life, was dropped in 1649.[34]

In the absence of relevant information it is not possible to state with any certainty the immediate source of the 1647 act. Possibly the basic principle was borrowed from Plymouth Colony, where after 1636 a widow received one-third of her husband's lands for life and one-third of his personal property absolutely.[35] Several achievements of Plymouth in the legal field appear to have been borrowed by Massachusetts Bay, for instance, the principle of partible inheritance,[36] the requirement of recording deeds,[37] and the device of codification.[38] However, the Plymouth provision is by no means so detailed as that in the Massachusetts act, and it apparently applied to property owned by the husband at his death and not to all property of which he had been seised during coverture. Whatever its immediate inspiration, the Massachusetts act seems clearly to have been modeled upon the rules of common law dower. No detailed comparison is required in the face of the striking similarities of the English and the Massachusetts laws.

A word must be said about dower by local custom in England. The right of a widow to share in her deceased husband's real property was universally acknowledged in English manorial law as well as by the common law courts. That right, known as freebench, varied in extent from place to place and might consist of one-fourth, one-third, one-half or the whole of her husband's realty.[39] With such customs the Massachusetts colonists were very likely familiar, for many of them had been recruited from the class of artisans and small farmers, whose knowledge of manorial customs was more extensive than their acquaintance with the common law of the king's courts. It should be noted, however, that freebench was the widow's right to a share of the realty of which her husband had *died seised* and hence in the nature of a right of succession, a survival perhaps from an age when a wife may have been her husband's heir.[40] At common law, the widow's right to one-third of the realty attached, as in Massachusetts, to all the lands of which her husband had been *seised during coverture*. Her right was one which accrued by virtue of the marital relationship and was one of which she could not be deprived by act of the husband; therefore it was not a right of succession. Freebench might entitle a widow to varying shares in her husband's estate, whereas in Massachusetts her rights attached to only one-third as at common law. In other words, the basic principles as well as the secondary characteristics of the Massachusetts law of dower are those of the English common law. It may not be without significance that it was in 1647 that the Massachusetts General Court voted to purchase several English law books, including a copy of Coke on Littleton.[41]

When we turn to the problem of how the Dower Act was administered by the courts, our conclusions must be less definite. It is not possible to determine how closely the courts observed the provisions of the act without detailed examination of the original court records. Many of the published records have been edited from the point of view of the antiquarian or the genealogist rather than for the purpose of exhibiting the law in action,[42] with the result that for present purposes they are often nearly useless. The reverse is true of the printed records of the Suffolk County Court, which provide a clearer picture of the law of dower in operation.

Several cases in the Suffolk records are concerned with claims for dower made by a widow against her husband's heir or grantee and show the courts disposing of the claims in accordance with the provisions of the 1647 act.[43] Other cases reveal that in the settlement of widows' claims the courts did not strictly adhere to the provisions of the Dower Act. It should here be noted that unlike contemporary England, where the administration of decedents' estates was in the hands of the ecclesiastical courts, probate jurisdiction in Massachusetts Bay belonged to the county courts.[44] Although dower rights were theoretically independent of other claims against a deceased's estate, whether those claims arose under a will or under the intestacy laws, the courts frequently concerned themselves with dower in the settlement of a decedent's estate. Hence the estate cases provide further evidence of the actual administration of the Dower Act by the courts. In many cases the distributions ordered by the courts indicate that they did not give literal effect to the wording of the act. Thus a widow sometimes received a portion of her husband's estate (either land or personalty) outright instead of for life, "in Lieu of her dowry."[45] In one case the court gave the widow all the deceased's land, including the house, for her life.[46] In another case the widow received one-half of her husband's houses and lands in fee simple and the other half for her life, ignoring the claim of the deceased's brother, who would have been the heir at common law.[47] In three cases, when the husband devised to his widow as large a share of his lands as she would have received by way of dower, she seems not to have been given her dower,[48] although in England at that time she would have been entitled to dower also unless the devise was expressly stated to be in lieu of dower.[49] Despite the provision of the Dower Act that the widow's interest should be free from the claims of the husband's creditors,[50] there are suggestions that creditors may sometimes have been given priority, provided the remainder of the estate was sufficient for the widow's needs.[51] In one case, the shares of the distributees of the estate, including the widow, were abated proportionately for the payment of creditors.[52]

Some distributions which disregarded the provisions of the Dower Act may have been the result of compromises between the widow and the other distributees of the estate, in which for the sake of simplicity or settlement or for other reasons the widow renounced her dower rights and was given a sum of money outright. Other cases seem to reflect a concern on the part of the courts for achieving fair results in particular cases.[53] Authority for modifying the words of the 1647 act might have been found in the 1641 act which allowed the General Court to relieve a widow who had been left an insufficient portion by her husband[54] and would presumably enable the county court to give a widow more than her thirds for life.[55] At least once the 1649 act, which gave the county court power to assign to the widow such part of her husband's estate "as they shall conceive iust and equall,"[56] was interpreted as applying to realty as well as personalty.[57] Such an interpretation did no violence to prevailing theories in Massachusetts, where in the administration of intestate estates the realty and personalty were valued together (contrary to the common law of England) and administered as one indiscriminate mass.[58]

It thus appears that although the Massachusetts Dower Act was based upon the rules of common law dower in England, it was interpreted by the courts in a manner which was in many instances at variance with the common law rules. With the legality of interpretations which were "contrary to the law of England" we are not here concerned. We are concerned with the various influences which shaped the early law of Massachusetts. It has been suggested elsewhere that the transplantation of customary law and local institutions was the basic fact in the colonial law of the seventeenth century, and considerable evidence has been advanced in support of the position that the law which the settlers brought with them was a curious mixture of religious ideas and of half-remembered customs from other lands.[59] The present examination of the Massachusetts law of dower points to another element in stressing the influence of the English common law and tends to confirm Professor Plucknett's statement that as early as 1648 "there had been a voluntary reception of a good deal of common law, freely modified to meet local conditions."[60] Nevertheless, although common law influences can be found in the substantive and procedural law of that century, it must be remembered that there were few professional lawyers in the colony and few English treatises and law reports. The answer to the question of the relative contributions of customary, common, and foreign law must await a detailed exposition of the "state of the law" in colonial Massachusetts. It may well prove true, as Professor Chafee has suggested, that the common law was present in some form at the start and that it "underwent a continuous reception as the growth of law libraries and serious legal students brought more and more case law and detailed doctrines from England."[61]

Professor Max Radin has observed pertinently that "the common law in the period between 1660 and 1776 certainly made great strides toward the domination of the law of America. But it never quite achieved it. Throughout the Colonial period it remained a subsidiary, supplementary law, . . . regarded some times with veneration and at others with suspicion and hostility."[62] In seventeenth-century Massachusetts the influence of the common law seems to have been less significant than other elements, such as local customs and practices of the ecclesiastical courts.[63] Because in the beginning the growth of the law was not overly hampered by traditional doctrines and rules it was possible for an indigenous law to develop in response to the social and economic conditions of the new American civilization.

COLONIAL AMERICA

FOOTNOTES

1. See, however, the excellent summary by Professor Zechariah Chafee in the Introduction to *Records of the Suffolk County Court 1671-1680*, Colonial Society of Massachusetts, *Publications*, XXIX (1933), xvii-xciv.
2. Paul S. Reinsch, "The English Common Law in the Early American Colonies," *Select Essays in Anglo-American Legal History*, 3 vols. (Boston, 1907), I, 367, 370.
3. Charles J. Hilkey, *Legal Development in Colonial Massachusetts*, Columbia University Studies in History, Economics and Public Law, Vol. XXXVII (New York, 1910), 68.
4. Reinsch, *op. cit.*, 385.
5. See discussion in Richard B. Morris, "Massachusetts and the Common Law," *American Historical Review*, Vol. XXXI (1926), 443-453.
6. Francis N. Thorpe, comp., *Federal and State Constitutions, Colonial Charters and Other Organic Laws, of States, Territories, and Colonies*, 7 vols. (Washington, 1909), III, 1849.
7. Julius Goebel, "King's Law and Local Custom in Seventeenth Century New England," *Columbia Law Review*, Vol. XXXI (1931), 416.
8. George L. Haskins, "The Beginnings of the Recording System in Massachusetts," *Boston University Law Review*, Vol. XXI, (1941), 281; George L. Haskins, "The Beginnings of Partible Inheritance in the American Colonies," *Yale Law Journal*, Vol. LI (1942), 1280.
9. Haskins, "The Beginnings of Partible Inheritance in the American Colonies," 1309-1311.
10. Haskins, "The Beginnings of the Recording System in Massachusetts," 289-291; Haskins, "The Beginnings of Partible Inheritance in the American Colonies," 1301-1302.
11. Hilkey, *op. cit.*, 5, 66ff., 144; Reinsch, *op. cit.*, 367 ff.
12. Max Farrand, ed., *Laws and Liberties of Massachusetts* (Cambridge, Mass., 1929); hereinafter, *Laws and Liberties of Massachusetts*. For a general discussion of the extent to which the common law was utilized, see George L. Haskins, *Law and Authority in Early Massachusetts* (New York, 1960), chapter X.
13. For the early history of dower, see Haskins, "The Development of Common Law Dower," *Harvard Law Review*, Vol. LXII (1948), 42.
14. Edward Coke, *The First Part of the Institutes of the Laws of England; Or a Commentary upon Littleton*, 3 vols. (Philadelphia, 1812), I, *30b: "Tenant in dower is, where man is seised of certeine lands or tenements in fee simple, fee taile generall, or as heire in speciall taile, and taketh a wife, and dieth, the wife after the decease of her husband shall be endowed of the third part of such lands and tenements as were her husband's at any time during the coverture, to have and to hold to the same wife in severalty by metes and bounds for terme of her life . . . ." Hereinafter *Coke on Littleton*. For purposes of this essay, no discussion of dower *ad ostium ecclesiae*, *ex assensu patris*, and *de la pluis*

beale is necessary. See Haskins, "The Development of Common Law Dower," *passim.*

15. After the Statute of Uses, 1536, 27 Hen. VIII, c. 10, an ante-nuptial settlement in the form of a jointure, if properly executed, would bar dower. *Coke on Littleton* *36b. See Charles H. Scribner. *A Treatise On the Law of Dower*, 2 vols. (Philadelphia, 1864-1867), chapter XV.
16. Devises were not permitted at common law until the enactment of the Statute of Wills, 1540, 32 Hen. VIII, c. 1. Certain interests in land, such as leasehold, and land held by burgage tenure, were excepted from the common law rule. See Frederick Pollock and Frederick Maitland, *History of English Law Before the Time of Edward I*, 2 vols. (Cambridge, 1911), 115 and 329-331.
17. *Coke on Littleton*, *36b.
18. *Coke on Littleton*, *32a; John Cowell, *The Interpreter* (Cambridge, 1607), under "Dower."
19. Henry Rolle, *Un Abridgment des plusiers cases et resolutions del Common Ley*, 2 vols. (London, 1668), I, 681.
20. *Coke on Littleton*, *34b, 35a.
21. *Ibid.*, 35a.
22. Pollock and Maitland, *op. cit.*, II, 349-351.
23. If a man were survived by a widow and children, his testament was effective as to one-third of his personal property; if he were survived by a widow or children, but not by both, it was effective as to one-half. Ranaulf de Glanville, *De Legibus et Consuetudinibus Regni Angliae*, VII, 5. The shares of the widow and children could be enforced by the writ *de rationabile parte bonorum. Ibid.*, 7.
24. For example, in York and London, where the system of forced shares was not abolished until 4, 5 Wm. and Mary, c. 2 (1692), and 11 George I, c. 18 (1724), respectively.
25. William S. Holdsworth, *A History of English Law*, (London, 1935), III, 552.
26. *Colonial Laws of Massachusetts Reprinted from the Edition of 1660, with Supplements to 1672* (Boston, 1889) 51; hereinafter *Massachusetts Colonial Laws 1660-1672.*
27. *Laws and Liberties of Massachusetts*, 17-18.
28. George F. Dow, ed., *Probate Records of Essex County, Massachusetts*, 3 vols. (Salem, 1916), I, 50, 67, 91, 196; hereinafter *Probate Records of Essex County, Massachusetts.*
29. Nathaniel B. Shurtleff, ed., *Records of the Governor and Company of the Massachusetts Bay*, 5 vols. (Boston, 1853-54), II, 281; *ibid.*, III, 170; hereinafter, *Records of Mass.*
30. *Massachusetts Colonial Laws 1660-1672*, 201.
31. *Acts and Resolves of the Province of Massachusetts Bay*, 21 vols. (Boston, 1869-1922), I, 48; hereinafter *Acts and Resolves of the Province of Massachusetts Bay.*
32. In the case of those already married in 1647, the rights accrued at once and were apparently retroactive except as to conveyances made by the husband to bona fide purchasers for value prior to Sept. 30, 1647.

33. That is, an estate in fee simple or fee tail. See, Haskins, "The Development of Common Law Dower."
34. *Records of Massachusetts*, III, 169-170: "Forasmuch as the printed lawe concerning dowries, upond second viewe and examinacion, appeares not so convenient as was formerly conceaved, in euery particuler thereof, itt is therefore hereby ordered, that the clawse toward the latter end of that order, that gives a wife a third parte of hir husbands mony, goods, and chattells, reall and personall, after hir husbands decease, shall henceforth be repealed and become voyd, and the rest of the said order to be, and remayne in full force and virtue."
35. William Brigham ed., *The Compact With the Charter and Laws of the Colony of New Plymouth* (Boston, 1836), 43. "That if the husband die the wife shall have a third part of his lands during her life and a 3d of his goods to be at her owne disposeinge."
36. Haskins, "The Beginnings of Partible Inheritance in the American Colonies," 1281.
37. Haskins, "The Beginnings of the Recording System in Massachusetts," 285 n. 19.
38. Goebel, "King's Law and Local Custom in Seventeenth Century New England," 418-419 n. 7; Haskins, *Law and Authority in Early Massachusetts*, chapter VIII; and Haskins, "Codification of the Law in Colonial Massachusetts: A Comparative Study," *Indiana Law Journal*, XXX (1954), 1.
39. Charles Watkins, *A Treatise on Copyholds*, 2 vols. (London, 1797-1799, II, 87-89. Freebench should be clearly distinguished from dower by special custom under which a widow might take a life interest in one-half, instead of one-third, of the lands of which her husband had been seised during coverture. See *Coke on Littleton*, *33b, *111a; Baker v. Berisford, Keble Reports, I, 509 (King's Bench, 1663).
40. See Gomme, "Widowhood in Manorial Law," *Archaeological Review*, Vol. II, (1888), 184. In some customals the wife is explicitly referred to as her husband's heir: H. B. Shillibeer, *Ancient Customs of the Manor of Taunton Deane* (Tiverton, 1821), 42; Matthew Imber, *The Case; or an Abstract of the Customs of the Manor of Merdon* (London, 1707), 47; see Martin v. Wentworth, Noy's Reports, I, (Queen's Bench, 1596). At common law a wife was never her husband's heir except in the rare instance where she happened to be related to him by blood and there was none nearer in degree than herself.
41. *Records of Mass.*, II, 212.
42. This statement is particularly true of the *Probate Records of Essex County, Massachusetts*. For a few examples, see Haskins, "The First American Reform in Civil Procedure," *Perspectives of Law: Essays for A. W. Scott* (Boston, 1964) 173.
43. Estate of Ellice, *Records of the Suffolk County Court 1671-1680*, Colonial Society of Massachusetts *Collections*, XXX (1933), 595-596 (1675); Vicars v. Joyliffe, *ibid.*, 755 (1676); Burnell v. Burnell, *ibid.*, 1096 (1679). See Estate of Gross in *Records of the Court of*

Assistants of the Colony of Massachusetts Bay 1630-1692, 3 vols., (Boston, 1928), III, 90 (1655); and*Records of Mass.*, III, 385.

44. See Haskins, "The Beginnings of Partible Inheritance in the American Colonies," 1284.
45. Estate of Walker, *Records of the Suffolk County Court 1671-1680*, Colonial Society of Massachusetts *Collections*, XXX (1933), 869 (1677). In this case the estate amounted to £950, of which the widow received £490 and the only child £460. In Estate of Ward, *ibid.*, II, 1069, the value of the estate was £413, of which the widow was given £113 outright in lieu of her dower. See also Estate of Shrimpton, *ibid.*, I, 438 (1674); Estate of Pratt, *ibid.*, 716 (1676); Estate of Davenport, *ibid.*, II, 1105 (1679).
46. Estate of Tibbot, in George F. Dow, ed., *Records and Files of the Quarterly Courts of Essex County, Massachusetts* 8 vols., (Salem, 1911-1921) (1650), I, 247; hereinafter *Records and Files of the Quarterly Courts of Essex County, Mass.*
47. Patten v. Dyer, *Records of the Suffolk County Court 1671-1680*, Colonial Society of Massachusetts *Collections*, XXIX (1933), 373; Patten v. Winsley, *ibid.*, 377. This case is discussed in detail by Zechariah Chafee, "Professor Beale's Ancestor," in *Harvard Legal Essays* (Cambridge, Mass., 1934), 39.
48. *Records and Files of the Quarterly Courts of Essex County, Mass.*, I, 127, 168, 239. The entries in these records are not always complete, so that any statements based on them may be open to question.
49. *Coke on Littleton*, *36b; J. G. Woerner, *American Law on Administration*, 2 vols. (Boston, 1899), 266.
50. "Freely discharged of and from all titles, debts, rents charges, judgements, executions and other incumbrances whatsoever had, made, or suffered by her said Husband during the said marriage between them." *Laws and Liberties of Massachusetts*, 17.
51. Estate of Walker, *Records of the Suffolk County Court 1671-1680*, Colonial Society of Massachusetts *Collections*, XXX (1933), 869 (1677).
52. Estate of Ward, *ibid.*, 1069 (1679).
53. For further discussion of that concern on the part of the courts, see Haskins, "The Beginnings of Partible Inheritance in the American Colonies."
54. *Massachusetts Colonial Laws 1660-1672*, 51.
55. This argument does not seem ever to have been made.
56. *Records of Mass.*, II, 281; *ibid.*, 170; and *Massachusetts Colonial Laws 1660-1672*, 201.
57. Patten v. Dyer, *Records of the Suffolk County Court 1671-1680*, Colonial Society of Massachusetts *Collections*, XXIX (1933), 373; *Records of the Court of Assistants of the Colony Massachusetts Bay*, I, 4. The original enactment in 1649 read "such a part of his personall estate as they shall conceive iust and equall." *Records of Mass.*, II, 281; *ibid.*, III, 170. The word "personall" was omitted in the 1660 edition of the Laws, *Massachusetts Colonial Laws 1660-1672*, 201. It

may be pertinent to note that after the clause giving the widow a third part of her husband's personalty was stricken from the Dower Act of 1649 (see *Records of Mass.*, III, 169-170), the question arose whether the widow's one-third interest attached only to realty, or to realty and personalty. It was resolved in the Court of Assistants that "by A third part for the wife to be ment a third part of the whole." *Records of the Court of Assistants of the Colony of Massachusetts Bay*, III, 91.

58. See Haskins, "The Beginnings of Partible Inheritance in the American Colonies," 1289. In England, at common law, the real estate passed directly to the heir and did not come within the jurisdiction of the probate court.
59. Goebel, "King's Law and Local Custom in Seventeenth Century New England," and Haskins, "The Beginnings of Partible Inheritance in the American Colonies."
60. Theodore F. T. Plucknett in a book review in *New England Quarterly*, III (1930), 157. For further examples and discussion see chapter 8 of Haskins, *Law and Authority in Early Massachusetts.*
61. Zechariah Chafee in a book review, *Harvard Law Review*, LVII (1944), 414.
62. Max Radin, "The Rivalry of Common-Law and Civil Law Ideas in the American Colonies," *Law, A Century of Progress* (New York, 1937), II, 427.
63. For a recent appraisal of the latter element, see Haskins, "Ecclesiastical Antecedents of Criminal Punishment in Early Massachusetts," Massachusetts Historical Society *Proceedings*, Vol. 72 (1963), 21.

THE MASSACHUSETTS VICE-ADMIRALTY COURT

L. KINVIN WROTH*

University of Maine Law School

THE MASSACHUSETTS Vice-Admiralty Court stood at the center of the clash between British constitutional orthodoxy and America's demands for greater autonomy in the decade before the Revolution. In this and other admiralty courts, royal officials enforced the Acts of Trade which did so much to arouse colonial antagonism. Admiralty courts, moreover, traditionally applied the civil law and sat without a jury. In suits under the Acts of Trade, the colonists were thus deprived of familiar and cherished common law safeguards. Reports of such suits in Massachusetts circulated throughout the colonies, and, with similar cases elsewhere, stirred feeling so strong that extension of the admiralty jurisdiction was listed as a major complaint in numerous American protests against British authority. The Declaration of Independence itself referred to the vice-admiralty courts when it charged George III with "depriving us in many cases of the benefits of Trial by Jury."[1]

Opposition to the admiralty jurisdiction was not a phenomenon unique to American colonial history. In England such opposition had existed on broader terms since the fourteenth century. By the time of the American Revolution, the English common law courts had imposed drastic restrictions upon admiralty's power to hear many ordinary civil maritime cases that logically would have seemed to lie within its competence. That these restrictions did not control the colonial vice-admiralty courts and so did not bind the federal district courts sitting in admiralty, has been a tenet of American constitutional construction. In *DeLovio v. Boit*,

*Portions of this paper appeared in somewhat different form in L. Kinvin Wroth, "The Massachusetts Vice Admiralty Court and the Federal Admiralty Jurisdiction," *American Journal of Legal History*, VI (July, Oct. 1962), 250-268, 347-367. Those portions are reproduced here with the permission of that publication.

the leading case in support of this position, Justice Joseph Story cited as authority the broad admiralty powers granted in the commissions of colonial governors and judges, adding that "In point of fact the vice-admiralty courts of Massachusetts before the Revolution, exercised a jurisdiction far more extensive than that of the admiralty in England."[2]

Much has been written about the political controversy aroused in Massachusetts and elsewhere by the vice-admiralty court's customs jurisdiction, but little is known about the relationship of this controversy to the older dispute between admiralty and the common law. Moreover, Story's conclusion that the latter dispute did not exist in Massachusetts has never been tested by a comparison of admiralty and common law practice. This essay is an attempt to throw some light on these issues on the basis of research in the court records of colonial and provincial Massachusetts.

Traditionally the admiralty courts of every seafaring nation had jurisdiction over all matters touching the sea and maritime commerce. In England, however, admiralty, which was a prerogative court, was restricted by two statutes passed during the reign of Richard II, limiting it to things "done upon the sea" and not "within the bodies of the counties."[3] The courts of common law, jealous for their own jurisdiction, used these acts to curb the High Court of Admiralty. When the statutory limits, as defined by the common lawyers, were exceeded, an aggrieved party could halt the proceedings by obtaining a writ of prohibition from the court of King's Bench. In the eighteenth century these limits were extensive and they were rigorously applied. The "instance" or civil jurisdiction of the High Court was in theory restricted to actions upon contracts made upon the high seas to be performed upon the high seas, and to actions in tort arising on the high seas. Moreover, admiralty could proceed only *in rem*, that is, against the vessel for which the liability sued upon had been incurred. As a practical matter, however, the High Court was permitted to act *in personam* as well as *in rem* in a number of cases theoretically forbidden, where for one reason or another the common law could not adequately serve the interests involved. On the prize side of the court, admiralty's power was virtually unchallenged.[4]

The admiralty jurisdiction in England also extended to certain offenses under the Acts of Trade. Violations of the requirement in the Navigation Act of 1660 that the vessels be English-or-colonial-built, owned, and manned, could be sued upon in "the court of admiralty" if the offending vessel were taken at sea by a naval officer.[5] Vessels which failed to give bond that they would not transport certain enumerated colonial goods to ports outside England and Wales, or which transported such goods elsewhere, could, under this Act as supplemented in 1671, be proceeded against "in the court of the high admiral of England, or of any of his vice admirals."[6] The English common law courts had concurrent jurisdiction of cases under the latter provision, however, as well as exclusive jurisdiction under all other Acts. In fact, virtually all customs and revenue litigation in England was carried on in the Court of Exchequer, which sat with a jury.[7]

In the American colonies there had been great confusion as to the proper court for trial of offenses against the Acts of Trade. The Act of Frauds, passed in 1696 only partly remedied the situation. It gave jurisdiction over violations of the requirements as to construction, ownership, and manning of vessels to "any court" in the colonies — language which was held to mean courts of admiralty as well as common law.[8] The Act also provided that "all penalties and forfeitures before mentioned, not in this act particularly disposed of," could be recovered "in the court of admiralty held in his Majesty's plantations."[9] There was much dispute as to whether this clause covered only certain provisions concerning the power to detect and punish offenders, made in the preceding section of the Act,[10] or whether it was meant to incorporate the forfeiture provisions of the earlier Acts of Trade, which had been recited in the preamble. If the earlier provisions were not included under the Act of 1696, it was argued that their somewhat ambiguous language nevertheless conveyed admiralty jurisdiction.[11]

Statutory jurisdiction in other cases was unambiguous. An Act of 1708 provided that prizes were to be tried in the colonial admiralty courts and laid down a procedure for such cases. The

Naval Stores Act of 1722 made clear that suits for breaches of the White Pine Acts, which reserved to the Crown all trees of a size suitable for use as masts or for other naval purposes, were also within the colonial admiralty jurisdiction.[12]

Prior to the passage of the Navigation Act of 1696 there had been no coherent system of admiralty courts in the colonies. Governors of royal provinces had had vice-admiralty powers by virtue of their commissions, but there was no consistency or uniformity in the way they exercised their authority.[13] In the chartered colonies the situation had bordered on the chaotic. The Massachusetts Bay Colony, for example, had exercised admiralty jurisdiction almost from the time it was first settled. During the early years of the Colony, special committees of arbitration sat to try maritime cases, applying principles of maritime, rather than common, law. A sophisticated maritime code, based on European sources, was enacted in 1668.[14] Under an act of 1674 the Court of Assistants was empowered to hear "all cases of admiralty," calling a jury only when it deemed it necessary.[15] The court, usually sitting without a jury, tried disputes over masters' wages, shipbuilding contracts, contracts for the sale of a vessel, and breach of charter party, all of which were matters then or later barred to the admiralty in England. When Edward Randolph and other customs officials appeared to prosecute violations of the Acts of Trade, the court called a jury, with the result that the royal litigants enjoyed a notable lack of success.[16]

Randolph and his colleagues preferred to sue in admiralty (outside Massachusetts at least) because widespread colonial opposition to the customs system meant that local juries were invariably hostile to the Crown. These customs officers had long recommended reform, and it was largely through Randolph's efforts that the Act of 1696 was finally passed. To implement the jurisdiction given by the act, Randolph set up a new system of colonial vice-admiralty districts, with judges and other officers commissioned by the Lords of Admiralty. The Massachusetts Vice-Admiralty Court was constituted under this system, with power to act also in matters arising in New Hampshire, and, after 1701, Rhode Island.[17]

In its first year, the court was involved more in politics than in adjudication. After the Massachusetts charter had been revoked in 1684, the powers of admiralty had been used by royal officials to enforce the Acts of Trade, creating a natural distaste in the Puritans for prerogative courts.[18] Nathaniel Byfield, Randolph's original nominee as judge, was thus superseded almost at once by Wait Winthrop, a leader of the Massachusetts Puritans, who had gained the favor of Lord Bellomont, the royal governor of New York, Massachusetts, and New Hampshire. The new commission covered all three provinces. Upon the failure of a plan under which Winthrop was to keep Massachusetts, with another judge to be appointed for New York, William Atwood was commissioned in 1701 as judge of admiralty in all of the colonies from West Jersey to New Hampshire. Atwood delegated his powers in New England to a deputy, Thomas Newton, who exercised the jurisdiction until 1704. Byfield was then reappointed through the machinations of Joseph Dudley, now governor of Massachusetts, and managed to hold the office until 1716.[19]

Amidst this political turmoil, the Massachusetts Vice-Admiralty Court began to develop into a judicial institution. Even when the Court of Assistants had sat in admiralty, the common law courts had exercised concurrent jurisdiction in many maritime matters.[20] From 1686, when the local admiralty courts ceased to sit, until 1699, when the new Vice-Admiralty Court began to operate, all maritime litigation seems to have been carried on at common law. After 1699, the inhabitants were understandably slow to bring civil cases before a court created primarily to benefit the Crown. The first matters tried were thus mainly customs and prize cases, which seemed to lead inevitably to controversy. Atwood became involved in a squabble over a customs matter that led to the first use of the writ of prohibition in Massachusetts.[21] Byfield was in difficulty because of the fees which he charged in prize.[22] In 1706 Paul Dudley, the governor's son and royal advocate in admiralty, summed up the situation, urging larger fees for the court's officers, because "We have not had above 8 or 10 prizes this warr, and indeed the whole business of the Admiralty is so very small, and the court itself being by commission from the Crown, so obnoxious to some of our Gentlemen."[23]

The "Gentlemen" of Massachusetts and Rhode Island, however, gradually overcame their reluctance to bring civil maritime cases before the Vice-Admiralty Court. Indeed, since Thomas Newton's time there had been a steady trickle of seamen's wage actions, which seemed to know no other home but admiralty.[24] There are no records for the year prior to 1718, but file papers and other sources show that some time after 1706 the court began to hear other civil cases as well.[25] For reasons that are obscure, the old distrust had abated by 1718 to a point where the court was exercising jurisdiction in a great number and variety of complicated maritime matters.

The records of the Massachusetts Vice-Admiralty Court are preserved in the Office of the Clerk of the Supreme Judicial Court for Suffolk County in Boston. Only a scattering of file papers remains. But three volumes of records provide enough information to permit a rough understanding of the points of law and procedure involved in most of the cases heard by the court from 1718 to 1733, and from 1740 to 1745. The materials available for later years are less satisfactory. One source is a book of accounts of sales covering the years 1760 to 1765, which contains full records of the sale and distribution of proceeds of each vessel condemned under the Acts of Trade during the period. Unfortunately this account book gives no information as to the ordinary business of the court. The minute book of the court for 1765-1772 contains terse docket entries, which give only the most general idea of the nature of the court's business.[26] No records or papers for any other period are known to exist. Presumably all were lost in the Stamp Act Riot of August 26, 1765, when the Boston mob broke into the house of William Story, Deputy Register of the court, and destroyed his public and private papers. The years have doubtless consumed anything that escaped the mob.[27]

Other writers, such as Judge Francis C. Lowell, have demonstrated that the first surviving volume of Massachusetts Vice-

Admiralty records, entitled "Volume II," contains numerous examples of the exercise of a jurisdiction beyond that allowed to the English High Court.[28] The following analysis of the second volume of records, "Volume III", shows that the court continued to act in this fashion from 1726 until at least 1733.

Procedure. The colonists' principal guide to admiralty procedure was Francis Clerke's *Praxis Curiae Admiralitatis*, first published in 1667 from notes made by the author at the end of the preceding century.[29] Clerke described what was essentially an *in personam* process, in which goods or vessels "upon the Sea or within the Flux and Reflux of the Sea," belonging to the "defendant" could be arrested only if he could not be reached personally. This procedure was more like foreign attachment than what had come to be admiralty's traditional *in rem* process. Any of the defendant's possessions could be taken, because the purpose was security for a personal obligation rather than satisfaction of the liability of a particular vessel. By the eighteenth century the common law's prescription of the admiralty *in personam* action had worked a major change in English practice. Clerke's forms were still followed when a claimant *in rem* had filed a stipulation, thus submitting his person to the court, but generally all proceedings were in the first instance against a vessel which had incurred liability. The ship was arrested by a warrant posted to her mast citing all who had an interest to appear. The suit proceeded *in rem*, executing in effect what today would be called the maritime lien created by the vessel's obligation.[30]

Trial procedure in the eighteenth century High Court was complex and ponderously slow. In an *in rem* action the libellant (equivalent of the plaintiff at common law) first had to enter four appearances on successive court days even if no claimant appeared. If there was an appearance, or if the suit were *in personam* in the first instance, complicated security arrangements were necessary before the libel was produced in court. Pleadings then followed, much as at common law, but there was no trial as such. Witnesses appeared at stated times and gave their testimony in secret on interrogatories, written questions previously prepared by counsel and administered before an examiner. The evidence was then read to the court and the case was argued. After a decree *in rem*, the *res* was technically subject to the owner's claims for a year, although this rule was often evaded by the fiction that the ship was in perishable condition. The court would order her sold on a summary hearing and distribute the proceeds among the interested parties. Procedure was greatly simplified and speeded up for seamen's wage actions and in certain other cases, but usually the ordained forms were observed. Reports of contemporary cases suggest that under these forms time was distinctly not of the essence.[31]

The practice in Massachusetts, in its relative simplicity, bore greater resemblance to that described by Clerke than it did to anything that went on in the High Court in the eighteenth century. As far as can be determined in the absence of file papers, the Massachusetts court drew no formal line between *in rem* and *in personam* actions, at least in civil proceedings. In the majority of cases, the process seems to have been *in personam* in the first instance. In many actions entitled *in rem*, recovery was decreed against the owner personally, with no indication that he had filed any formal stipulation. The action *in rem* seems to have been relied upon primarily in cases in which no respondent to an *in personam* suit could be found within the jurisdiction, or in customs matters. As cases discussed later will show, however, when the Massachusetts court did act *in rem*, it was proceeding directly against the vessel on an obligation for which she was liable. This process closely resembled the High Court's *in rem* action founded upon a maritime lien.

As in other colonies, trial procedure in Massachusetts was far simpler than that employed in the High Court.[32] As a fundamental simplification, the proceedings were carried on in English from the earliest date, a practice which did not overtake Doctors' Commons until 1733.[33] The language used was far from the highly technical vocabulary of the civilians, but it was not inconsistent with that in the English translation of Clerke's *Praxis* made in 1722. Thus, "libellant," "complainant," "appellant," and "proponent," are all found in the records, but the most common usage was the reliable and familiar "plaintiff," the term used in the 1722 translation of Clerke for the civil law's "actor." Counsel were known as "attorneys," or "advocates" in contrast to Clerke's "proctor" (for "procurator"). Technical terms such as "porrect" (produce, for example, a bill of costs) and "impugnant" (respondent), in use in the eighteenth-century High Court, do not appear either in Massachusetts or in Clerke, but the basic words "libel," "citation," and "monition" were part of the vocabulary.[34]

The course of an action in the Vice-Admiralty Court was also simpler. In both *in rem* and *in personam* proceedings, the action was initiated by the reading and filing of the libel before the court. If the judge "allowed" the libel, any vessel in suit was arrested and all parties were cited to appear. On the day set for trial, the parties were called three times. If anyone appeared, the action proceeded forthwith, with witnesses ordinarily testifying in open court. If all claimants or respondents defaulted, a decree was issued for the libellant. In form, these proceedings resembled an action in the High Court, but the lengthy preliminaries, the series of formal defaults, and the civil law requirement of extensive security were all but discarded.[35] The emphasis was upon a speedy proceeding designed to dispose of all claims at a single sitting.

Little can be learned of appeal procedure in the absence of file papers. The records show that appeals were infrequent, being generally confined to customs cases. Where appeals were allowed, they seem to have been taken to the High Court of Admiralty.[36]

Seamen's Actions. The English courts of common law recognized the right of a seaman seeking his wages to pursue in admiralty his time-honored triple remedy against master, owner, or vessel. One or several sailors could sue *in rem* or *in personam*, on the theory that admiralty had a duty to protect its "wards," and that it was the most convenient court for all concerned. The English practice was followed in Massachusetts, and the great number of such actions suggests that the court made its chief contribution to the maritime community in hearing these suits.[37]

Jurisdiction over wage actions was only one aspect of a general supervision which admiralty exercised over the affairs of seamen. In Massachusetts the court, in effect, served as arbiter of all disputes concerning the ship's articles. Thus, in a wage action a seaman might find himself ordered to continue his voyage, perhaps on altered terms, sometimes with part payment of wages, sometimes not. A seaman could also complain of ill-usage, barbarous or cruel treatment, and assault. If the master's action had exceeded "due correction," he might be fined and the seaman discharged from his contract. The court was available to the master too, however, and actions against seamen for refusing to proceed on the voyage, neglect of duty, desertion, and mutiny were common. In such cases the offender was usually penalized with confinement and forfeiture of wages and then ordered to rejoin his ship.[38]

Most of the Massachusetts wage suits were brought *in personam* against the owners, or against the master having in his hands the funds, goods, or credit of the owners. Thus, John Read, master and owner of the *Mary* galley, which had been condemned for violation of the Acts of Trade, was not allowed a libel *in rem* on behalf of the crew and himself, when the vessel had brought a substantial freight. Read obviously sought to take advantage of the priority of a lien for wages over the claims of those entitled to the proceeds on condemnation, but he was ultimately held liable *in personam* for the crew's wages, presumably on the basis of the freight.[39] Recovery as well as action was thus generally *in personam*, but the true nature of the obligation was not forgotten. If those personally liable seemed reluctant to satisfy a decree for wages, the court would threaten sale of the vessel unless payment was made within a certain time.[40] When the owners did not appear and the master had no funds, the action was brought *in rem*, and the vessel might be ordered sold to pay the wages of both master and crew.[41]

Although the term has not been found in the Massachusetts records, something very like the modern maritime lien appears in these cases. Whatever the form of the action, the vessel was the ultimate source and measure of liability. If no other funds were available to meet seamen's claims, she would be sold, and those claims would have priority over all others in the division of her proceeds.[42] While no case of a lien against a ship in the hands of a bona fide purchaser has been found, in at least one case the crew was allowed to follow the proceeds of sale into the hands of a former part-owner.[43] The right *in rem* granted to the seaman was thus more than the right to attach the owner's goods; it was a right against a specific vessel for services performed for her.

Possession and Part-Ownership. The traditional admiralty jurisdiction extended to petitory and possessory suits — the former being an action to try the title to a vessel, the latter, merely a plea for restoration of possession pending determination of title. The common law held that title could not be tried in admiralty, but allowed jurisdiction over suits for possession.[44] The Massachusetts Court of Vice-Admiralty generally observed this distinction, although it occasionally heard suits by a master for a promised share of the vessel.[45]

A related type of action allowed to admiralty by the common law was that seeking to compel part-owners of a vessel who wanted to put to sea to give security for the voyage for those who did not. The maritime law held that in the case of ultimate obstinacy, uncooperative owners might be forced to sell for the benefit of all.[46] The common law courts ruled that admiralty could not compel a sale, but only a stipulation for the voyage, the ground being that a sale was a proceeding *in personam*, whereas the requirement of security was a proceeding *in rem*.[47] In several cases the Massachusetts Vice-Admiralty Court exceeded this limitation, ordering a sale.[48]

Tort. Few cases in tort appear in the Massachusetts admiralty records. For one thing, the seaman had no action for his injuries comparable to that given him by statute today, and no instance has been found of the application of the doctrine of unseaworthiness in a case of personal injury.[49] Although there were frequent actions for assault on the high seas, they were criminal in nature, resulting in fines payable to the Crown.[50] Thus, in *Fall v. Smith* the court, while fining a master for assaulting a seaman, noted that the seaman's remedy for his damages was at common law.[51]

Actions for collision were unaccountably few. Perhaps the court observed the common law restrictions and took no jurisdiction in accidents occurring in rivers and harbors. Collisions at sea, in an era of better seamanship and smaller and slower craft, were undoubtedly a rarity. Only one case of collision is to be found in Volume III.[52] There were, however, occasional actions for damage to cargo and for the loss of or damage to personal property.[53]

Contract. In England the common law restrictions on jurisdiction over contracts were relaxed not only for seamen's wages, but also in the case of an express hypothecation of the vessel by the master in foreign parts for ships' necessaries (bottomry).[54] Jurisdiction of other contracts which today give rise to maritime liens was denied to the High Court of Admiralty.

Actions upon bottomry bonds were not common in the colonial vice-admiralty courts, and none have been found in the Massachusetts records, but the court heard numerous cases on contracts that the common law would have deemed outside the jurisdiction of admiralty. In *Palatines v. Lobb*, the court took jurisdiction of a libel for the breach of a transportation agreement brought by a company of Palatine immigrants against the master of the vessel. The contract of transportation had bound the vessel to performance, and the court based its jurisdiction upon that "hypothecation." The existence of something like a maritime lien was recognized here, not only as a basis for jurisdiction, but as an incident of the remedy. The court's decree ordered the master to pay various damages and provided that in the event of default the vessel should be sold and payment made out of the proceeds. Since the performance bond involved was not technically an hypothecation, the court was clearly entering an area where prohibition would have been possible.[55]

Except for foreign bottomry bonds, jurisdiction over the maritime lien arising for goods or services furnished to the master on the credit of the vessel was denied to the admiralty court on the ground that such contracts were made on land. In Volume III of the records, there are three such cases that were "agreed" (settled). In a fourth case, a libel *in personam* against a master for work done aboard ship, the court found for the "defendant" on the ground that the agreement upon which the action was based did not include the items for which recovery was sought.[56]

The master's contract for his wages was always withheld from the admiralty jurisdiction, and even today the master has no lien, although he may bring an *in personam* action against the owners. That the Massachusetts court was willing to recognize the master's lien for his wages and charges appears in cases already noted, in which he was allowed to join the crew in *in rem* proceedings.[57] In many instances part of the consideration which the master was to receive for the voyage was a portion of the proceeds based on a share in the vessel herself. The division of the shares not only concerned a contract made on land, but necessitated determination of title to all or part of the vessel. Nevertheless, the Massachusetts court took jurisdiction, not only of claims for wages and profits, but also of actions over the nature of the performance required.[58]

The Massachusetts court heard at least one libel *in rem* on a contract to build a ship, a matter that even today is held to be altogether outside of the admiralty jurisdiction.[59] A suit on a charter party, an action for cargo, actions for pilotage, and a libel on a passage contract also appear in Volume III.[60] It should be noted that nowhere in the Massachusetts records, nor in the published vice-admiralty records of the other colonies, has there been found an action on a marine insurance policy, the subject matter of Story's decision in *DeLovio v. Boit*.[61]

Statutory Actions. Suits under the Acts of Trade and other regulatory legislation made up the next largest category on the court's docket after seamen's actions.[62] Such suits were usually brought by information *in rem* in the name of the customs officer who had seized the offending vessel or goods. Officers also sued *in personam* for fines which the acts placed upon certain offenses. Since the proceeds were ordinarily to be divided among the seizing officer, the governor, and the Crown, these were known as *qui tam* actions, from the Latin form of the phrase commonly used in the information, "who as well for himself as for [the King and governor] sues."[63]

Despite doubts as to the scope of the statutory grants of jurisdiction, actions brought included suits for fines against masters for various violations; suits for forfeiture of unlawfully imported goods and the vessels importing them; and suits for forfeiture of vessels for not carrying a proper register, or for being foreign-built, owned, or manned.[64] There were also occasional actions to recover penalties under the White Pine Acts.[65] In several cases the court overruled pleas to the jurisdiction based on the arguments that an importation took place within the body of a county, or that the court lacked power to try the matters sued upon.[66] That the court sought to apply the acts fairly appears in cases in which it showed leniency toward violations caused by mistake or stress of weather.[67]

Other Matters. During the years 1726 to 1733 the court also took jurisdiction in a variety of other maritime matters. There were actions for average and salvage, petitions for the survey of damaged vessels and cargo, litigation over drift whales, and actions for the "droits of admiralty."[68] Prize cases, a major source of business for the High Court and the other vice-admiralty courts, are not found in Volume III, because the colonies were at peace during the period which it covers. When occasion demanded, however, the Massachusetts court was active in such cases.[69] Volume III also includes the proceedings of a statutory special Court of Admiralty called for the trial of cases of piracy.[70]

The preceding analysis of the substance of the Massachusetts Vice-Admiralty practice shows that the court exercised jurisdiction in almost every type of case that has ever been claimed for the admiralty.[71] Furthermore, through flexible procedure and the ready use of the *in personam* process, speedy and efficient justice was done. Yet, as Judge Lowell has pointed out, in assuming as broad a jurisdiction as the circumstances would permit, the Vice-Admiralty Court was doing no more than the English High Court, which even in the eighteenth century would occasionally brave the wrath of the common law and exercise its ancient powers when no objection was raised by the parties. Admiralty judges obeyed the writ of prohibition not because they accepted the limits it set, but because it was the order of a more powerful court.[72] The real significance of the Vice-Admiralty Court must be sought not in the extent of its practice, but in the attitudes toward admiralty and the maritime law expressed by the colonial courts of common law.

Although Justice Story urged that the limiting acts of Richard II were not in force in the colonies, there is no doubt that from the earliest years of the vice-admiralty system the writ of prohibition was used against it, both in Massachusetts and elsewhere.[73] The Massachusetts colonists argued that their Superior Court of Judicature, having by statute the full powers of the King's Bench, was empowered to issue the writ. The argument was supported by specific reference to the acts and to the history of the struggle between the common law and admiralty, of which the colonists were well aware.[74]

Relatively few prohibitions are to be found in the Massachusetts records. The Superior Court did not lead the kind of active fight against the admiralty which the King's Bench had carried on, and the principal use of the writ seems to have been as a delaying tactic. A temporary prohibition would be granted on the plaintiff's "suggestion" until a full hearing could be had on the jurisdictional question, usually at the next term of court. In four of the five non-customs cases in Volume III where prohibition issued, delay seems to have been enough, because no final hearing was had at common law.[75] The fifth case, *Gray v. Travisa*, was a seaman's action for wages in which the prohibition was made final. The ship's articles had been signed while "in the river" bound out from London, and were under seal. The Superior Court's decision was in accord with the common law rule that a prohibition would lie even in a wage action when suit was brought on a sealed instrument.[76]

Prohibitions also were issued in suits brought under the Acts of Trade. The parties always asserted the statutes of Richard II as the basis for seeking the writ, but surviving papers in three such cases found in the period covered by Volume III indicate that the Superior Court based its decisions primarily on construction of the customs acts involved, rather than on any finding that the activities in question occurred within the body of a county.

In the first of these cases, *Jekyll v. Sloop Sea Flower*, the information, filed in August 1728, alleged that the vessel had cleared out at St. Christopher in the West Indies without giving bond or obtaining a sufferance (permit to load) for 55 hogsheads of molasses and a barrel of sugar. The suggestion for a prohibition urged that under the applicable Acts of Trade: (1) want of a sufferance could be tried only in a court of admiralty in the colony from which the vessel had cleared, (2) want of a bond could be tried only at common law, (3) no bond was needed for sugar shipped as ship's stores or for molasses, and (4) there was no penalty for landing goods shipped without a sufferance. Final prohibition issued after a hearing at which the mate testified that the sugar had been used as stores.[77] The next day a new information was filed against the molasses alone, alleging only the failure to obtain a sufferance. The court rejected a plea that the former prohibition was a bar, as well as a plea to the jurisdiction, and decreed the molasses forfeit.[78] The master meanwhile sought a second prohibition, arguing again that the matter could be tried only in St. Christopher and that no sufferance was required on landing. He further urged that the first prohibition had been decided upon these grounds. The Superior Court dismissed his petition, probably because the earlier prohibition had been based upon the inclusion of the sugar and the allegations as to bond in the first information.[79]

In 1732 the sloop *Defiance* was libelled under the Act of 1696 as being partly foreign-owned and for not having a register showing a change of name and ownership. The ownership and registry provisions of the act had been construed in 1702 by the Attorney General in England as being within the admiralty jurisdiction, but the opinion was not binding on the courts and might even have been unknown in Massachusetts. It thus seems probable that the prohibition which issued was based on the ground that the statute did not confer admiralty jurisdiction over these offenses.[80] A clue to the reasoning may appear in *Durell v. Bardin*, a suit later in the same year by the commander of a naval vessel to recover statutory penalties for luring seamen away from the King's service. The suggestion urged that the acts complained of occurred within the body of the county of Suffolk, and, more important, that the penal act in question gave "diverse things to the cognizance of the admiralty but in the branch whereupon this Libel is grounded no mention is made of the admiralty, but the cognizance of it is given to any Court in his Majesty's Dominions which words always by a necessary legal understanding mean one open to try the facts mentioned at least not expressly prohibited." The court granted a temporary prohibition and the petitioner finally discontinued.[81] The argument seems to proceed upon the theory that the statutes of Richard II could be avoided only by an express grant of jurisdiction to the admiralty.

It was only natural for litigants and the courts to take advantage of such statutory ambiguities in preference to larger questions. Moreover, in all likelihood, the Superior Court would have rejected a broader attack on the jurisdiction. Under orthodox British constitutional theory, as developed in the eighteenth century, Parliament was the legal sovereign. Since it had restricted admiralty in the first place, no lawful power could prevent it from abrogating the restrictions in particular cases. The Superior Court apparently accepted this view, questioning the extent of the abrogation, but not the existence of the power to abrogate.[82]

A statistical summary of the Massachusetts Vice-Admiralty records suggests one reason for the apparently limited use of the writ of prohibition. Even in the court's most active period, the number of cases it heard in which the common law might have claimed the power to interfere was small in proportion to its total business. Between 1718 and 1733 the court heard 105 cases of breaches of the Acts of Trade or other suits which were within its jurisdiction by act of Parliament. Of the remaining 542 actions, 412 were cases affecting seamen, or other matters clearly of admiralty cognizance, such as prize and survey. Only 130 cases, or about 20 percent of the court's business, were even arguably within the disputed area, and many of these, such as actions for possession and torts on the high seas, probably would not have been subject to prohibition. Thus, on the average there were but seven cases a year in which the jurisdiction might have been contested.

Against this picture of an admiralty court concerned primarily with wage and customs actions, stands the busy and varied maritime practice of the common law courts, a continuation of the

Puritan tradition of competence in such matters. A comparison of admiralty and common law business during the arbitrarily chosen year 1732 suggests the extent of the common law practice. Admiralty heard 49 cases, of which 37 were actions for seamen's wages or otherwise concerned mariners. Two of the remaining cases were petitions for the survey of a vessel and five were statutory suits. Only five civil cases came before the court that were not within the jurisdiction generally allowed to admiralty.[83] In the Superior Court of Judicature, at its Suffolk County term in August 1732, at least ten civil maritime actions were heard that might have drawn prohibitions if tried in admiralty.[84] These actions do not by any means reflect the total heard at common law in that year. In the first place, the Superior Court also sat in Suffolk County in February, and had terms in the five other maritime counties. Secondly, the actions heard in the Superior Court were appeals from the Inferior Court of Common Pleas, and only one out of four cases docketed there was carried to the higher court.[85] Finally, many actions that may have been maritime in nature cannot be identified as such because the facts of the case do not sufficiently appear in the records or files.

The Massachusetts Vice-Admiralty Records show a significant drop in the number and variety of actions brought in the court after 1733, perhaps in part as a reaction to Parliament's unequivocal grant of admiralty jurisdiction over evasions of the duties imposed by the Molasses Act of that year. In 1741, the busiest year in Volume V of the records, only 38 cases were heard. Of a total of 118 cases in that volume, six might have drawn a prohibition. Fifty-seven were wage or other seamen's actions, 45 were customs suits, and the remainder were prize or other matters clearly within the jurisdiction.[86] The court may well have flourished in the years after 1747, for which there are no records. In the period covered by the Vice-Admiralty Minute Book (1765-1772) its civil business almost vanished, however, and only a steady flow of customs actions kept it open at all.

The decline in the decade preceding the Revolution was a direct reflection of changes made in the British customs system.

In 1760 England abandoned a policy of lax enforcement which had contributed greatly to harmonious colonial relations since about 1725. William Pitt, disturbed by the illicit colonial trade with the French during the Seven Years' War, insisted that existing customs regulations be strictly applied.[87]

At the close of the war, England decided to raise revenue by laying duties on imports into the colonies. The American Act of 1764, which established the new duties, also tightened the regulatory provisions, added new and heavier penalties, and made clear for the first time that violations of this and all of the Acts of Trade could be sued upon in the vice-admiralty courts. Customs officers were given increased procedural advantages in these suits, and a new superior court of admiralty was authorized in which cases from any province could be tried.[88] At about the same time Benning Wentworth, Surveyor General of the Woods, was prodded into a stricter enforcement of the White Pine Acts in admiralty.[89]

The Stamp Act was also enforceable in admiralty, despite the fact that offenses against it unquestionably occurred on land. In the aftermath of the Stamp Act's repeal, the American Act duties were reduced without change in the enforcement provisions.[90] The Townshend Acts in 1767 laid additional duties upon colonial imports, and further strengthened enforcement by creating an American Board of Customs Commissioners to supervise the system from Boston. Parliament also authorized the establishment of four new district courts of admiralty, one of which sat at Boston, with both original and appellate jurisdiction over surrounding provinces.[91] The uproar following the Boston Massacre in 1770 led to the removal of all duties except that on tea, but once again the enforcement powers were left intact.[92] The vice-admiralty courts thus had jurisdiction of violations of the Tea Act of 1773, of the Boston Port Act of 1774, and of other repressive measures which the British imposed upon the colonies in the desperate months between Lexington and the Declaration of Independence. All of the revenue measures aroused great opposition, not only on account of the tax burden imposed, but because of the added indignity of an admiralty trial for matters which in England were tried by the Court of Exchequer.[93]

The records of the Massachusetts Vice-Admiralty Court for this period are not comparable to those found for earlier years. Fortunately, however, other sources provide many additional details about the procedure of the court and the cases tried before it.

Procedure. Robert Auchmuty, judge of the court from 1767 to the Revolution, and members of the bar were well aware of admiralty's civil law background. Notes and minutes made by John Adams in several admiralty cases which he tried at this time contain extensive citations to Roman law texts, as well as elaborate arguments based upon these authorities.[94] In one customs case Adams contended that under the civil law, oral testimony that a witness was a fugitive from justice could be admitted to impeach him. At common law a written record of conviction was necessary for impeachment on this basis. Auchmuty's "Interlocutory Decree," recorded by Adams, held the testimony inadmissible on the alternative grounds that the construction of the civil law urged was erroneous, and that, in any event, the common law controlled in a statutory proceeding.[95]

Adams' notes also show that in a number of *in rem* customs actions, delivery of the vessel on stipulation for her value was allowed.[96] At least one case was heard on what Adams from his common law experience called a "demurrer." The comparable device in admiralty practice was actually known as an "exception."[97] Interrogatories were administered to the principal witnesses in the outlying counties by commissioners in at least one civil suit. Counsel agreed that depositions taken for use in an earlier common law action between the same parties could be used in evidence as well.[98] Interrogatories administered by the register of the court, were also used in suits under the Acts of Trade; Judge Auchmuty himself on occasion examined the witnesses, both in chambers and in court.[99] In several important customs cases, Auchmuty incorporated in his decrees lengthy opinions which summarized the arguments of counsel and gave the authorities and reasoning supporting his decision.[100]

In March 1769 Auchmuty's commission as judge of the new District Court of Admiralty was read in court.[101] Little change in practice seems to have resulted. Auchmuty retained his position as judge for the province and apparently heard most, if not all, matters brought before him in the first instance in this capacity. The register of the court continued to use the same minute book, docketing cases without regard to the court in which they were formally brought. Thus, a libel to be filed in the "Province of Massachusetts Bay/Court of Vice Admiralty," and addressed to "the Judge Commissary, Deputy and Surrogate of the Court of Vice-Admiralty of Boston in the Province of Massachusetts Bay," was drafted by Adams for use in a case which appears in the same volume with the entries of the first appeals heard by Auchmuty in his new capacity.[102] These appeals were brought in 1772. In view of Auchmuty's dual status as district and province judge, the right to appeal apparently had been deemed to be without value in prior cases. The decision in these suits had been rendered by Auchmuty's deputy sitting in New Hampshire, however.[103]

Appeals to England were taken in several instances during this period. In one case in which Adams did not participate, on appeal to the High Court of Admiralty the question whether a certain act had been an "importation" within the meaning of the statute was decided in the Crown's favor.[104] One of Adams' clients in a later customs case also appealed to the High Court, apparently without success.[105] In 1773 an appeal was allowed to the Privy Council from a decision adverse to the Crown in a proceeding under the White Pine Acts, but no decision had been reached by the time of the Revolution.[106]

Civil Actions. About one-third of the suits heard in admiralty between 1765 and 1772 were civil matters. The majority of these suits were probably wage actions, but few of them can be identified.[107] Adams' minutes and other documents have survived for *Doane v. Gage*, a dispute between two whaling men over title to a whale taken at sea in the Straits of Belle Isle between Newfoundland and Labrador. The location and subject matter would certainly seem to put such a matter properly within even a narrow view of the admiralty jurisdiction, but the fact that title was involved might have served as a basis for an attack upon the jurisdiction at common law. No such issue arose. Adams had originally brought suit at law in Barnstable County, but, perhaps to avoid a biased local jury, that action was withdrawn and proceedings instituted in the admiralty court at Boston in January 1768. In April 1769 the parties agreed to submit the matter to arbitration. A lengthy hearing on interrogatories and depositions was held before the arbitrators in October, but the result is not known.[108]

Statutory Actions. Two-thirds of the cases docketed in the Vice-Admiralty Court between 1765 and 1772 were customs matters, or arose under the White Pine Acts. Adams' notes in several such proceedings show the close relationship between the Vice-Admiralty Court and the political controversy surrounding the customs system. The first test of the American Customs Commissioners' power occurred in *Folger v. Sloop Cornelia.* Timothy Folger had been appointed a "searcher and preventive officer" by the Surveyor General of the Customs, an officer whose functions were abolished when the Commissioners were established. Folger seized the *Cornelia* with a cargo of contraband tea, but she was seized again by the collector of Boston, an official commissioned by the Crown. In February 1768 each man brought suit in the admiralty against the vessel, with the Crown intervening on the collector's behalf. Judge Auchmuty resolved complicated questions of authority in the collector's favor, thus lending important support to the new Commisioners' power over the customs establishment.[109]

The most significant admiralty proceedings in Boston before the Revolution were those arising out of the seizure of John Hancock's sloop *Liberty* in June 1768 for unlawfully unloading a cargo of dutiable wine before entry. An ensuing riot drove the Customs Commissioners to Castle William in Boston Harbor, where they remained until troops which they had urgently requested were garrisoned in Boston. The *Liberty* was condemned for the unloading and sold.[110] Upon the Commissioners' return in November, *in personam* suits for heavy penalties were commenced against Hancock and others under provisions of the Act of 1764. After a lengthy trial, the Crown withdrew the actions in March 1769. Not only had the Commissioners failed to get their man, but charges of oppression circulated by the radical press throughout the colonies served to impair permanently both the Commissioners' position and that of the admiralty courts.[111]

Other Adams cases show that offenses against many provisions of the Acts of Trade, both technical and substantial, were brought to trial in the Vice-Admiralty Court.[112] The court, moreover, remained active virtually until the British evacuation of Boston in March 1776. In 1773 John Wentworth, Surveyor General of the Woods, brought suit in admiralty under the White Pine Acts, challenging the Kennebec Company's claim to exclusive property in the logs on its lands. The Company successfully defended its title.[113] Adams was at least present in court to make brief minutes of a proceeding brought under the Boston Port Act for violation of its provision against remaining in the harbor after June 15, 1774.[114] Documentation in a later Adams case shows the Massachusetts Vice-Admiralty Court exercising jurisdiction in the fall of 1775 over a vessel seized for violation of the Restraining Act of that year.[115]

Other Matters. During the decade prior to the Revolution, two special courts of admiralty for the trial of felonies committed at sea were convened. Crimes other than petty offenses and contempts were beyond the power of the Vice-Admiralty Court. The special courts, which included the judge of admiralty as well as other civil and naval officials, were called under a standing commission from the Crown issued pursuant to statute.[116] Their procedure was in part dictated by the statute and in part resembled that of a naval court-martial, but they were essentially admiralty courts, applying the civil law and sitting without a jury. In the more important of these cases, *Rex v. Corbet*, tried in 1769, Adams and James Otis, counsel for the prisoners, first moved for a jury, arguing that the statutes creating the court required it. Defeated on this issue, Adams then filed a plea to the jurisdiction based on the same statutes, which was also unsuccessful. The location of the crime presumably forestalled any attack based upon the acts of Richard II. After a lengthy trial at which numerous witnesses were examined orally, the prisoners were acquitted.[117]

The attitude of the common law courts toward the ordinary civil jurisdiction of admiralty seems to have remained unchanged during the period 1760-1775.[118] In *Scollay v. Dunn*, the libellant, mate of the brigantine *Peggy*, had agreed to go as hostage to ransom the vessel from her French captors. When he brought suit in admiralty in 1763 to recover the compensation which he alleged that the master had promised him, the owners sought a prohibition, arguing that the *Peggy* had not been sued *in rem* and that they could not be held personally liable. After full argument in which a variety of maritime treatises and contemporary English common law cases were cited, the prohibition was made final. The court's position seemed to be that while the master's contract might bind the vessel *in rem*, no action *in personam* could be had against the owners, apparently on the theory that their personal liability, if any, stemmed from their employment of the master, a relationship entered into upon land.[119] In a similar case filed in the Vice-Admiralty Court in 1769, the libellant alleged that the ransom contract had been made with the owners' consent. A temporary prohibition nevertheless issued, and admiralty proceedings were halted. The action remained on the docket of the Superior Court until it was dismissed in 1777, having halted the original suit without a determination on the merits.[120]

After the American Act of 1764 had expressly extended the admiralty jurisdiction to all cases under the Acts of Trade, the only grounds for a prohibition in such a suit (other than technical jurisdictional flaws) would have been that admiralty was barred in matters arising within a county by virtue of the statutes of Richard II. No prohibition was issued in a customs case after 1764 on these or any other grounds, and, as far as can be determined, none was sought. The Superior Court presumably would have adhered to the constitutional doctrine that one act of Parliament could supersede another, and the bar, whatever the private feelings of some of its members, recognized the futility of pressing the point.

Arguments based on the acts of Richard II were made against the court in a political context, implying a view that these statutes established a fundamental right which Parliament could not abrogate.[121] It is interesting however, that in the most articulate attack on the court which Massachusetts produced, John Adams took higher ground. His argument for Hancock in the *in personam* suits arising out of the case of the sloop *Liberty*, was used for political purposes, but it probably was originally drafted for use in court. In it Adams first attacked the American Act on the ground that it was made without Hancock's consent, then argued that the provision for admiralty trial was vicious because it violated Magna Carta's requirement that no man be condemned except by a jury.[122] This was a much more telling attack on the court than one based upon the statutes of Richard II, because it focused attention not on the location of the facts, but on the nature of the suit. Proceedings without a jury which could deprive a man of his liberty or property were invalid under this theory, whatever their cause.

An analysis of the entries in the court's Minute Book between 1765 and 1772 reveals few cases in which a prohibition would have been needed. Admiralty's popularity as a forum for the trial of ordinary maritime actions, never high in this period, declined steadily as the court became more involved in political controversy. From 1765 through 1767 there were only three to five customs cases a year out of a total of 15 to 20 cases entered annually.[123] In 1768, the first full year of the Customs Commissioners' operations in Boston, 24 out of 33 entries in the Minute Book were *in rem* or *in personam* proceedings under the Acts of Trade. In 1769 there were 55 entries. Only six of them were ordinary civil cases, 21 of the remainder being prosecutions under the White Pine Acts, and the other 28, customs matters. Total entries dwindled to 13 in 1770, six of which were civil matters. The following year only two out of 17 cases entered were on the civil side. The figures for 1772 are incomplete, but through March, 16 actions had been entered, at least 10 of which were customs cases. Subsequent passage of the Tea Act and the Boston Port Act would suggest a similar pattern in the remaining years before the Revolution.[124]

Although the brevity of the entries makes a comparison with the maritime business of the common law courts difficult, it is nevertheless revealing. In 1766, a year chosen arbitrarily, but presumably one more normal than subsequent years, only six out of 21 entries in admiralty can be positively identified. There were three revenue cases, one suit under the White Pine Acts, and two actions for seaman's wages. The 15 unidentified actions in all probability were suits for wages or other relief that would not be questioned.

In the Superior Court, cases were few because the courts of the province did little or no business between November 1765 and May 1766 as a result of the Stamp Act crisis. Shipping was probably reduced somewhat by the lack of stamped paper also.[125] A check of the records for all 1766 terms in the maritime counties reveals, nevertheless, that eleven actions were heard at common law which would have been prohibited in admiralty.[126] The factors already noted for the year 1732 indicate that in 1766 the maritime business of the common law courts must have been at least twice that of the Vice-Admiralty Court.

In summary, the principal function of the Massachusetts Vice-Admiralty Court, even in its busiest period, was that of trying seamen's actions and other matters in which the common law courts could not or would not give adequate relief. In no sense did it serve all the judicial needs of a maritime community. It heard civil maritime cases in the great range which admiralty courts have traditionally claimed, but such exercises of jurisdiction were coincidental and sporadic, occurring only when the party sued failed to seek a prohibition. Probably the role of the High Court of Admiralty in England in this period was similar, even though in the eighteenth century common law domination was at its peak. The common law courts of the province filled the gap thus created, trying many more maritime cases of the kind in which the jurisdiction was contested. In the 1770's when resentment over the Vice-Admiralty Court's political role was high, its civil business disappeared almost entirely, leaving the common law in possession of the field. In short, the accepted rule in eighteenth century Massachusetts was that in civil cases the admiralty jurisdiction was limited by the statutes of Richard II, as those acts had been interpreted by the English common law courts, and that observance of the limits could be enforced by writ of prohibition from the Superior Court. Most litigants in fact preferred the common law.

There was a difference of opinion as to the jurisdiction of the

Vice-Admiralty Court in customs and revenue cases. The orthodox view as represented by the Superior Court seems to have been that, since the power of Parliament was absolute, the statutes of Richard II could not defeat later parliamentary grants of admiralty jurisdiction, even in cases arising within the body of a county. Thus, when prohibitions were issued, the court usually took the position that under the statutes involved there was no power to act in the case before it. The opposing view, which had no standing in the courts but became the position of the patriot faction in Massachusetts, was based on the theory that Parliament must yield to fundamental right. It is not clear that the statutes of Richard II were considered as embodying fundamental right, but trial by jury in cases in which the sovereign sought to deprive a man of his property certainly had this status. Thus, the grants of jurisdiction in customs cases were considered beyond the power of Parliament and became a major grievance among American patriots. This disagreement over parliamentary power was so profound that it could not be resolved in the courts. It was, in fact, one manifestation of a constitutional question which was settled only by the American Revolution.

COLONIAL AMERICA

FOOTNOTES

1. Carl Ubbelohde, *The Vice-Admiralty Courts and the American Revolution* (Chapel Hill, 1960), 63-64, 78, 142-147, 189-190, 209-211; David S. Lovejoy, "Rights Imply Equality: The Case Against Admiralty Jurisdiction in America, 1764-1776," *William and Mary Quarterly*, 3d Ser., XVI, (Oct. 1959), 466-467, 483-484.
2. DeLovio v. Boit, 7 Fed. Cas. 418, 442-443 (No. 3776) (C.C.D. Mass. 1815). See Insurance Co. v. Dunham, 78 U.S. (11 Wall.) 1, 35 (1871); Grant Gilmore and Charles L. Black, Jr., *The Law of Admiralty* (Brooklyn, 1957), 10, 19-20.
3. 13 Rich. 2, c. 5 (1389), *The Statutes at Large*, ed. Danby Pickering (Cambridge, Eng., 1762-1807), II, 312; 15 Rich. 2, c. 3 (1391), *ibid.*, 340 341. Sanctions were imposed by 2 Hen. 4, c. 11 (1400), *ibid.*, 412-413, providing an action for double damages for those sued wrongfully in admiralty, and a fine of £10 against the offender. See Sir William Holdsworth, *A History of English Law*, 7th rev. ed. (London, 1956), I, 548-549.
4. Holdsworth, *History of English Law*, I, 552-559; William Blackstone, *Commentaries on the Laws of England*, 8th ed. (Oxford, 1778), III, 106-107; Arthur Browne, *A Compendious View of the Civil Law, and of the Law of Admiralty*, 2d ed. (London, 1802), II, 71-122, 202, 208.
5. 12 Car. 2, c. 18, §1, (1660), *Statutes*, VII, 453.
6. 22 & 23 Car. 2, c. 26, §11 (1671), *Statutes*, VIII, 388. See, however, Pidgeon v. Trent, 3 Keble 640, 84 Eng. Rep. 926 (K. B. 1676) (prohibition *nisi*, where goods sold in Ireland from vessel that had not broken bulk).
7. See Lawrence A. Harper, *The English Navigation Laws* (New York, 1939), 109-115. For the practice generally, see Elizabeth E. Hoon, *The Organization of the English Customs, 1696 - 1786* (New York, 1938), 274-280. For cases showing the jury in action, see Bradley, qui tam, v. Long, Bunbury 78, 145 Eng. Rep. 601 (Exch. 1721); Attorney General v. Woodmass, Bunbury 247, 145 Eng. Rep. 662 (Exch. 1727). Actually, many minor violations were tried without a jury before Commissioners or Justices of the Peace. See Blackstone, *Commentaries*, IV, 281; Felix Frankfurter and Thomas G. Corcoran, "Petty Federal Offenses and Trial by Jury," *Harvard Law Review*, XXXIX (1926), 922-934.
8. 7 & 8 Will. 3, c. 22, §2, *Statutes*, IX, 429. See Opinion of Attorney General Northey, Aug. 21, 1702, *Opinions of Eminent Lawyers*, ed. George Chalmers (Burlington, Vt., 1858), 499-502.
9. 7 & 8 Will. 3, c. 22, §7, *Statutes*, IX, 432.
10. Provisions of 13 & 14 Car. 2, c. 11 (1662), *Statutes*, VIII, 78-94, incorporated by reference in 7 & 8 Will. 3, c. 22, §6.
11. See, for example 12 Car., c. 18, §1 (1660), *Statutes*, VII, 453 (ownership, etc. and enumerated goods in "any court of record"); 15 Car. 2, c. 7, §6 (1663), *Statutes*, VIII, 162 (illegally imported European

goods in "any of his Majesty's courts" in colonies, "any court of record" in England); 22 & 23 Car. 2, c. 26, §11 (1671), *Statutes*, VIII, 388 (enumerated goods to be seized and sued for "in any of the said plantations, in the court of the high admiral of *England*, or of any of his vice-admirals, or in any court of record in *England*"). It was presumably clear that the duties laid upon enumerated goods when shipped from one colony to another which were to be enforced "as for nonpayment of or defrauding his Majesty of his customs in *England*," could not be sued for in the colonial admiralty courts. 25 Car. 2, c. 7, §2 (1673), *Statutes*, VIII, 399. The argument against admiralty jurisdiction in the case of the first three acts cited was strengthened by the fact that they all provided for trial in a court, "wherein no essoin, protection, or wager of law shall be allowed." These procedural devices were unique to the common law, so, it was argued, the statute could refer only to a common law court. Moreover, the admiralty was not a "court of record." For these and the other arguments on both sides of the question, see Opinion of Northey, *Opinions*, ed. Chalmers, 499-502; Opinion of Sir John Cooke, July 23, 1702, *ibid.*, 504-507; Opinion of Richard West, June 20, 1720, *ibid.*, 518-519; Joseph H. Smith, *Appeals to the Privy Council* (New York, 1950), 93n, 178, 181. See also Bernhard Knollenberg, *Origin of the American Revolution* (New York, 1960), 266-267.

12. 6 Anne, c. 37, §§1-8 (1708), *Statutes*, IX, 433-438; 8 Geo. 1, c. 12, §5 (1722), *Statutes*, XIV, 387-388. The latter act was expressly incorporated in 2 Geo. 2, c. 35, §2 (1729), *Statutes*, XVI, 103-104.
13. See Smith, *Appeals*, 88-95; Charles M. Andrews, "Introduction," *Records of the Vice Admiralty Court of Rhode Island, 1716-1752*, ed. Dorothy S. Towle, *American Legal Records*, Vol. III (Washington, 1936), 9.
14. *Records of the Governor and Company of the Massachusetts Bay*, ed. Nathaniel Shurtleff, (Boston, 1854), Vol. IV, pt. II, 388-393.
15. *Ibid.*, 575.
16. See Michael G. Hall, *Edward Randolph and the American Colonies, 1676-1703* (Chapel Hill, 1960), 55-62. See also cases and other materials cited in Wroth, "Mass. Vice Admiralty Court," *American Journal of Legal History*, VI, 253-255. As to this period generally, see Helen J. Crump, *Colonial Admiralty Jurisdiction in the Seventeenth Century* (London, 1931).
17. See Hall, *Edward Randolph*, 138-171; Michael G. Hall, "The House of Lords, Edward Randolph, and the Navigation Act of 1696," *William and Mary Quarterly*, 3rd Ser., XIV (Oct. 1957), 494-515; Smith, *Appeals*, 90, 183n, 184-185; Wroth, "Mass. Vice Admiralty Court." *American Journal of Legal History*, VI, 257-259.
18. See Hall, *Edward Randolph*, 100-111; Wroth, "Mass. Vice Admiralty Courts," *American Journal of Legal History*, *VI*, 255-257.
19. See Richard S. Dunn, *Puritans and Yankees* (Princeton, 1962), 269-281; Wroth, "Mass. Vice Admiralty Court," *American Journal of Legal History*, VI, 259-261, 263.

20. By virtue of a "saving clause" in the jurisdictional statute cited in note 15 above. See Zechariah Chafee, Jr., "Introduction," *Records of the Suffolk County Court, 1671-1680*, Colonial Society of Massachusetts, *Publications*, XXIX (1933), lxxii-lxxiv.

21 .See *Winthrop Papers*, Vol. VI, Massachusetts Historical Society, *Collections*, 6th Ser., V (1892), 98-99, 101; *Calendar of State Papers, Colonial, 1701* (London, 1910), §§974, 1122 ii, iii, vi; Records of the Superior Court of Judicature, 1700-1714, fols. 70, 84, 100 (MS volumes in the office of the Clerk of the Supreme Judicial Court for Suffolk County, Boston, Mass.; hereinafter Superior Court of Judicature will be abbreviated "S.C.J."). Wait Winthrop tried several customs cases. See *Winthrop Papers*, Vol. IV, Massachusetts Historical Society, *Collections*, 5th Ser., VIII (1882), 562; *Cal. State Papers, Col., 1699*, §890; *ibid., 1700*, §953 xxv. Thomas Newton had both customs and prize cases. *Cal. State Papers, Col., 1702-1703*, §§301, 543. See also Philopolites, *Memorial on the Present Deplorable State of New England* (Boston, 1707), 26, facsimile in *Sewall Papers*, Vol. II, Massachusetts Historical Society, *Collections*, 5th Ser., VI (1879), 55*.

22. See Marguerite Appleton, "Rhode Island's First Court of Admiralty," *New England Quarterly*, V (1932), 151-157; *Cal. State Papers, Col., 1704-1705*, §§1274 xvi, 1300, 1424; *ibid., 1706-1708*, §§ 511, 553 i.

23. *Cal. State Papers, Col., 1706-1708*, §535. See also Byfield's similar remark, *ibid., 1704-1705*, §884.

24. Philopolites, *Memorial*, 27, *Sewall Papers*, II 55*; *Cal. State Papers, Col., 1704-1705*, §1 iv; Andrews, "Introduction," *R. I. Vice Admiralty Records*, 27n.

25. See Patterson v. Dixon, Massachusetts Vice Admiralty File Papers, Nos. 1d-3d (1715); Fix v. Skeel, *ibid.*, No. 4d (1716); John Noble, "A Few Notes on Admiralty Jurisdiction in the Colony and Province of Massachusetts Bay," Colonial Society of Massachusetts, *Publications*, VIII (1906), 167; Robert Moody, "The Last Voyage of the *Province* Galley," *ibid.*, XXXII (1934), 131. Cases concerning drift whales also were heard in the court's early days. See Andrews, "Introduction," *R. I. Vice Admiralty Records*, 72-73.

26. The volumes are entitled as follows: Court of Admiralty Records, 1718 to 1726 Vol. II; Court of Admiralty Records 1726 to 1733 Vol. III; Court of Admiralty Records 1740-1745 Vol. V; Admiralty Book of Accts. of Sales; Court of Vice Admiralty Province of Massachusetts Bay AD 1765 to 1772. The few surviving file papers, ranging from 1715 to 1754, are found in separate envelopes numbered 1d-22d. The materials will be cited in the following manner: 2, 3, 5 Mass. Adm. Recs.; Mass. Adm. Min. Bk.; Mass. Adm. Acct. Bk.; Mass. Adm. Pap. For the history of the Massachusetts records, see Noble "Notes", Colonial Society of Massachusetts, *Publications*, VIII, 169. A thin volume in the Price papers at the Boston Athenaeum, containing receipts for the

proceeds of vessels seized and sold by the court in 1772 and 1773, is of some value in the interpretation of the Minute Book.

27. Josiah Quincy, Jr., *Reports of Cases Argued and Adjudged in the Superior Court of Judicature*, Samuel Quincy, ed. (Boston, 1865), 169. See Story's own account of his losses in a copy of his petition for relief to the Crown in the files of the Superior Court. Suffolk County Early Court Files, No. 102146. (MS in the office of the Clerk of the Supreme Judicial Court for Suffolk County, Boston, Mass.). A tradition that the remaining Massachusetts papers were carried off to Halifax or England in 1776 by the departing loyalists has never been verified. Quincy, *Reports* 387n; *Reports of Cases in the Vice Admiralty of the Province of New York*, ed. Charles M. Hough (New Haven, 1925), 257.
28. See Judge Lowell's scholarly opinion in *The Underwriter*, 119 Fed. 713 (D.C. Mass. 1902); see also Noble, "Notes," Colonial Society of Massachusetts, *Publications*, VIII, 170-185.
29. Francis Clerke, *Praxis Curiae Admiralitatis Angliae*, Latin and English ed. (London 1722), tits. 1-24, 31-32; see T. L. Mears, "The History of the Admiralty Jurisdiction," *Select Essays in Anglo-American Legal History* (Boston, 1908), II, 343-349. As to use in the colonies see Anthony Stokes, *A View of the Constitution of the British Colonies in North America* (London, 1783), 271. The Harvard Law School Library's copy of the 1722 edition reputedly belonged to John Adams. Clerke's was the standard work on admiralty practice until the publication in 1798 of the first edition of Browne's *Civil Law*. See Holdsworth, *History of English Law*, XII, 628; compare Blackstone, *Commentaries*, III, 108n.
30. Browne, *Civil Law*, *II*, 396-404. See Mears, "History of Admiralty," *Select Essays*, II, 349-352n.
31. Browne, *Civil Law*, II, 403-428. See Fell v. *The Dorothy*, Burrell 9, 167 Eng. Rep. 447 (High Ct. Adm. 1766).
32. See *N. Y. Vice Admiralty Reports*, ed. Hough, xiii, 218n; Frederick B. Wiener, "Notes on the Rhode Island Admiralty, 1727-1790," *Harvard Law Review*, XLVI (Nov. 1932), 44; Andrews, "Introduction," *R. I. Vice Admiralty Records*, 15-16.
33. See Burrell 231, 167 Eng. Rep. 549.
34. For the High Court terminology, see Browne, *Civil Law*, II, 395-430; Voguel v. Tomlinson, Burrell 314, 167 Eng. Rep. 588 (High Ct. Adm. 1734).
35. While security for appearance may have been a part of the procedure in Massachusetts, only three cases in Volume III of the records refer to bond of any kind. D'Carteret v. Chevalier, 3 Mass. Adm. Recs. 72b (1730); Powell v. Walker, *ibid.*, 37b, 40b (1728); Grace v. Cunningham, *ibid.*, 49a (1728).
36. See Rex. v. Brig't *Mary*, *ibid.*, 22b (1727); Rex. v. Norton, note 78 below; Dunbar v. Wyre, 3 Mass. Adm. Recs. 79a (1730). Of greater significance to the jurisdiction were appeals to the Privy Council from the common law courts on prohibitions. See Andrews, "Introduction,"

R. I. Vice Admiralty Records, 20-24, 73n; Wiener, "Notes," *Harvard Law Review*, XLVI, 49-50; Smith, *Appeals*, 90-92, 177-192, 514-520; Knollenberg, *Origin*, 267-268.

37. From 1718 to 1733, out of 647 actions entered in the court, 263 were for wages, and 101 concerned other claims by and against seamen. For the common law practice, see Charles Molloy, *De Jure Maritimo et Navali*, 6th ed. (London, 1707), bk. 2, c. 6, §8; Browne, *Civil Law*, II, 103-105, 157.

38. See, for example, Tregoe v. Rodier, 3 Mass. Adm. Recs. 134a (1733) (wages not yet due; seaman to continue voyage and jailed as security for his doing so); Lewis v. Russell, *ibid.*, 83b (1730) (articles not sufficiently clear as to voyage, as required by statute; crew to proceed only on voyage now planned); Sailors v. Guy, *ibid.*, 93a, 93b (1731) (half wages decreed; crew to continue); Moulton v. Sailors, *ibid.*, 84a (1730) (master's action for neglect of duty; wages ordered to be paid and crew to proceed); Fonds v. Sailors, *ibid.*, 83a (1730) (crew jailed after refusing to obey court's order to proceed); Marlow v. Gutteridge, *ibid.*, 6b (1726) (seaman's libel against master for "pinching and starving"); Rex v. Winkley, *ibid.*, 39b (1720) (master fined for ill-treating and stranding seaman); Pitcher v. Sailors, *ibid.*, 100b (1731) (mutiny; wages forfeit and crew jailed for 48 hours). There was extensive statutory regulation of these relationships. See, for example, 7 & 8 Will. 3, c. 21 (1696), *Statutes*, IX, 419-428. See also Molloy, *De Jure*, bk. 2, c. 3, §12; Browne, *Civil Law*, II, 202.

39. Rex v. The *Mary* Galley, 3 Mass. Adm. Recs. 52b (1728); Read v. The *Mary* Galley, *ibid.*, 53a; Sailors v. Read, *ibid.*, 54b. The form of execution in the case of Serjant v. Coffin, set out at length in the records, *ibid.*, 23b, makes clear that *in personam* decrees were executed against the defendant's person only.

40. See, for example, The Sloop *Ann*, *ibid.*, 63a, 63b (1729); Byrn v. Ship *Rebecca*, *ibid.*, 135a (1733). Compare Sloley v. Watson, *ibid.*, 91a (1731); Mackie v. Powell, *ibid.*, 129b, 130a (1733).

41. For example, The Sloop *Rainbow*, *ibid.*, 9a (1726). Compare Sailors v. Ship *Oistin's* Wreck, *ibid.*, 73a, 74b-76a (1730) (wages and salvage).

42. Chamberlain v. Sloop *Hannah*, *ibid.*, 89a (1730) (proceeds subject first to wages, then to common law judgment).

43. Sailors v. Pepperill, *ibid.*, 87b (1730).

44. Molloy, *De Jure*, bk. 1, c. 6, §12; bk. 2, c. 1, §§2, 11; Browne, *Civil Law*, II, 114-118. See Adams v. Crouch, Burrell 110, 167 Eng. Rep. 496 (High Ct. Adm. 1771); Meeke v. The *Lord Holland*, Burrell 145, 167 Eng. Rep. 513 (High Ct. Adm. 1774).

45. For possessory actions, see Fairweather v. Lupton, 3 Mass. Adm. Recs. 30b (1727); Littlefield v. Webber, *ibid.*, 143a (1733).

46. Molloy, *De Jure*, bk. 2, c. 1, §3; Browne, *Civil Law*, II, 131-132.

47. Ousten v. Hebden, 1 Wils. K. B. 101, 95 Eng. Rep. 515 (K. B. 1745); Dimmick v. Chandler, Fitz-G. 197, 94 Eng. Rep. 717 (K. B. 1730).

48. McLeister v. Brigantine *Victory*, 3 Mass. Adm. Recs. 63a (1729). See also Pilkington v. Monk & Marsh, *ibid.*, 142b. (1733).
49. There are, however, cases in which the court awarded the eighteenth century equivalent of maintenance and cure — "doctor's bill and sickness charges." Maddox v. Russell, 3 Mass. Adm. Recs. 93a (1731); See Molloy, *De Jure*, bk. 2, c. 3, §2; Andrews, "Introduction," *R. I. Vice Admiralty Records*, 31.
50. See, for example, Rex v. Harlow, 3 Mass. Adm. Recs. 3b (1726); Wingfield v. Lobb, *ibid.*, 68b (1729); Webber v. Tresahon, *ibid.*, 108a (1732); Adv. Gen. v. Ingerson, *ibid.*, 31a (1727).
51. *Ibid.*, 62a (1729). If the action were purely civil in nature, the only relief which the Vice-Admiralty Court would grant was an award of wages and liberation from the articles. Wills v. Legall, *ibid.*, 35b (1728); see Rex v. Winkley, *ibid.*, 39b. The common law, however, allowed to the admiralty *in personam* suits for assault at sea as an exception to the usual restrictions. Browne, *Civil Law*, *II*, 109-110. The Massachusetts court on occasion refused to act in other cases with a maritime flavor that were clearly common law causes of action. See Savage v. Davies, 3 Mass. Adm. Recs. 47a (1728) (defamation of marshal by bringing unfounded suit for taking exorbitant fees, "if actionable is alterius fori to redress").
52. Patten v. Dockes, *ibid.*, 40a (1728). See Browne, *Civil Law*, II, 110-111; Molloy, *De Jure*, bk. 2, c. 2, §2; Andrews, "Introduction," *R. I. Vice Admiralty Court Records*, 31.
53. Newman v. Mackidon, 3 Mass. Adm. Recs. 10b (1727). See also Scandrett v. Matthews, *ibid.*, 5b (1726); McClean v. Barrick, *ibid.*, 66a (1729); Westcott v. Young, *ibid.*, 82b (1730). In a case involving a misappropriated cable and anchor, return of the property in specie was awarded. Sailors v. Hewson, *ibid.*, 103a (1731).
54. See Browne, *Civil Law*, II, 80, 84-85, 196; Molloy, *De Jure*, bk. 2, c. 11, §11; Johnson v. Shippen, 2 Ld. Raym. 982, 92 Eng. Rep. 154 (Q. B. 1703).
55. 3 Mass. Adm. Recs. 106a (1732). For the libel, see Suff. Files, No. 33260. As to actions on performance bonds, see *Select Pleas in the Court of Admiralty*, Vol. I, ed. Reginald G. Marsden, Selden Society, *Publications*. VI (1892), lxxii; Molloy, *De Jure*, bk. 1, c. 6, §12; bk. 2, c. 4, §4. See also Johnson v. Shippen, note 54 above.
56. Wakefield v. Cloude, 3 Mass. Adm. Recs. 96b (1731). See Parker v. Sloop *Hester and Hannah*, *ibid.*, 97b (1731); Gibbs v. Ship *Christiana*, *ibid.*, 110a (1732); Wells v. Sloop *Molly*, *ibid.*, 145b (1733). For the common law position see Molloy, *De Jure*, bk. 1, c. 6, §12; bk. 2, c. 3, §8, Browne, *Civil Law*, II, 80; Justin v. Ballam, 2 Ld. Raym. 805, 92 Eng. Rep. 38 (K. B. 1702).
57. See cases cited in note 41 above. See also Benjamin v. Smith, 3 Mass. Adm. Recs. 63b (1729). For the common law position, see Molloy, *De Jure*, bk. 1, c. 6, §12; Browne, *Civil Law*, II, 87; Gilmore and Black, *Admiralty*, 512-513.

58. Jones v. Mountfort, 3 Mass. Adm. Recs. 114a (1732); Powell v. Walker, *ibid.*, 40b (1728). See Molloy, *De Jure*, bk. 2, c. 1, §4; *ibid.*, c. 2, §15; Adams v. Crouch, note 44 above.
59. Alfrey v. The Snow *Charming Molly*, 3 Mass. Adm. Recs. 86a (1730). See Gilmore and Black, *Admiralty*, 15.
60. Cheever v. Willey, 3 Mass. Adm. Recs. 19b (1727) (charter party); Bowdoin v. Wills, *ibid.*, 123b (1733) (cargo); Manning v. Cresty, *ibid.*, 148a (*1733*) (passage contract). Pierce v. Dutch, *ibid.*, 103b (1731) (pilotage). However, the court refused to grant relief against the drawee of a bill of exchange given to seamen for their wages. Sailors v. Apthorp, *ibid.*, 109a (1732).
61. See note 2 above. The records of the colonial common law courts contain many actions on marine insurance policies. See, for example, cases cited in note 126 below. As to similar English practice, see *Select Pleas in the Court of Admiralty*, Vol. II, ed. Reginald G. Marsden, Selden Society, *Publications*, XI (1897), lxxx; Molloy, *De Jure*, bk. 2, c. 8, §18, *et. seq.*
62. There were 105 such actions out of 647 entered in the court between 1718 and 1733.
63. See William Hawkins, *A Treatise of the Pleas of the Crown*, 4th ed. (London, 1762), Vol. II, c. 26, §17.
64. See, for example, Jekyll v. Powes, 3 Mass. Adm. Recs. 15a (1726) (fine for refusal to answer collector's questions as to ownership of goods shipped); Rex v. Brigantine *Friendship* and Cargo, *ibid.*, 4b (1726) (sugar, cotton, and pimiento forfeit for non-payment of duties at Jamaica; ship discharged in view of circumstances); Jekyll v. Brandy, *ibid.*, 103b (1731) (French brandy and cloth forfeit as illegally imported); Jekyll v. *Mary* Galley, *ibid.*, 52b (1731) (vessel condemned for lack of register); Jekyll v. *Serving Mallet* and 78 Casks of Molasses, *ibid.*, 94b (1731) (foreign-built, unregistered vessel condemned).
65. See, for example, Dunbar v. Urin, *ibid.*, 78b (1730); Dunbar v. Wyre, *ibid.*, 79a (1730).
66. See, for example, Jekyll v. Belcher, *ibid.*, 87b (1730) (plea overruled in case of seizure of unlawfully imported goods in claimant's house); Jekyll v. Brig. *James and Mary* and Cargo, *ibid.*, 118a (1732) (plea overruled in case of illegally imported goods under 15 Car. 2, c. 7, §6; jurisdiction supported by language of Act — "any court" — and under 7 & 8 Will. 3, c. 22); Lambert v. Schooner *Society*, *ibid.*, 110a (1732) (plea asserting that importation was within the body of a county overruled, but information dismissed because vessel entered port in distress).
67. See, for example, Lambert v. Ship *True Love*, *ibid.*, 28a (1727) (suit for having foreign crew dismissed on showing of necessity); Fairfax v. Ship *St. Cecilia*, *ibid.*, 145a (1733) (suit for not having register dismissed because no fraud intended; master to give bond to obtain register); Lambert v. Schooner *Society*, note 66 above.
68. See, for example, The Ship *Rebecca*, *ibid.*, 122a, 123b (1732) (average); Sailors v. Wellington, *ibid.*, 70-72a (1729) (salvage); Nich-

oll's Petition, *ibid.*, 27a (1727) (survey); Advocate General v. Anchor, *ibid.*, 38b (1728) (droits of admiralty); Sergeant v. Glover, *ibid.*, 11a (1727) (whale). As to droits of admiralty, see Holdsworth, *History of English Law*, I, 559-561.

69. As to prize generally, see Holdsworth, *History of English Law*, I, 563-564. For the colonial practice, see Andrews, "Introduction," *R.I. Vice Admiralty Records*, 35-42. A few Massachusetts cases appear in "Volume V" of the records.

70. Rex v. Snow *Elizabeth*, 3 Mass. Adm. Recs. 1a (1726). See note 116 below.

71. Similar conclusions have been reached about the practice in other vice admiralty courts. See *N. Y. Vice Admiralty Reports*, ed. Hough, xviii; Wiener, "Notes," *Harvard Law Review*, XLVI, 44; Andrews, "Introduction," *R. I. Vice Admiralty Records*, 2, 67.

72. *The Underwriter*, 119 Fed. 713, at 735-736 (D. C. Mass. 1902). Our knowledge of the High Court's eighteenth-century practice is incomplete, but see Fairless v. Thorsen, Burrell 130, 167 Eng. Rep. 506 (High Ct. Adm. 1774); Mackenzie v. Ogilvie, Burrell 134, 138, 167 Eng. Rep. 508 (High Ct. Adm. 1774); See Browne's similar view, with examples from his experience in admiralty in Ireland, 1795-1799, where the prohibition was less frequently used than in England. Browne, *Civil Law*, II, 71-72, 122, 530-557. Admiralty defied the common law in the seventeenth century also. See Holdsworth, *History of English Law*, I, 556-557; *Select Pleas*, Marsden ed., Vol. II, lxxix.

73. See DeLovio v. Boit, note 2 above. Early uses of the writ in Massachusetts have already been mentioned. See note 21 above. As to the colonies generally, see Andrews, "Introduction," *R. I. Vice Admiralty Records*, 70-75. In 1720, Richard West, counsel to the Board of Trade, expressly held that the statutes of Richard II extended to the colonies and could be the basis of prohibitions there. *Opinions*, ed. Chalmers, 515-518.

74. Jeremiah Dummer, *A Defense of the New England Charters* (London, 1721), 49-54. Compare Scollay v. Dunn, Quincy, *Reports*, 82 (S.C.J. 1763). The leading maritime treatise used in the colonies made explicit reference to the common law's victory over admiralty. Molloy, *De Jure*, xv-xvi. See Smith, *Appeals*, 514-515.

75. See Best v. Bath, 3 Mass. Adm. Recs. 8b (1726); Wylie v. Perkins, *ibid.*, 69b (1729), Recs. S.C.J. 1725-1730, fol. 338 (1730); Bethune v. Shaw, 3 Mass. Adm. Recs. 43b (1728), Recs. S.C.J. 1725-1730, fol. 182 (1728); Rex v. Burden, 3 Mass. Adm. Recs. 43a (1728).

76. 3 Mass. Adm. Recs. 56a (1728); Recs. S.C.J. 1725-1729, fol. 326 (1730); Suff. Files, Nos. 29775, 30199. For the common law view, see Browne, *Civil Law*, II, 86, 96-97. Compare Gawne v. Grandee, Holt 49, 90 Eng. Rep. 925 (Q. B. 1706).

77. Norton v. Jekyll, Recs. S.C.J. 1725-1730, fol. 184 (Suffolk Co., Sept. 1728). The information was never formally entered in the admiralty records. It, the suggestion, and the mate's testimony are in Suff. Files, No. 21957.

78. Rex v. Norton, 3 Mass. Adm. Recs. 48a. See Suff. Files, No. 164598. The contents of the information are recited in the second suggestion, discussed, note 79 below. Norton (the master) appealed, apparently to the High Court of Admiralty, but failed to prosecute and forfeited his bond. Jekyll v. Norton, 3 Mass. Adm. Recs. 66a (1729).

79. Norton v. Jekyll, Recs. S.C.J. 1725-1729, fol. 214 (Bristol Co., Sept. 1728). See the suggestion in Suff. Files, No. 21957. See also Suff. Files, No. 164596. There was authority to the effect that no prohibition lay after a decree in the admiralty or in favor of one who had pleaded there. Molloy, *De Jure*, bk. 1, c. 6, §12. The Superior Court seems to have issued prohibitions after decree in other cases, however. See Gray v. Travisa, note 76 above.

80. Bardin v. Lambert, Recs. S.C.J. 1730-1733, fol. 135 (Suffolk Co., March 1732). This information was also never formally entered in admiralty records. See a copy of it in Suff. Files, No. 33539. Lambert, the comptroller of the port of Boston, proceeded against Bardin in the Superior Court, in one of the few such actions found in the Suffolk Files. The proceedings were apparently based on the practice of the Exchequer in revenue cases. Before trial, the vessel was taken and appraised under a warrant of appraisement. After a verdict that the master was "guilty," judgment of forfeiture was entered for the comptroller. See cases cited in note 7 above, and Johnson, qui tam, v. Sower, Bunbury 30, 145 Eng. Rep. 585 (Exch. 1718). The Superior Court had Exchequer powers by statute. Act of 26 June 1699, c. 3, §1, *Acts and Resolves of the Province of Massachusetts Bay*, ed. Ames and Goodell (Boston, 1869-1922), I, 370. After judgment, the crew came into court seeking their wages, and the court ordered a sale of the vessel, declaring the proceeds liable for wages and costs. Lambert prevailed on review before a second jury, and Bardin appealed to the Privy Council with a result that is not known. Recs. S. C. J. 1730-1733, fol. 202 (Suffolk Co., Aug. 1732); fol. 238 (Suffolk Co., Feb. 1733); Suff. Files, No. 34701. See the common law information, warrant of appraisement, Bardin's unsuccessful prayer for a writ of delivery and numerous depositions, in Suff. Files, Nos. 33654, 33657, 33674, 33837, 33896, 33914, 34045, 34443, 34455.

81. Bardin v. Durrell, Recs. S.C.J. 1730-1733, fol. 272 (Suffolk Co., March 1733); Minute Book No. 19, Suffolk Superior Court of Judicature, Aug. 1733, continued No. 13. (MS in the office of the Clerk of the Supreme Judicial Court for Suffolk County, Boston, Mass.). The suggestion, quoted in the text, appears in Suff. Files, No. 35687. The information is in *ibid.*, No. 34484. For the admiralty proceedings, see Durrell v. Bardin, 3 Mass. Adm. Recs. 126b (1732). The statute involved was 6 Anne, c. 37, §10 (1708), *Statutes*, XI, 438. Apparently the same Richard Bardin was involved in this action and in Lambert v. Bardin, note 80 above, but the incidents seem to be unrelated.

82. The Privy Council's 1743 decision in Kennedy v. Sloop *Mary and Margaret*, upholding a prohibition to the New York Court of Vice Admiralty in a case of unlawful importation of European goods under 15

Car. 2, c. 7, similarly seems to have turned on a construction of the jurisdictional grant in that act (note, 11 above) as not conveying jurisdiction to the admiralty. See Smith, *Appeals*, 515-517; compare Knollenberg, *Origin*, 267-268. As to the power of Parliament, see Blackstone, *Commentaries*, I, 90-91; J. W. Gough, *Fundamental Law in English Constitutional History* (Oxford, 1961), 174-191; Edward McWhinney, *Judicial Review in the English-Speaking World*, 2d ed. (Toronto, 1960) 31-48. Beginning with 3 & 4 Vict., c. 65 (1840), Parliament passed a series of statutes extending the civil jurisdiction of admiralty to cover most matters, whether arising at sea or on land, traditionally considered to be within the court's competence. See Gilmore and Black, *Admiralty*, 10.

83. Palatines v. Lobb, note 55 above (performance bond); Gibbs v. Ship *Christiana*, note 56 above (materialman's suit; settled); Jones v. Mountfort, note 58 above (part-ownership); Parrot v. Sloop *Carolina*, 3 Mass. Adm. Recs. 110a (1732) (average); The Ship *Rebecca*, note 68 above (average).

84. Baptist de la Place v. Boutineau, Recs. S.C.J. 1730-1733, fol. 178 (master's contract); Gould v. Jepson, *ibid.*, fol. 217 (ships' necessaries); Bath v. Clark, *ibid.*, fol. 219 (ships' necessaries); Barrell v. Stoddard, *ibid.*, fol. 184 (loan secured by vessel); Dupé v. Stoddard, *ibid.*, fol. 179 (conversion of vessel); Elliot v. Ellery, *ibid.*, fol. 199 (conversion of cargo); Atkinson v. Ingersoll, *ibid.*, fol. 202 (conversion of part interest in a vessel); Gunter v. Pym, *ibid.*, fol. 194 (enticing away seamen); Tilley v. Bowers, *ibid.*, fol. 218 (contract for work on a vessel under construction). See also Lambert v. Bardin, note 80 above, in which the court ordered a vessel to be sold after condemnation under the Acts of Trade, in order to satisfy the crew's claim for its wages.

85. The Inferior Court minute books for 1732 are missing, but a comparison of the Inferior Court dockets found in the legal papers of John Adams and the Minute Books of the Superior Court indicates that in 1769 the Inferior Court had 1037 cases in its four terms in Suffolk County, while the Superior Court, sitting twice in the same county, had only 258 cases. Adams Papers, Microfilms, Reel 184; Min. Bk., Suffolk S.C.J., March and Aug. 1769.

86. Molasses Act, Geo. 2, c. 13, §3 (1733), *Statutes*, XVI, 375. See Knollenberg, *Origin*, 138-149; Thomas C. Barrow, "The Colonial Customs Service, 1660-1775" (Harvard Univ. doctoral dissertation, 1961), ch. VII. The apparent collapse of the court reflected in the fact that only four cases appear in Volume V for the years 1745-1747 may be illusory. A number of pages at the end of the volume are taken up with orders and plans relating to the Louisburg expedition of 1745, suggesting the possibility that the court may have done some business that was recorded elsewhere.

87. See Lawrence H. Gipson, *The British Empire before the American Revolution* (New York, 1961), X, 111-131. The course of British trade policy as reflected in the history and development of colonial

customs regulation is admirably summarized in Barrow, "Colonial Customs". The new policy in 1760 provoked a series of common law actions against the officers of the vice-admiralty courts and the customs-service, in which damages for their role in enforcement were sought. James Otis' famous argument against the issuance of writs of assistance was a further consequence. See Gipson, *British Empire*, X, 111-131; Barrow, "Colonial Customs," 357-358; Quincy, *Reports*, 541-556; Petition of Lechmere, *Legal Papers of John Adams*, ed. L. Kinvin Wroth and Hiller B. Zobel (Cambridge, Mass., in press), Case No. 44 (S.C.J. 1761); hereinafter *Legal Papers of John Adams*.

88. 4 Geo. 3, c. 15 (1764), *Statutes*, XXVI, 33-52. The admiralty provivisions are in §§41-47, *ibid.*, 44-52. Offenses in England were to be tried in the Exchequer under §40, *ibid.*, 44. See Barrow, "Colonial Customs," 376 - 390; Knollenberg, *Origin*, 150 - 152, 176 - 181; Ubbelohde, *Vice-Admiralty Courts*, 44-54. Appeals from the provincial courts were given to the new superior court by a provision of the Stamp Act, 5 Geo. 3, c. 12, §58 (1765), *Statutes*, XXVI, 202-203.

89. See Knollenberg, *Origin*, 135-137. Robert G. Albion, *Forests and Sea Power* (Cambridge, Mass., 1926), 253.

90. The Stamp Act, 5 Geo. 3, c. 12, §58 (1765), *Statutes*, XXVI, 202-203. Repeal was effected in 6 Geo. 3, c. 52 (1766), *Statutes*, XXVII, 275-287. See Barrow, "Colonial Customs," 443-444.

91. The Townshend Acts, 7 Geo. 3, c. 41, c. 46 (1767), *Statutes*, XXVII, 447-449, 505-512. The new admiralty courts were established pursuant to 8 Geo. 3, c. 22 (1767), *ibid.*, XXVIII, 70-71. See Ubbelohde, *Vice-Admiralty Courts*, 130-133.

92. 10 Geo. 3, c. 17 (1770), *Statutes*, XXVIII, 294-295.

93. Tea Act, 13 Geo. 3, c. 44 (1773), *Statutes*, XXX, 74-77; see Benjaman W. Labaree, *The Boston Tea Party* (New York, 1964), 70-73, 126-127. Boston Port Act, 14 Geo. 3, c. 19 (1774), *Statutes*, XXX, 336-341. For other repressive legislation of this period, see John C. Miller, *Origins of the American Revolution* (Palo Alto, 1959), 355-376. For the later legislation, see 15 Geo. 3, c. 10 (1775), *Statutes*, XXXI, 4-11; 15 Geo. 3, c. 18 (1775), *ibid.*, 37-43; 16 Geo. 3, c. 5 (1776), *ibid.*, 135-154. See generally Arthur M. Schlesinger, *The Colonial Merchants and the American Revolution* (New York, 1918), 538-540. For the colonial reaction to the admiralty jurisdiction generally, see sources cited in note 1 above.

94. Doane v. Gage, *Legal Papers of John Adams*, Case No. 43 (V. Adm. 1768); Sewall v. Hancock, *ibid.*, Case No. 46 (V. Adm. 1769); Rex v. Corbet, *ibid.*, Case No. 56 (Special Ct. Adm. 1769); Rex v. Nickerson, *ibid.*, Case No. 57 (Special Ct. Adm. 1773). That the bar considered a knowledge of the civil law part of a well-trained lawyer's equipment appears from Adams' own early studies. See *Diary and Autobiography of John Adams*, ed. Lyman Butterfield *et al.* (Cambridge, Mass., 1961), I, 44, 55-57, 173-174. See also *ibid.*, II, 56.

95. Sewall v. Hancock, *Legal Papers of John Adams*, Case No. 46 (V. Adm. 1769).
96. Dawson v. Sloop *Dolphin*, *ibid.*, Case No. 51 (V. Adm. 1772); Harrison v. Schooner *Chance*, Mass. Adm. Min. Bk., 10 March 1769. In Harrison v. Sloop *Liberty*, *ibid.*, 22 June 1768, negotiations between owner John Hancock and the customs officers for a stipulation fell through. See Sewall v. Hancock, *Legal Papers of John Adams*, Case No. 46.
97. Surveyor General v. Logs, *ibid.*, Case No. 55 (V. Adm. 1773). See Browne, *Civil Law*, II, 362.
98. Doane v. Gage, *Legal Papers of John Adams*, Case No. 43 (V. Adm. 1768).
99. Folger v. Sloop *Cornelia*, *ibid.*, Case No. 45 (V. Adm. 1768); Sewall v. Hancock, *ibid.*, Case No. 46 (V. Adm. 1769); Harrison v. Sloop *Liberty*, Mass. Adm. Min. Bk., 22 June 1768.
100. Folger v. Sloop *Cornelia*, *Legal Papers of John Adams*, Case No. 45 (V. Adm. 1768); Dawson v. Sloop *Dolphin*, *ibid.*, Case No. 51 (V. Adm. 1772); Dawson v. Lighter and Molasses, Suff. Files, No. 101809, Mass. Adm. Min. Bk., 22 April 1768.
101. Mass. Adm. Min. Bk., 25 March 1769. As to his appointment, see Ubbelohde, *Vice-Admiralty Courts*, 133-140.
102. Surveyor General v. Logs, Mass. Adm. Min. Bk., 1 May 1769; *Legal Papers of John Adams*, Case No. 54. See also Dawson v. Sloop *Dolphin*, *ibid.*, Case No. 51 (V. Adm. 1772).
103. Cutt v. Meservey, Mass. Adm. Min. Bk., 23 Jan. 1772; Baker v. Meservey, *ibid.*, 9 March 1772. See *Diary and Autobiography of John Adams*, II, 56; Ubbelohde, *Vice-Admiralty Courts*, 157.
104. Bishop v. Brig *Freemason*, Quincy. *Reports*, 387 (V. Adm. 1763); The *Freemason* v. Bishop, Burrell 55, 167 Eng. Rep. 469 (High Ct. Adm. 1767).
105. Folger v. Sloop *Cornelia*, Mass. Adm. Min. Bk., 4 Feb., 12 Feb. 1768; *Legal Papers of John Adams*, Case No. 45 (V. Adm. 1768).
106. Surveyor General v. Logs, *ibid.*, Case No. 55 (V. Adm. 1773); *Acts of the Privy Council of England*, *Colonial Series*, ed. James Munro (London, 1908-1912), Vol. V, §304.
107. Of 175 entries in the Minute Book, eight have been identified as wage actions and 50 are unidentified, but presumably are other civil actions.
108. Doane v. Gage, Mass. Adm. Min. Bk., 6 Jan., 28 Nov. 1768; *Legal Papers of John Adams*, Case No. 43.
109. Folger v. Sloop *Cornelia*, Mass. Adm. Min. Bk., 4 Feb. 1768; Harrison v. Sloop *Cornelia*, *ibid.*, 12 Feb. 1768; *Legal Papers of John Adams*, Case No. 45.
110. Harrison v. Sloop *Liberty*, Mass. Adm. Min. Bk., 22 June 1768. It has been argued that the *Liberty* was condemned for the technical violation of having loaded oil and tar without giving the required bond. No bond had been given, because the goods were only being stored in the vessel. Oliver M. Dickerson, *The Navigation Acts and*

the American Revolution (Philadelphia, 1951), 237-238. The fact that the oil and tar were released when the vessel was condemned, and that this factor was not mentioned in contemporary accounts, indicate that the actual cause of condemnation was the more serious offense of unloading wine before entry. See *Boston Post-Boy*, 22 Aug., 1768; *Legal Papers of John Adams*, Case No. 46, note 21.

111. Sewall v. Hancock, Mass. Adm. Min. Bk., 29 Oct. 1768; *Legal Papers of John Adams*, Case No. 46. Accounts of the trial with accompanying criticisms appeared in "A Journal of the Times," a running narrative of events in Boston from the patriot standpoint, which was published in various newspapers. The "Journal" has been printed in full in *Boston under Military Rule, 1768-1769*, ed. Oliver M. Dickerson (Boston, 1936). As to the long-range effect of this and other cases on the admiralty jurisdiction, see sources cited in note 1 above.

112. See Dowse v. 33 Hogsheads of Molasses, *Legal Papers of John Adams*, Case No. 47 (V. Adm. 1768) (landing without payment of duties); Sheaffe v. Brigantine *Triton*, *ibid.*, Case No. 48 (V. Adm. 1768) (unloading before entry); Dowse v. 19 Casks of Molasses, *ibid.*, Case No. 49 (V. Adm. 1768) (landing without warrant and payment of duties); Butler v. Brig *Union*, *ibid.*, Case No. 50 (V. Adm. 1769) (unloading before entry; authority of locally commissioned officer); Dawson v. Sloop *Dolphin*, *ibid.*, Case No. 51 (V. Adm. 1772), (failure to endorse change of ownership on register); Dawson v. Schooner *Jenny*, *ibid.*, Case No. 52 (V. Adm. 1773) (importation of European goods not loaded in England).

113. Surveyor General v. Logs., *ibid.*, Case No. 55 (V. Adm. 1773).

114. Ross' Case, *ibid.*, Case No. 53 (V. Adm. 1774).

115. De La Touche v. Brigantine *Industry*, (V. Adm. Sept. 1775). File papers in the case, including the decree, are in National Archives Microcopy No. 162, "The Revolutionary War Prize Cases: Records of the Court of Appeals in Cases of Capture, 1776-1787," Case No. 30, Docs. 37-58. See Penhallow v. Brigantine *Lusanna*, *Legal Papers of John Adams*, Case No. 58, (N.H. Ct. Maritime, 1777).

116. 11 & 12 Will. 3, c. 7 (1700), *Statutes*, X, 320-326, made perpetual by 6 Geo. 1, c. 19, §3 (1719), *ibid.*, XIV, 260-261. See also 28 Hen. 8, c. 15, §§1, 2 (1536), *ibid.*, IV, 441-443; 4 Geo. 1, c. 11, §7 (1717), *ibid.*, XIII, 475. The commission in force in Massachusetts at this period appears in Book of Charters, Commissions, Proclamations, etc., 1628-1763, fols. 231-238 (MS, Massachusetts Archives, Boston).

117. Rex v. Corbet, *Legal Papers of John Adams*, Case No. 56. The other case was Rex v. Nickerson, *Legal Papers of John Adams*, Case No. 57 (Sp. Ct. Adm. 1773).

118. Prohibitions are found in the years between 1733 and 1763. See, for example, Shide v. Sloop *Mary*, 5 Mass. Adm. Recs. 13a (1742) (prohibition in suit by mate and pilot for their wages). See also later cases in which the Superior Court allowed at least temporary

writs. Min. Bk., S.C.J. Suffolk Co., Aug. 1754, following new No. 121; Recs. S.C.J. 1755, fol. 149 (Suffolk, Aug. 1755).

119. Quincy, *Reports*, 74 (S.C.J. 1763). See Browne, *Civil Law*, II, 72-85, 100-107. Dunn was not allowed an appeal on the grounds that the sum in controversy was less than £300. *Ibid.*, 80-83. See Dunn's subsequent unsuccessful common law action, *ibid.*, 187 (S.C.J. 1765). The court here was acting more strictly than did the common law in England. See *ibid.*, 79n; Holdsworth, *History of English Law*, I, 557n.

120. Jones v. Odiorne, Mass. Adm. Min. Bk., 10 April 1769; Min. Bk., Suffolk S.C.J., March 1769, new No. 97; *ibid.*, York, June 1777, continued No. 4; Suff. Files, No. 131785.

121. See, for example, "A Journal of the Times," 7 Jan. 1769, *Boston under Military Rule*, ed. Dickerson, 46; Ubbelohde, *Vice-Admiralty Courts*, 189-190; Henry Laurens, *Extracts from the Proceedings of the Court of Vice-Admiralty in Charles-Town, South Carolina* ([Philadelphia], 1768), 18-19. Jared Ingersoll, judge of the district court established at Philadelphia, was attacked more broadly under the statutes of Richard II, on the basis of the traditional jurisdiction granted in his commission. He denied that he actually had such power, admitting the right of the common law courts to issue prohibitions, Ubbelohde, *Vice-Admiralty Courts*, 182-188.

122. Sewall v. Hancock, *Legal Papers of John Adams*, Case No. 46.

123. In the period May 1760 to June 1765 covered by the court's Book of Accounts of Sales, 24 forfeitures of vessel or goods were decreed, 13 of them in 1760 and 1761. There were two forfeitures in 1762 and three each in 1763-1765. There were also 16 compositions (settlements without forfeiture), 14 of which occurred in 1764 as part of the controversy surrounding James Cockle, collector at Salem. See Barrow, "Colonial Customs," 406-408; Ubbelohde, *Vice-Admiralty Courts*, 58-60. The number of cases prior to the beginning of the Minute Book in which forfeitures did not result, and the number of civil cases, have not been determined. For the first three years covered by the Minute Book, the figures are: 1765 (Oct.-Dec.), two customs entries out of a total of five; 1766, three customs and one White Pine entry out of a total of twenty-one; 1767, one customs and two White Pine entries out of a total of fifteen.

124. Ezekiel Price's "Receipts from Seizures of Ships" (MS, Price Papers, Boston Athenaeum) shows that between May 1772 and September 1773 nineteen seizures of vessels and goods resulted in forfeitures, and there was one composition. A search of the Boston newspapers after September 1773 shows ten notices of seizures, five of which resulted in sales. See *Massachusetts Gazette and Boston Newsletter*, Sept. 23, 1773; Sept. 30, 1773; Nov. 18, 1773; Oct. 6, 1774; Dec. 22, 1774; Feb. 16, 1775; March 2, 1775; March 9, 1775; April 6, 1775 (two items); April 13, 1775; April 20, 1775 (two items); May 25, 1775; Feb. 22, 1776. That these figures do not represent the complete revenue business of the court is demonstrated by the

fact that the cases cited in notes 114 and 115 above were not found in the newspapers. Moreover, no mention is made of several Port Act cases from the fall of 1774 cited in "Letters of John Andrews," Massachusetts Historical Society, *Proceedings*, VIII (1864-1865), 378, 386. There is no evidence as to the court's civil business at this time.

125. As to the effect of the Stamp Act, see *Diary and Autobiography of John Adams*, I, 264, 292; Knollenberg, *Origin*, 236-237; Edmund S. and Helen M. Morgan, *The Stamp Act Crisis* (Chapel Hill, 1953), 130-143, 159-168. Of the 21 actions docketed in admiralty, 13 were settled, and only one of the remainder was entered earlier than 16 August, suggesting a rather careful approach to the court at this time.

126. Baker v. Hallowell, Recs. S.C.J. 1766-1767, fol. 92 (ships' necessaries); Glazier v. Jennessa, *ibid.*, fol. 64 (carpentry done aboard ship); Hill v. Boorn, *ibid.*, fol. 148 (master's wages and disbursements); King v. Kinlock, *ibid.*, fol. 4 (master's action against owner for indemnity); Coffin v. Vernon, *ibid.*, fol. 176 (marine insurance); Hancock v. Bowes, *ibid.*, fol. 91 (marine insurance); Masters v. Dowse, *ibid.*, fol. 172 (marine insurance); Robins v. Turner, *ibid.*, fol. 34 (work done in fitting out); Broden v. Robinson, *ibid.*, fol. 44 (assault aboard ship in foreign harbor, alleging fictitious venue); Goodwin v. Brimshire, *ibid.*, fol. 174 (assault aboard ship in foreign harbor, alleging fictitious venue); Jones v. Barker, *ibid.*, fol. 33 (conversion of goods aboard ship in harbor by sheriff). In Jan. 1773 an action of replevin for a ship hypothecated under a bottomry bond was brought in the Suffolk Inferior Court with an unknown result. Since such suits were considered to be within admiralty's exclusive jurisdiction because of the *in rem* nature of the obligation, this may have been an attempt to bend the common law's forms to achieve the same result. See Mercer and Ramsay v. Moffat, Suffolk Inferior Court Files, Jan. 1773, No. 268 (MS in Office of the Clerk of the Suffolk Superior Court for Civil Business, Boston); *Legal Papers of John Adams*, Pleadings Book, Form XXIV.

THE ADVENT OF COMMON LAW IN COLONIAL NEW YORK

HERBERT ALAN JOHNSON

Hunter College in the Bronx

ONE OF the most perplexing questions in the legal history of the American colonies is posed in determining the reasons underlying the transition from a seventeenth-century system of local law to an eighteenth-century legal system in which English common law became the established mean. While historians and lawyers have generally approached the problem seeking continuity and evolutionary development, it is here contended that this change, at least as far as the Province of New York was concerned, was abrupt, calculated, and dictated by the legal development which had occurred during the proprietary period from 1664 to 1685.

To understand the wholesale acceptance of English common law after 1691, it is necessary to review the legal institutions of New York as they developed during the relative calm of the years 1664 to 1685. During the period of the Dominion of New England and the military tribunals of Leisler's revolt, the political turmoil was such as to discourage normal legal development. Hence those years are excluded from this study. A further limitation on the scope of this essay is imposed by the need to compare the disparate legal systems of proprietary New York without becoming involved in the intricacies of minute differences in substantive or procedural law. For these reasons, this essay will consider the jurisdiction of courts to be the basis upon which the New York legal systems may be compared, and shall restrict its analysis to the colonial courts in the New York counties as far north as Westchester.

The mode of settlement of New York determined the manner in which its laws were to be formed during the seventeenth century. Dutch traders at New Amsterdam brought with them the highly developed civil law system of their homeland, and this Roman-Dutch law continued to govern the relations between the people of New York City long after the flag of the Dutch West India Company was lowered at the fort on the Battery.[1] Migration of settlers from Connecticut across Long Island Sound and overland from western Connecticut, resulted in the introduction of "Bible Codes" in the areas of their settlement in Westchester and Suffolk Counties.[2] Superimposed on these two indigenous systems of law was the English common law, preferred by the proprietor and the Crown. These three disparate legal systems supplied law to the inhabitants of proprietary New York. Considering the large elements of the population who owed loyalty to the two indigenous systems, it is remarkable that the institution that survived into the eighteenth century was English common law.

How did it happen that New Yorkers permitted twenty-seven years of precedent under the proprietary government to be discarded in exchange for the wholesale importation of English common law? What had so weakened the indigenous legal systems that they fell easy victims to the externally imposed institution? Where are the vestiges of Roman-Dutch civil law and the "Bible Codes" in the eighteenth century? What, in short, worked this remarkable transformation in such a short period of time?

One of the most striking characteristics of New York law during the proprietary period was its complexity. The complexity resulted not only from the attempt to apply three systems of law within one political subdivision, but also from the very confused situation concerning the jurisdiction of courts. Both the complicated nature of the law and the conflicting court jurisdictions, in turn, may be attributed to the precarious hold of the English conquerors over the Dutch and Puritan province. Faced with the problem of governing a colony where the majority of the population was non-English and non-Anglican, English governors refrained from making sudden changes; rule by diplomacy rather than by force resulted in the continued application of Dutch and Puritan law in the proprietary province of New York.

After the conquest of New Netherland, the English governor, Richard Nicolls, was faced with the formidable task of ruling a population composed of Dutch-speaking inhabitants and Puritan dissenters. Both groups had evolved their own legal systems, and promised to offer strong resistance to the imposition of English common law. Consequently the Duke's Laws, promulgated in the spring of 1665 did not apply to the Dutch settlers, and appeased the Puritans of Long Island by substantially restating their town laws, which were based upon the Bible Codes of New England. Representatives of the Westchester and Long Island towns met at Hempstead, in March of 1665, and gave reluctant approval to this new code of laws. One major reason behind the resistance to the Duke's Laws at the meeting was that the governor's approval was required for the election of townsmen to serve as constable and overseers in local communities. The institution of a system of courts based upon the local justice of the peace and triennial Courts of Sessions, also was unpopular. Such restrictions upon the previous self-government of the towns were bound to cause resentment.[3]

Surprisingly the delegates to the Hempstead assembly did not realize that the Duke's Laws, despite their ostensible reaffirmation of the Long Island Bible Codes, actually provided procedural devices whereby the extinction of Puritan law was guaranteed. There is no question that the jurisdiction of the Courts of Constable and Overseers, the successors to the independent town courts of Long Island, was sharply restricted. Hitherto such courts had general jurisdiction to try all matters; now their authority was reduced to where they could try only small causes where the amount in controversy did not exceed £5. Furthermore, appeals from the Courts of Constable and Overseers, were to be heard by the Courts of Sessions. The Sessions Courts, composed of justices of the peace appointed by Nicolls, reviewed the decisions of the local courts and also confirmed the appointment of the constable and overseers of the towns on behalf of the governor.[4] In this way, the Duke's Laws guaranteed not only the close local supervision of the town courts in their judicial capacity, but also enabled the governor to verify the political reliability of a town official before his election was confirmed. It seems clear that a continuance of some vestige of the New England codes was being tolerated, but only under close supervision. Nicolls had begun to lay the foundation for a centralized judicial system based upon the authority of the governor.

Despite the efforts of Nicolls and his advisers, the system of courts established in Long Island and Westchester proved to be a cumbersome arrangement. The lower courts were to have jurisdiction only over those areas within town limits. Town boundaries in the seventeenth century were imprecise, not only because of conflicts in land grants, but also because Long Island towns had refused to submit their patents, Dutch land briefs, and Indian deeds to the governor for confirmation.[5] These efforts to deny jurisdiction of the Duke of York over the Long Island settlements made it impossible to determine just where the bounds of those towns actually were. For this reason the jurisdiction of the Courts of Constable and Overseers was constantly open to challenge upon the basis of some disputed town boundary.

The Court of Sessions, according to the Duke's Laws, was to be a tribunal of general jurisdiction throughout Long Island and Westchester. To this court were assigned civil cases where the amount in dispute did not exceed £20, all cases concerning title to real property, and those causes appealed from the Courts of Constable and Overseers. The Courts of Sessions, in addition, were empowered, at least in theory, to try all criminal matters, including those punishable by death. In practice, however, nearly all prosecutions for felonies were instituted before the Court of Assizes.[6] Further inroads into the general jurisdiction of the Courts of Sessions were made possible by provisions in the Duke's Laws which conferred concurrent jurisdiction upon the Court of Assizes in civil cases where the amount in litigation exceeded £20.[7] Because of this situation, any party wishing to pay the higher costs in the Court of Assizes could avoid the jurisdiction of his local Court of Sessions. To the extent that the substantive law applied in the Court of Assizes might differ from the local law applied in the Court of Sessions, the opportunity to select a more favorable court presented an unfair advantage to the plaintiff.

Not surprisingly, there are numerous instances where the Court of Assizes transferred cases originally commenced before it, to the Courts of Sessions for trial.[8] The short term during which the Court of Assizes met, coupled with the inconvenience of assembling juries from distant counties in New York City, made such transfers desirable. However, had the Courts of Sessions been permitted a general jurisdiction in their various ridings, the Court of Assizes could have functioned more efficiently as a tribunal of appellate jurisdiction.

From the foregoing description, it may be seen that, intentionally or otherwise, the jurisdiction of the Courts of Sessions was left in an amorphous state. In cases where the amount in litigation was less than £20, the jurisdiction was clearly vested in the Sessions Court; in cases where the cause involved more than £20, and in all criminal cases, the Sessions Court exercised whatever authority the Court of Assizes was willing to permit. Litigants selected their court without any clear-cut guide lines concerning whether the case would be heard by the court in which it was commenced or transferred to some other court. Added to this uncertainty was the possibility of selecting a court that would apply the legal system most favorable to a party's position.

The dynamic force behind the judiciary in proprietary New York was the General Court of Assizes, the highest court in the Province. Composed of the governor, his Council, and all of the justices of the peace of the Province, this court met annually in October, usually in New York City, the capital of the Province. Because of its composition, the Court of Assizes exercised both legislative and judicial authority, much like the English House of Lords.[9] While we need not be concerned with the legislative authority of the court in this essay, it is important to realize that the plenary power of the Court of Assizes resulted in procedures quite different from those in the inferior courts. Particularly noteworthy in this regard was the rule that should the Court of Assizes be confronted with a criminal case where the offense had not been prohibited by the Duke's Laws, the court itself was empowered to try the offense after deciding whether it was a punishable trangression. Professor Julius Goebel has noted the large number of crimes that were not enumerated in the Duke's Laws, including manslaughter and rape. In these and other like offenses, the Court of Assizes apparently fixed the penalty after convicting the accused.[10]

In its capacity as the highest court in New York, the Court of Assizes possessed the power to resolve conflicts of jurisdiction between the various lower courts. For example, in 1667 a judgment of a Westchester town court was vacated, presumably for lack of jurisdiction, and the case was referred to the local Court of Sessions for the North Riding.[11] In its supervisory capacity, the Assizes Court was frequently plagued by the petitions of unsuccessful litigants who demanded that the local judges be censured or removed because of decisions adverse to the petitioners. To put a stop to this practice, the Court of Assizes in 1681 declared its support for the judges and thereafter enforced a policy that relief from adverse judgments could be had only by way of appeal.

Appellate procedure before the Court of Assizes was formal in nature, and was begun by a petition filed by the applicant. This petition was the basis upon which the appellant argued his case before the court. Prior to filing such a petition the appellant was required to post a bond to secure the costs of the appeal and to file a notice of appeal with the clerk of the Court of Assizes. Failure to post the bond or to file the notice of appeal was adequate ground for a non-suit.[12] An interesting departure from this procedure occurred in 1682 when the clerk of the Assizes Court was instructed to prepare the case for a group of Indians who were claiming an injustice at the hands of their local Court of Sessions.[13] Such an extraordinary step gives evidence of the importance the New York governors attached to amicable Indian relations.

According to the Duke's Laws, the Assizes Court could hear new evidence only in those cases where a material witness was not heard by the court of original jurisdiction. This rule was amended in 1666 to confer upon the court the power to hear appeals on the facts, as well as the law, whenever "... the Court shall see Cause."[14] After this change, review by the Court of Assizes of facts on appeal was virtually unlimited and its control over inferior courts vastly increased. Usually the Court of Assizes remitted cases to a Court of Sessions for retrial. However, in those causes bearing upon public policy, such as the titles to township lands and Indian affairs, a new hearing of the evidence normally occurred before the Court of Assizes.[15] In at least one of these cases, the Court of Assizes overruled the verdict of a seven-man jury rendered in the lower court.[16]

With the establishment of the office of justice of the peace in the Province of New York, English common law practices began to intrude on the local level. On the provincial level, the impact of English common law was made evident in the Court of Assizes. The preference for trying felonies before the Court of Assizes closely paralleled the tradition in England where felony prosecutions pending before the Courts of Quarter Sessions of the Peace would be held for the arrival of the justices on the assize instead of having such causes tried by the local justices of the peace, who in Quarter Sessions, possessed the requisite jurisdiction.[17] Before the Court of Assizes, there was a conscious attempt to duplicate the English writ system, and the minutes of that Court's proceedings contained references to the English forms of action.[18] Apparently the authorities were attempting to introduce English modes of practice through the provisions of the Duke's Laws and the activity of the Court of Assizes. Yet the numerous departures from the English common law norm emphasize the strong resistance to English legal institutions that still prevailed in seventeenth-century New York.

If the judicial system established by the Duke's Laws had been the sole basis of legal development in proprietary New York, it is possible that the conflicting jurisdictions referred to above may have been resolved, and the Province might have started down the path toward a gradual reception of English common law. That such was not the case was due to the continued existence of the Dutch courts, left relatively unchanged by the conquest in 1664, and to the creation of a system of private manorial courts. Both these courts functioned outside the court system established by the Duke's Laws.

Dutch civil law survived in the province of New York primarily because the population of the colony was predominantly Dutch and any inroads into Dutch institutions might prove particularly dangerous. Estimates for the years 1672 and 1673 indicate that approximately three-fifths of the people in the Province were Dutch and one-fifth were composed of disaffected Englishmen on Long Island, who, because of their Puritan inclination, desired to become a part of the corporate colony of Connecticut. While the Englishmen were more vocal in proclaiming their rights, the Dutch remained secure in their preponderance of numbers. Despite the occasional protests from Long Island, the Puritan towns gradually lost their independence as the Duke's Laws began to take effect. The Dutch, on the other hand, became taciturn under English rule and succeeded in resisting English legal institutions for several decades. Accepting the superficial changes made in their traditional Court of Burgomaster, Schepens and Schout, which was renamed the Mayor's Court of the City of New York, they continued to operate the court according to Dutch rules.[19]

One of the more bizarre results of the English attempt to alter the Dutch court, was the compromise reached in regard to jury trials during the proprietary period. In complying with the English insistence upon jury trials, the Dutch were ostensibly more conscientious than required by the Duke's Laws. The Mayor's Court of New York always utilized a twelve-man jury, while in those areas where the Duke's Laws were applied, a seven-man jury was usually employed.[20] Having thus complied with the conqueror's whim, the Mayor's Court proceeded to use a trial jury in a suit for separation from bed and board. This may well have been the only time that a jury was used in an English matrimonial case. In this suit for separation, as in a criminal case that followed, the court rendered its decision, and then as if an afterthought, requested the jury to ratify the verdict already given by the court.[21] In still another case, the trial jury was asked to rule on whether a party should be non-suited for failing to produce a document before the court.[22] Whether these unorthodox practices were the result of Dutch intransigence, or whether they resulted from a complete ignorance of the proper function of a trial jury is difficult to assess. However, the English towns of New Netherland had been permitted to use trial juries under the Dutch government, and this past familiarity with jury trials indicates that the Mayor's Court was employing the trial jury as a protective device by which it could shield itself from a charge by the governor that the court was exceeding its powers. After the Mayor's Court was called before the Court of Assizes in 1681 to answer a charge of treason concerning its alleged denial of a jury trial, the Court's attitude toward the "formality" of jury trial seems to have been substantially altered.[23]

Although the Mayor's Court of New York reluctantly accepted the English system of jury trials, it nevertheless continued to exercise its traditional probate jurisdiction under Dutch law. Furthermore, the Mayor's Court possessed a criminal jurisdiction equivalent to, or perhaps even greater than, the penal authority of the Courts of Sessions. One of the lasting vestiges Dutch law left upon the New York legal system was its extensive use of arbitration in the settlement of law suits.[24]

While the first English commission to the Mayor's Court confined its territorial jurisdiction to Manhattan Island, the court had traditionally exerted its authority beyond those limits. From the cases heard by the court, it would appear to have been the rule that the court would entertain any cause arising in adjacent territory provided that there was no court functioning in that area. Consequently, a contract of sale executed in New Jersey in 1668 was the subject of litigation in the Mayor's Court, as were other cases involving "bronx-Land" and the town of Fordham.[25] While in each instance the presence of the parties gave jurisdiction to the Mayor's Court, there can be little doubt that the doctrine of *forum non conveniens* played a small role in early Manhattan jurisprudence.

The Mayor's Court under the English also continued to exercise its maritime jurisdiction. Before the appointment of a judge of admiralty in 1683, the court frequently received a commission from the governor to sit as a court of admiralty in a particular cause.[26] There were, however, a number of instances in which the Mayor's Court of its own volition heard suits concerning seamen's wages and maritime contracts.[27] It is almost impossible to ascertain those cases tried solely upon the basis of a special commission and those cases which determined solely upon the existence of certain inherent powers of the court. We can only conclude from the evidence that the Mayor's Court exercised independent admiralty jurisdiction, subject to the prohibition of the governor in certain cases.[28]

Of all the courts in the judicial system of proprietary New York, the Mayor's Court of New York City was most clearly the one that took a hybrid form. Retaining a large part of its jurisdiction from the Dutch period, it gained new powers by grant of the English governors, or by various provisions of the laws enunciated by the governor and Council. Neither entirely statutory nor entirely customary in its source of authority, the Mayor's Court derived its power from both sources. For this reason it is nearly impossible to determine the limits of the Mayor's Court jurisdiction during the proprietary period. However, once the majority of the population was no longer Dutch and the English authorities could move with greater assurance against the independence of the Mayor's Court, its unique characteristics began to disappear. It became, in fact, a court of common pleas for New York City.

Contrary to the policy of *laissez-faire* evidenced by the English concerning the Dutch court system in New York City, the governors of the Province of New York took positive steps with regard to the establishment of private manorial courts. Although these courts in themselves were merely appendages to the manorial land grants, they served to further complicate and confuse the already complex system of courts within the Province.

As historians have long noted, the New York manors were created to serve two principal functions: defense and social control. Along the shores of Long Island and the outlying settlements in the Hudson River valley, the manorial grants were made in strategically located areas to guarantee the loyalty of leading citizens in the event of Dutch revolt or Indian attack. In the case of the manorial grants on Long Island, a class of large landowners with aristocratic privileges was formed to curb the extreme republican tendencies of the Puritan townspeople. To this extent the manorial lords of New York served a useful function in making possible a stronger political control of the Province by English governors.[29]

By far the most extensive grant of privileges made by the Duke of York was that to Thomas Mayhew, who, at the age of eighty, was made governor for life of Martha's Vineyard. Simultaneously Mayhew was made lord of Tisbury Manor, but his jurisdiction as governor extended far beyond the boundaries of this manor. As governor, he presided over the annual general court for Martha's Vineyard and Nantucket, which exercised civil jurisdiction without appeal in all cases below £50. This court also served in a legislative capacity, and its laws were binding upon the people under its control, subject only to confirmation by the governor in New York City. In the exercise of criminal jurisdiction, all transgressions other than those punishable by forfeiture of life or limb, or banishment, could be heard before Mayhew's general court.[30] The authority granted to Mayhew was subject only to judicial review by the New York Court of Assizes, and to confirmation of legislative acts as noted above. For most purposes, Martha's Vineyard continued to be substantially independent of New York until it, along with Nantucket, was re-annexed to the Bay Colony by the Massachusetts charter of 1691.

The extent to which private jurisdictions, such as that of Mayhew and the manorial lords, were used to avoid the authority of provincial courts is difficult to determine. We know that at least one manor lord was quite jealous of his prerogatives. John Archer, lord of Fordham Manor, refused to accept service of process from the Mayor's Court of New York, and erected a manorial court to rule the town of Fordham. According to a petition to the Mayor's Court, he fined an opponent in a lawsuit pending in the Mayor's Court the sum of £20 when he found that unfortunate man in the town of Fordham and hence subject to the jurisdiction of his manorial court.[31] Another manor lord, John Pell of Pelham Manor, was also challenged for avoiding the power of the provincial courts by utilizing his own jurisdictional privileges.[32] In the long run, however, the impact of these private jurisdictions upon the development of New York law was probably very slight. What is of importance, is the fact that these manorial grants weakened the power of the provincial courts. They made equal justice under the law unavailable when one's adversary was a manor lord and undermined the power and prestige of the courts held under the authority of the governor. In this way, manorial grants originally made to secure military and political objectives, worked against the governor's efforts to establish a sound judiciary in the Province.

As a result of the inroads of private jurisdictions and the persistence of Puritan "Bible Codes" and Dutch civil law institutions, the Province of New York during the proprietary period presented an intricate patchwork pattern of local law. While the government gave clear indications of its desire to impress an English pattern upon the court system, the implementation of the Duke's Laws resulted in a jumble of jurisdictions between the town courts, the Court of Sessions, and the Court of Assizes. The situation was only compounded by the continued existence of the indigenous legal systems which continued to function to a greater or lesser degree after the English conquest.

When in 1683 the English population of New York had reached a point where a General Assembly could safely be called, the people of the Province began to pay more attention to the court system. The result was a bill to revise the judiciary passed in 1683. Characteristically the jurisdiction of the local town courts was again reduced, and the Courts of Sessions were placed under the immediate supervision of Courts of Oyer and Terminer. Appeals from the Courts of Oyer and Terminer could be prosecuted to the High Court of Chancery at New York, consisting of the governor and Council, or to the Privy Council in England.[33] Once this new system of courts was in operation the old Court of Assizes was abolished.[34]

The court system erected under the Judiciary Act of 1683 enjoyed but a short tenure and was superseded in rapid succession by the courts of the Dominion of New England and the military tribunals of Leisler's revolt. Practice under the 1683 Act was so brief that it could not have been of much assistance to the lawyers who became engaged in setting up the Supreme Court of Judicature in 1691. Nevertheless, the example of the 1683 Judiciary Act, coupled with the declining influence of the Long Island town courts and the New York City Mayor's Court, provided a rare opportunity to completely revise the system of law in the Province of New York. With the establishment of the Supreme

Court of Judicature, the day of redemption for English common law in the Province of New York was at hand.

Mere alteration of a court system does not of itself indicate a change in the substantive law of a region. Indeed, it is possible that some remnants of the old indigenous legal systems formed a part of the New York law during the opening decades of the eighteenth century. However, with the confusing state of jurisdiction in the seventeenth century it is most likely that the substantive law was in an equally disheveled state by 1691. The era was one of drastic change in the political life of the mother country, and the trend was toward greater simplification and efficiency in government. New York lawyers having long suffered from the diversity of laws in the Province, no doubt welcomed an opportunity to eliminate from New York law all of the precedents based upon local law and were glad to substitute instead a legal system deriving its precedents and procedures from English common law.

This supposition is supported by the tradition among eighteenth-century New York lawyers, that the law of the Province prior to 1691 was to be considered identical with the common law of England.[35] For the eighteenth-century attorney, this rule meant that he could substitute the readily available materials of English common law for the seventeenth-century colonial precedents which were available only in manuscript. In addition, had such a rule been applied in 1691, it would have saved New York lawyers of that day from the frustrating experience of attempting to ascertain any consistent pattern in the precedents of the proprietary province. Either by agreement in 1691, or by the established practice of the bar in the following decades, the complex system of local law that prevailed in proprietary New York was relegated to the limbo of "pre-history," and the years from 1664 to 1685 became, in fact, the "dark age" of New York's legal history.

If the foregoing be true — that in 1691 a revolutionary change in New York law resulted in the elimination of precedents created during the proprietary period — the lawyer may well question the value of spending time in the study of proprietary law. Since the rules developed before 1691 have no binding effect upon future courts, they possess what many might consider to be merely an antiquarian interest. Yet a careful study of various aspects of New York law in the seventeenth century promises to yield large dividends to those who have the tenacity to pursue the subject. In addition to having the opportunity to study the legal development of the Province during its most inventive period, the legal historian approaching proprietary New York finds a clash of legal systems that serves as an antecedent for similar events that occurred later in American legal history. What happened in proprietary New York is, I submit, not substantially different from the adjustments that had to be made in later years when English common law came into contact with different legal systems. Examples of such conflicts may be found in the development of legal institutions in the states of Louisiana, Missouri, Texas and California. A study of New York in the proprietary period provides a fascinating introduction to the study of clashing legal systems; such an entree into this subject of laws in conflict, has too long been neglected and deserves closer attention in the years ahead.

LAW AND AUTHORITY

FOOTNOTES

1. Dutch practice in the New Amsterdam Court of Burgomaster, Schepens and Schout, established in 1653, closely paralleled the laws of the Netherlands and particularly the customs of the city of Amsterdam, Richard B. Morris, ed., *Select Cases of the Mayor's Court of New York City, 1674-1784*, in *American Legal Records*, II (Washington: 1935), at 42; Berthold Fernow, ed., *Records of New Amsterdam from 1653 to 1674 Anno Domini*, 7 vols. (New York, 1897), IV, 122. For notarial practice see Edmund B. O'Callaghan, trans., Register of Solomon Lachaire, Notary Public of New Amsterdam 1661-1663, City Clerk, New York City, and Edmund B. O'Callaghan, trans., Register of Walewyn van der Veen, Notary Public of New Amsterdam, 1662-1664, City Clerk, New York City. It is notable that the Dutch permitted English settlers within their province to use a trial jury, see *Minutes of the Town Court of Newtown 1656-1690*, in Historical Records Survey, *Transcripts of Early Town Records of New York* (New York: 1940), 27. Appeal from New Netherland courts was to to the Director-General and Council, see Fernow, ed., *Records of New Amsterdam*, IV, 251.
2. George L. Haskins and Samuel E. Ewing, "The Spread of Massachusetts Law in the Seventeenth Century," *University of Pennsylvania Law Review*, CVI (1958), 414-417.
3. The Long Island settlers wished complete independence or political attachment to Connecticut; both Richard Nicolls and his successor, Francis Lovelace, resorted to every art of diplomacy to gain their support. It was to no avail, for the Puritans persisted in resistance to the the Governor's authority. The numerous retreats by the governors in the face of Long Island intransigence are striking examples of what groups exercised political power in the Province. Edmund B. O'Callaghan, ed., *Documents Relating to the Colonial History of the State of New York*, 15 vols. (Albany: 1856-1883), III, 157, 158; XIV, 542, 545, 551, 620, 681. Victor Hugo Paltsits, ed., *Minutes of the Executive Council of the Province of New York . . . 1668-1673*, 2 vols. (Albany: 1910), I, 80, 81; Josephine C. Frost, ed., *Records of the Town of Jamaica, Long Island, New York 1656-1751*, I (Brooklyn: 1915), 29, 47, 48. See also Julius Goebel, Jr., "Some Legal and Political Aspects of the Manors in New York," Order of Colonial Lords of Manors in America, *Publications*, No. 19 (1928), 4.

   For brief period of Dutch resistance, and the use of gifts and offices to palliate them see Fernow, ed., *Records of New Amsterdam*, V, 145; VI, 198; Paltsits, ed., *Minutes of the Executive Council*, I, 329-330.
4. The preamble to the Duke's Laws cites its New England heritage, *The Colonial Laws of New York from the Year 1664 to the Revolution*, I (Albany: 1894), 7. For parallel texts and a narrative account of the enactment of the Duke's Laws see Morton Pennypacker, *The Duke's Laws: Their Antecedents, Implications and Importance*, in Paul M. Hamlin and Richard B. Morris, eds., *Anglo-American Legal History*

Series, 1st ser., No. 9, 30-31. The results of requiring the governor to have a veto over the selection of town officials are discussed in Richard M. Bayle, *Historical and Descriptive Sketches of Suffolk County* (Port Jefferson, N.Y.: 1874), 34, 35, and Henry J. Scudder, "The Formation of the Civil Government of Suffolk County," in *Bicentennial: A History of Suffolk County* (Babylon, N.Y.: 1885), 24. In at least one case local resentment resulted in the beating of a constable, see O'Callaghan, *Documents . . . Colonial History*, XIV, 582. For jurisdiction, personnel and supervision of Court of Constable and Overseers, see applicable provisions of the Duke's Laws, at *Colonial Laws New York*, I, 7, 44, 48, 55, 63, 88, 90, 91; criminal jurisdiction see *ibid.*, I, 63; power of justice of peace to preside over town courts, see *ibid.*, I, 31.

5. An example of a contested town boundary is that of Jamaica, which was challenged by Newtown, Hempstead, and Flushing, see Frost, ed., *Town Records of Jamaica*, I, 33, 86, 190. The Southold-Southampton line was one of many settled by the Court of Assizes, O'Callaghan, ed., *Documents . . . Colonial History*, XIV, 599.
6. For jurisdiction of Sessions Courts see *Colonial Laws of New York*, I, 7, 23, 25, 27, 31, 75. The allocation of criminal jurisdiction is discussed at length by Julius Goebel, Jr. and T. Raymond Naughton, at *Law Enforcement in Colonial New York: A Study in Criminal Procedure 1664-1776* (New York: 1944), 61.
7. See cases at Paltsits, ed., *Minutes Executive Council*, I, 132-133 (Jamaica), 115 (Gravesend), Fernow, ed., *Records New Amsterdam*, VI, 151 (Mayor's Court, N.Y.C.).
8. Paltsits, ed., *Minutes Executive Council*, I, 131, 132, Fernow, ed., *Records New Amsterdam*, VI, 175.
9. *Colonial Laws New York*, I, 44.
10. *Ibid.* See also Goebel and Naughton, *Law Enforcement*, 61.
11. Orville C. Ackerly, Calendar of the Proceedings of the Court of Assizes 1665-1672 (in the New York State Library), Manuscript Division, New York Public Library, New York City, 20. When the Court of Assizes was not in session the conflicts were resolved by the governor and Council, Goebel and Naughton, *Law Enforcement*, 299.
12. *Colonial Laws New York*, I, 12, 75, 76; Fernow, ed.,*Records New Amsterdam*, V, 151; Mayor's Court Minutes 1677-1682, Division of Records, New York County Clerk, Hall of Records, New York City, 24. See *Osborne* v. *Tuder*, at Proceedings of the General Court of Assizes Held in the City of New York, October 6, 1680 to October 6, 1682, New York Historical Society *Collections*, XLV (New York: 1913), 20. But if tender to the clerk should be shown, appellant could renew at the next term, *Martinoe v. Latten*, *ibid.*, 20, 23.
13. *Tackapowsha v. Town of Hempstead*, *ibid.*, 32
14. *Colonial Laws New York*, I, 11, 90.
15. Paltsits, ed., *Minutes Executive Council*, I, 42, 326.
16. O'Callaghan, ed., *Documents . . . Colonial History*, XIV, 572; *Tacka-*

powsha v. *Town of Hempstead*, Proceedings General Court Assizes, New York Historical Society *Collections*, XLV, 32, 33.

17. Bertram Osborne, *Justices of the Peace 1361-1848* (Shaftesbury, Eng.: 1960), 83; Michael Dalton, *The Country Justice: Containing the Practice Duty and Power of the Justices of the Peace* (London: 1746), 83, 84. Appellate procedure under the Duke's Laws seems to have followed English precedents, see Dalton *ibid.*, 63, 66; Charles A. Beard, *The Office of the Justice of the Peace in England: Its Origin and Development* (New York: 1904), 77, 78, 153; Osborne, *ibid.*, 35, 51.
18. For example the court minutes contain references to an " . . . action of trover and Conversion", *Archer* v. *Orchard*, an " . . . action of assault and battery", *Coursen* v. *Orchards*, and the notation that the defendant craved a nonsuit and the court adjudged that the plaintiff did not have a cause of action and granted the request, *Osborne* v. *Tuder*, all at Proceedings General Court Assizes, 19, 20.
19. The 1672 and 1673 population figures have been graphically presented in Herbert A. Johnson, *The Law Merchant and Negotiable Instruments in Colonial New York 1664-1730* (Chicago: 1963), 48. The figure for Suffolk County is from *History of Suffolk County New York* (New York: 1882), 62, for the year 1673. Under their own Dutch governors, the Dutch were not slow in asserting their rights, see Fernow., ed., *Records of New Amsterdam*, V, 60.
20. *Ibid.*, V, 267; *Colonial Laws New York*, I, 42, 91 (Sessions Courts used twelve man juries only when trying capital crimes.)
21. Fernow, ed., *Records of New Amsterdam*, V, 282; VI, 16.
22. *Ibid.*, VI, 75, 78.
23. Use of jury in English towns under Dutch, see *Newtown Court Minutes*, 27. Procedure against Mayor's Court recorded in case of *Tuder* v.*Rumbouts, et al.*, Proceedings . . . General Court of Assizes, New York Historical Society *Collections*, XLV, 13, 22.
24. Probate jurisdiction, see Morris, ed., *Select Cases Mayor's Court*, 46; Mayor's Court Minutes, 1675-77, 208 for appointment of curators in accordance with Dutch practice. For penal jurisdiction see Goebel and Naughton, *Law Enforcement*, 66, 67; that this practice was a continuation of the Dutch practice, cf. Fernow, ed., *Records of New Amsterdam*, V, 93, 96 with *ibid.*, VI, 11, 35, but also see *ibid.*, V, 287, 288, where one accused of assault and battery was held for the Court of Assizes. On use of arbitration see Morris, *ibid.*, 44, for a 1670 arbitration see Fernow, ed., *Records New Amsterdam*, VI, 271.
25. Fernow, ed., *Records New Amsterdam*, V, 249, 326, VI, 7, 213, 234-235, 325 [bronx-Land and Harlem], see also *ibid.*, VI, 120 [Bergen in "New Garsie"], and Mayor's Court Minutes, 1675-77, 253-254.
26. Paul M. Hamlin and Charles E. Baker, eds., *Supreme Court of Judicature of the Province of New York 1691-1704*, I (New York: 1959), 25-27; see also Fernow, ed., *Records New Amsterdam*, VI, 304, 341, and Mayor's Court Minutes, 1675-77, 76.
27. *Ibid.*, VI, 185-188; 305-341.

28. O'Callaghan, ed., *Documents . . . Colonial History*, III, 264, XIV, 617-619, 625; Fernow, *ibid.*, VI, 117; Paltsits, ed., *Minutes Executive Council*, I, 76.
29. Goebel, "Some Legal and Political Aspects of . . . Manors", Order of Colonial Lords of Manors in America, *Publications*, No. 19, 11, 12, 15. See also John Henry Livingston, "The Minor Manors of New York," Order of Colonial Lords of Manors in America, *Publications*, No. 12 (1923), 14, and Howland Pell, "The Pell Manor," Order of Colonial Lords of Manors in America, *Publications*, No. 5 (1917), 5.
30. *Colonial Laws New York*, I, 1; Paltsits, ed., *Minutes Executive Council*, I, 361, 367, 375; John M. Wightman, "The Mayhew Manor of Tisbury," Order of Colonial Lords of Manors in America, *Publications*, No. 10 (1921), 29.
31. Harry C. W. Melick, *The Manor of Fordham and its Founder* (New York: 1950), 80, 81, 84, 89; see also Fernow, ed., *Records New Amsterdam*, VI, 325, 326. See petition of Johannes Vervelen, Mayor's Court Minutes 1675-77, 75 — this is probably the paper noted in Goebel, "Some Legal and Political Aspects of . . . Manors," at p. 19.
32. Goebel, "Some Legal and Political Aspects of . . . Manors," 14.
33. *Colonial Laws New York*, I, 125; Hamlin and Baker, eds., *Supreme Court of Judicature*, I, 14, 15; Julius Goebel, Jr., *Cases and Materials on the Development of Legal Institutions* (Brattleboro, Vt.: 1946), 525.
34. *Colonial Laws New York*, I, 172.
35. The rule was enunciated by William Smith and Daniel Horsmanden shortly before the Revolution, Hamlin and Baker, eds., *Supreme Court of Judicature*, I, 378-379. For the disruptive effect of the year 1691 see Fred S. Hall, "Common Law Marriage in New York State," *Columbia Law Review*, XXX (1930), 2-3, and Johnson, *The Law Merchant*, 35.

THE FOUNDATIONS OF LAW IN MARYLAND: 1634-1715

Joseph H. Smith

Columbia University Law School

LEGAL historians have made little effort to identify and evaluate the various elements that constituted the foundation for law and authority in colonial Maryland prior to the resumption of proprietary rule in 1715. The records contain references to the "constitution," the "laws and constitution," "the laws and usages," the "fundamental and known laws," "the laws and precedents" of the Province, the "laws of the country" and the "common law of the province," but contemporary exposition of these terms is not to be found. In recent years, writers have tended to concentrate on specific elements such as the provisions of the 1632 charter, the extension of various acts of Parliament to the Province, the putative manorial court system, or certain aspects of law enforcement. The purpose of this essay is to present some general conclusions as to law and authority in a period comprising proprietary rule (1634-1689) and royal government (1692-1715), based primarily upon study of the records of the Assembly, the Council, the Court of Appeals, the Provincial Court, the Court of Chancery and certain county courts.[1]

There were nine important elements of law and authority during the years 1634 to 1715.[2] For the proprietary period, the basic source was, of course, the royal charter, as implemented by proprietary commissions, instructions and "conditions of plantation." The comparable instrument for the period of royal government was the governor's commission, as supplemented by royal instructions, and less frequently, by Orders in Council, directions from the Board of Trade, and commissions or instructions from such participants in imperial administration as the High Court of Admiralty and the Commissioners of the Customs. A second consisted of the numerous acts, both public and private, of the provincial Assembly, plus occasional ordinances and resolutions (the latter being used at times to provide interpretations of earlier acts).

A third was made up of the various acts of Parliament, both pre-settlement and post-settlement, that were regarded as extending to the Province. The fourth consisted of the common law of England (including equity, local custom, and the law merchant) to the extent it was received in the colony. The fifth was local custom and usage, including the bylaws of towns or cities and manorial customs and usages. The sixth was composed of judicial commissions and instructions and commissions to administrative officers such as sheriffs, coroners, and constables. The seventh comprehended judicial practice in procedural matters, including the rules of court promulgated at various times. The eighth may be characterized as the decisional law of the various courts of the Province. The ninth took the form of proclamations and conciliar orders issued by the executive authority, or in a few instances, royal proclamations extended to the Province. Sources of private law such as contracts, leases, writings obligatory, bills of exchange, conveyances, wills, and trusts are considered as being beyond the scope of the present essay.

The 1632 charter from Charles I to Cecilius Calvert, the first proprietor of the Province, in many respects provided the broadest foundation for law and authority in Maryland.[3] Numerous acts of the Assembly stemmed from its grant of power to enact laws with the advice and assent of the freemen or their delegates. Exercise of this power was subject to the usual proviso that the laws should be consonant to reason and not repugnant or contrary but, so far as conveniently might be, agreeable to the laws, statutes, customs, and rights of the kingdom of England. Although the liberal charter failed to provide for any legislative review by the King in Council, the records disclose no case in which this omission ever became significant.[4] The power to make ordinances for the conservation of the peace and better government of the Province, subject to certain restrictions, was seldom resorted to, except to the extent that it served as the basis for proclamations and conciliar orders.

The charter also conferred broad powers on the proprietor to administer justice and to establish a system of courts with both civil and criminal jurisdiction. While some obscurity surrounds the establishment of the Provincial Court and the earliest county courts, they and the Court of Chancery and the Prerogative Court undoubtedly owed their origin and continued existence to this power. The same may be said of the issuance of process in the name of the proprietor.

As to a land system, the charter in effect provided for tenure by free and common socage, estates and interests in land as in England, and subinfeudation free from the restrictions of *Quia Emptores* (18 Edward I, c.1).[5] In practice, however, the proprietary land-grant policy was characterized by a resort to quit rents, fines on alienation, and broad claims to escheat.[6]

License to erect manors with courts baron and courts leet resulted in the granting of a number of manors but there was no extensive introduction of a system of manorial courts.[7] The power to incorporate boroughs and cities took on significance only in the case of the several charters to the city of St. Mary's.[8] The somewhat enigmatic provision that the settlers and their descent should be regarded as English subjects and have all the privileges, franchises, and liberties of the kingdom of England in the same manner as subjects within the kingdom became a rallying point in the struggle of the inhabitants against proprietary pretensions. However, upon some occasions the settlers relied upon an inherent right or birthright theory, or upon the extension of the provisions of Magna Carta to the Province by an act of Assembly.[9] The well-known clause granting rights comparable to those possessed by the Bishop of Durham in the County Palatine of Durham, prior to the parliamentary abridgment of 1536, may have authorized the appointment of a council and the establishment of counties, as well as vesting in the proprietary as *jura regalia* the right to waifs, estrays, wreck and treasure trove.[10] As far as the power to tax was concerned, the proprietary collector was to be "wholly guided by the Rules and Directions of our Royall Charter and the known Laws of our Kingdom of England."[11]

During the period of royal government the charter was in effect suspended, although rights to the soil and to certain revenues remained in the proprietor, and the governor's commission became the "constitution" of the Province. Introduction of royal government brought with it some institutional changes — in its law-making, the Assembly, although more active and independent, was now subject to the royal prerogative and, after 1696, to effective legislative review by the King in Council. The Anglican Church became the established church of the colony and a moral element was introduced into law enforcement. A Court of Appeals was instituted and appeals to the Privy Council provided for. The governor became head of the Court of Chancery and the administration of justice in other courts was centralized to some extent and tightened up. New admiralty courts were established. Certain controls were asserted over the legal profession and Council members became less identified with the administration of justice.

Yet in many respects, the institutions spawned under proprietary rule remained untouched during the period of royal rule. Much of the legislation followed closely the pattern of laws passed in the proprietary period. Although process now issued in the King's name, the practices of the courts showed no cleavage with the past. The county and the hundred remained the significant administrative units with many matters handled by the commissioners and by the sheriff, coroner, and constable as in the past. Nor did the corpus of law administered by the courts change to any significant degree.[12]

While the acts of the Assembly constituted one of the principal elements of law and authority in early Maryland, no comprehensive system of local legislation existed before the first years of the Restoration. Maryland's early legislative history was characterized by a constitutional tug of war between the proprietor and the House of Delegates as to the locus of the power to initiate legislation. Moreover, there was a lack of legislative continuity as events in England or in neighboring Virginia brought about changes in Maryland's government. No collected laws appeared in print until 1700.[13] Throughout most of the period, lawyers and litigants alike were beset by the uncertainty inherent in a system of temporary laws, with numerous acts reviving or repealing legislation. The passage of successive laws on the same subject, with little or no change in substance, resulted in a staggering volume of legislation — almost 1,000 public acts for the period 1638-1715, in addition to nearly 150 private or petitionary acts. Less than one-half the public acts and about one-fifth of the private acts were enacted in the proprietary period.

Much of the legislation concerned itself with subjects peculiar to the circumstances of the colony and afforded little room for resort to the laws and customs of England. Some of the laws in this category were acts raising and disbursing revenues, fixing or regulating the fees of public officers, maintaining the militia, governing Indian relations, defining proprietary rights, and encouraging and regulating the growth and sale of tobacco — the crop upon which the economy of the Province was based. Others were concerned with providing economic regulation of various sorts, regulating the conduct of servants and slaves, regulating the keeping of domestic and control of wild animals, establishing new counties, ports and towns, and the keeping of various records. Laws were also passed regulating the fencing of cultivated lands, providing for the establishment and maintenance of highways and bridges, regulating ordinaries, and encouraging trade and agriculture other than tobacco-raising. Legislation also regulated the use of commodities as currency; tobacco being the common medium of exchange, little use was made of sterling. Finally, acts were passed encouraging the building of watermills, regulating departures from the Province, authorizing the purchase of lands and erection of buildings for public use, and ascertaining the bounds of counties and, as a royal province, of parishes.[14]

A number of these statutes contemplated enforcement by so-called popular actions (*qui tam* actions) in the Provincial Court or the county courts for breach of a penal statute. A few were remedial statutes providing for "actions upon a statute" in which the right to sue was limited to the aggrieved or injured party or parties.[15] Despite the fact that the popular action was frequently provided as a means of law enforcement in Maryland, relatively few such actions appear in the court records examined and the abuses incident to its use in England were avoided in the Province.[16] The extent to which draftsmen may have been influenced by English legislative models or by the lack of a strong system of proprietary public prosecutors is not apparent.

Apart from a few early statutes, the Assembly made little attempt to deal with serious criminal offenses or to regulate procedure in criminal matters.[17] Generally speaking, the colony relied upon the laws of England in such matters. However, provincial laws, at various times, did provide punishment for such offenses as drunkenness, profane cursing and swearing, hog-stealing, adultery and fornication, divulging false news, theft or stealing, fence burning, perjury and subornation of witnesses, blasphemy, and altering or defacing tobacco marks. Punishments in most cases were fines or whipping, standing in the pillory, or the payment of punitive damages.[18]

Acts of the Assembly played no significant role in the fields of contract or tort law. As to real property matters, the legislature sought to integrate security and certainty of holdings with the proprietary land grant system. One late development was the substitution of commissioners for common law actions in determining disputed metes and bounds.[19] In the area of probate and administration, a succession of provincial acts: (1) regulated in some detail the early jurisdiction of the Provincial Court in such matters and, after 1671, the duties of the Commissary General and the deputy commissaries, as well as the conduct of executors and adminstrators; and (2) sought to afford protection to the rights and properties of orphans.[20]

The Maryland legislature made no comprehensive attempt to regulate procedure in civil actions in any court, apart from a group of laws passed in 1642.[21] Subsequent acts passed from time to time were primarily concerned with such specific matters as the appointment of court days, the regulation of attachment and execution, appellate procedure, actions on accounts or on bills obligatory, arrest by *capias*, outlawry, amercements, special bail, the summoning of witnesses, the entry of actions, rules of evidence in certain actions, limitation of actions, stays and delays in execution, damage on protested bills of exchange, execution for public officers' fees, the reformation of jeofailes, proof of debts and discounts in bar, execution against defendants leaving the county, the recovery of small debts, and compelling the attendance of jurors and witnesses.[22] Virtually all changes in procedure introduced by the legislature were designed to correct specific evils or shortcomings. Closely related were the acts of the Assembly regulating the practice and charges of attorneys, establishing the fees incident to litigation, and regulating abuses by such officers as the sheriff.[23]

Maryland's charter made no provision for wholesale extension to the colony of the laws and customs of England, including acts of Parliament. At the time of settlement there was no judicial authority with respect to the extension of the laws of England to a territory such as Maryland, unsettled except for the Indians, yet not a conquered country.[24] The general attitude in the Province was that, by executive or legislative action, some or all of the laws of England might be received as the colonists saw fit, saving those privileges and rights guaranteed by the charter.[25] The distinction between acts of Parliament passed prior to Maryland's settlement and those later enacted was not current in the seventeenth century. In any event, it was generally accepted that, unless otherwise specifically provided, the courts should be guided in the first instance by acts of the Assembly or general usage. A divergence of views developed as to the "rule of judicature" if the laws of the Province were silent. At least four basic views appear in a succession of acts and in legislative debates during the proprietary period: (1) the court was free to exercise its discretion — but since the proprietary controlled the judiciary this view found little favor in the House of Delegates; (2) the court was free to exercise its discretion including due consideration of the applicable laws of England; (3) the court was to judge by those laws of England not inconvenient to the Province or not inconsistent with its condition; and (4) the court was to judge by the laws of England without any discretion as to applicability. The fourth view ultimately prevailed in the proprietary period and was adopted in the early years of royal government, although the exact scope of the rule is vague. However, by reason of repeals and disallowance, for much of the period of royal rule no statutory rule of judicature existed.[26]

Whether adherence to one rule of judicature or another resulted in significant variations in judicial standards in civil cases is difficult to ascertain from the surviving court records. However, in view of the few acts of Assembly of a substantive nature in the fields of private law, the rudimentary jury instructions seemingly in use during the period, and the many actions determined by a jury verdict on a plea of the general issue, such variations appear unlikely. Chancellor Kilty, in his extensive report on the English statutes in Maryland, concluded that, apart from those of a confirmatory nature, some 220 pre-settlement acts of Parliament and about 70 post-settlement but pre-1715 enactments were regarded as extending to the Province.[27] This is not to say that direct contemporary evidence exists as to each extension or that each statute played a day-to-day role. In evaluating the significance of these statutes it is perhaps of value to note that of the pre-settlement statutes almost 90 related to criminal law and its administration, almost 70 to civil procedure, about 50 to real property matters and 15 to probate and administration. The post-settlement statutes were divided as follows: criminal law and its administration — 15, civil procedure — 12, trade and customs — 17, religious matters — 15, real property — 9, and probate and administration — 2.

Many acts of Parliament appear to have been accepted by usage as part of the law of the Province. Despite the fact that a vast number of pre-settlement acts were tacitly rejected by the Province, the basis on which selection was made is hard to discern. Apart from prosecutions under the Acts of Trade and criminal proceedings, relatively few cases coming before the courts raised any issue of the force of particular acts of Parliament in the Province.[28] Attempts to clarify the situation by legislative action were largely abortive.[29] Yet by the period of royal government the better lawyers in the Province certainly possessed one or more of the available volumes containing selected acts of Parliament.

Those responsible for criminal prosecutions, the Attorney General in the Provincial Court and the clerks of the indictments in the county courts, obviously had familiarity with those statutes relating to criminal law and its administration. The earliest approaches to a substantive law of criminal offenses tended to limit the applicability of the laws of England, if invoked at all, to lesser offenses. For offenses extending to life or member, the laws of the Province constituted the rule of judicature — despite their deficiency in this respect. Ultimately, the distinction between greater and lesser offenses and that between civil and criminal jurisdiction was obliterated. Thus, when the laws of the Province were silent, the laws of England were constituted the rule of judicature.[30] As noted earlier, however, the statutory language was vague as to scope. In any event, no statutory rule of judicature existed for much of the period of royal government.

In the absence of reported decisions by the provincial judiciary it is difficult to assess the role of the common law of England in Maryland in areas of substantive law such as contracts, torts, bailments, wills and trusts, partnerships, and real property. However, from pleadings, from judicial rulings on demurrers, motions in arrest of judgment, writs of error, and appeals, and from a wide variety of legal documents, it would appear that the common law of England, together with acts of Parliament in some areas, constituted the governing law. As to the equity jurisdiction of the Court of Chancery, the surviving records are uninformative and in large part devoted to matters relating to proprietary land grants and escheats. Petitioners usually sought relief on broad grounds of equity and justice. With little guidance available in printed form and with the principles of equity still developing in England, there is no assurance that equity as administered in Maryland closely resembled that of Westminster Hall. While no "constitutional" opposition to the Court of Chancery developed in the Province, the role played by the Assembly in passing petitionary or private acts appears at times to have been quasi-equitable in nature and perhaps tempered such opposition.

The courts of Maryland in civil procedure adopted much of the common law, as modified by various acts of Parliament and as modified and supplemented by acts of the Assembly. While there was little use of original writs to commence an action (except for replevin and a few others in the Provincial Court), pleadings were based on a form of action concept and many followed closely the patterns of English form books. *Capias* was used as initial process, but attachment of personal property, based primarily upon acts of the Assembly, played a greater role than the custom of foreign attachment in England. Pleading in most cases did not proceed beyond the declaration, plea, replication stage, yet after some procedural maturity had been achieved in the colony, arrest of judgment or reversal on writ of error or appeal was sought in many cases for defective pleadings. The exact role of *scire facias juratores*, qualification and challenge of jurors, and use of *tales de circumstantibus* is obscure. The court records yield little information regarding trial procedure. From assignments of error in the Provincial Court it appears that, at least on the county court level, there were frequent clerical lapses in the rendering of verdicts, the entry of judgments thereon, the issuance of final process, and the proper demarcation of the respective functions of jury and bench. Transfer and appellate procedure was vague in its outlines; while writ of error and the record brought up for review followed English prototypes, no use appears of a bill of exceptions. Execution in personal actions was largely by *capias ad satisfaciendum* although *fieri facias*, *elegit* and *levari facias* were also found. *Scire facias* was used to revive judgments. Little use was made of attaint or *audita querela*. No evidence appears of use of *recordari facias*, although the courts held by one or two justices of the peace apparently were not regarded as courts of record.[31]

The Court of Chancery in procedural matters followed the English pattern. Little effort was made by the Assembly to govern its procedure; some supplemental rules of practice promulgated by the court appear in its records.[32]

The role of the English common law in defining criminal offenses in the colony has been noted above. Procedure in criminal matters followed closely the common law, as modified by various statutes. From an early date, the grand jury presentment or indictment was used in the Provincial Court and county courts; informations were used sparingly. *Venire facias* constituted process; arraignment, trial by a petty jury, the right to benefit of clergy, and sentencing followed English practice. The right to jury trial was apparently grounded upon Magna Carta and the privileges clause of the charter. From certain scattered judicial entries it is obvious that, at the Provincial Court level at least, the prosecutor, clerk, and court had available English form books detailing procedure in criminal causes step by step.[33] Whether all these procedural niceties were consistently followed, particularly in the trial of the seditious and malcontents, is doubtful. It should be noted also that the Assembly on several occasions intervened in criminal matters by acts of attainder, banishment or outlawry, and statutory fines.[34]

Legal historians of New England have tended to emphasize the influence of English local custom upon the course of legal development.[35] In early Maryland such custom probably played a role in the administration of manorial justice but the court baron, the court leet, and the "hundred court" were not significant factors in the development of the Maryland legal system.[36] The county courts, as they developed, owed little to their English counterparts. However, on the criminal side, there can be no doubt that the jurisdiction and practice of the justices of the peace in England exercised considerable influence.[37] Only two courts, (St. Mary's and Annapolis), were comparable to English borough courts. It may be that the early resort to attachment of personalty as initial process may be credited to the custom of foreign attachment found in London and other English cities, although Maryland's statutory form departed visibly from its putative counterpart.[38] In deprecating the impact of English local customs it should be noted that conditions of settlement in Maryland resulted in a scattered population. Manorial communities never developed in appreciable numbers; and there were few towns or cities. Thus there was no corpus of law made up of town regulations or a system of magistrates or town commissioners, as found in Massachusetts Bay under its first charter.[39]

The significance of the law merchant in Maryland law is a subject which still awaits investigation. References to the custom of merchants were commonly included in the declarations in the common law courts relating to protested bills of exchange. At least one book on the subject, Molloy's *De Jure Maritimo et Navali*, was owned by some lawyers in the Province.[40] That this body of law was resorted to by any city or admiralty court seems doubtful.[41]

Finally, it should be observed that the House of Delegates

from an early date drew upon the precedents of the House of Commons in asserting its rights and privileges. By 1682, however, the House of Delegates was ready to invoke the "ancient rules and Custome of this house."[42]

The importance of custom and usage in matters of substantive law is difficult to evaluate. Rarely is custom or usage found equated with acts of the Assembly, except in the commissions to the county courts, the Provincial Court, the Commissary General, and the Court of Chancery.[43] Custom certainly was important in the case of servants serving by "the custom of the country" in determining length of service and the right to freedom clothes, corn, and tools. Custom in this instance, however, received statutory support[44]. Judicial recognition of custom and usage also appears in connection with such subjects as the year and a day respite allowed administrators, the allowance to a widow from her deceased husband's estate, writs of partition, the compulsion upon a plaintiff to make oath to a debt sued for, and the levying of fines.[45] In at least one county, the usages on attachment went beyond the letter of the provincial act.[46] A close study of county court records might well reveal other usages of a similar nature. In the application of acts of Parliament within the colony, usage was perhaps the governing element in those instances in which reception was not attributable to some action by the provincial legislature or executive.

Some insight as to custom appears from the comment by Governor Nicholson in 1697 that:

> The People begin to pretend Custome, and claime it is their Common law, which if not timely prevented . . . may be a disservice, and prejudicial to his Majesty's Interest. For if they be allowed the benefit of their old Customs, t'will be in vain for me to prosecute illegall Traders, and forfeited Bonds etc. as also to endeavour to new modell the Country, whether in Church or State.

Nicholson later admonished the House of Delegates saying that it had no right "to insist upon any thing as matter of Custom in this Country which is not agreeable to the Laws of England."[47]

The commission from the governor was the principal device used to establish the jurisdiction of various courts and, to some extent, rules of judicature in Maryland from an early date. Acts of the Assembly, on the other hand, provided minimum jurisdictional standards for the Provincial Court, Court of Chancery, and county courts, conferred limited jurisdiction upon one or two justices of the peace, and regulated procedural matters. Although such acts infringed upon the proprietary or royal prerogative, they were never seriously challenged. When in 1707 Governor John Seymour, in accordance with directions from the Board of Trade, sought to impose an assize system upon the Provincial Court, as part of his attempts to centralize the administration of justice, the Assembly's refusal to grant allowances to the assize justices frustrated the change and left the "country party" triumphant.[48]

The earliest grants of judicial authority were in the form of commissions to local commanders and conservators of the peace investing them with designated jurisdiction and included in most cases the powers of a justice or justices of the peace in England.[49] Commissions issued at a later date to the justices or commissioners of the county courts were patterned after the commissions to justices of the peace in England. These commissions conferred limited civil jurisdiction in real and personal actions (later commissions excluded actions involving title to real property) to be exercised according to the laws, orders, and reasonable customs of the province — or in part of the royal period, according to the laws, orders, and customs of England and the province. At the same time, such commissions conferred criminal jurisdiction not extending to life or member and comparable to that of quarter sessions in England.[50]

No commissions have been found for the early years of the Provincial Court. Proprietary commissions to this court from 1665 onward authorized the holding of all pleas relating to the conservation of the peace, all pleas touching upon proprietary rights and revenues, and common pleas, as well as the determining of all matters of equity.[51] The earliest commission of the royal period followed the proprietary model, except for the omission of equitable jurisdiction. Subsequent commissions followed in large part the format of the English commission to the justices of the peace and granted broad powers to hold pleas touching upon the conservation of the peace and common pleas, according to the laws and customs of England and of the province.[52]

From time to time commissions were granted to hold special courts of oyer and terminer and special civil courts comparable to county courts.[53] Two Chancery commissions, to a Lord Keeper of the great seal of the Province and two assistant judges (1695-96), provided for exercise of judicial powers according to equity and good conscience and according to the rules and customs of England and of the Province.[54] Several proprietary commissions to the Commissary General provided for proceedings according to the laws and the usage and customs of the Province.[55] The vice-admiralty courts of the royal period were also held by virtue of commissions from the governor as vice-admiral.[56]

Commissions, sometimes following a statutory mandate, were used early to define the powers of administrative officers such as the sheriff, coroner, and constable, at times incorporating by reference powers under the laws and customs of England.[57] At a later date, as the office declined in dignity and importance, commissions were not used in the appointment of constables. However, the oath of office might still refer to the governing laws and customs of England and of the province instead of spelling out the duties of the incumbent.[58]

Judicial practice in a sense may be considered as part of "custom and usage," discussed above. In establishing the procedures for their courts, the judges and justices, taking account of the circumstances of the province and of their courts, relied primarily upon the diverse and complex elements of the common law of England, acts of Parliament, and acts of Assembly. The fashioning of such procedures was a continuing process. Although changes, apart from those resulting from legislation or executive direction, are difficult to pinpoint, there can be no doubt that by 1715 the procedures of the Provincial Court and county courts had attained levels well in advance of those of the early decades of the colony. Legal historians tend to use conformity to the laws and customs of England as the criterion in appraising the procedures of colonial courts, but perhaps judicial adherence to established procedural norms, fair and efficient in their operation, whatever their origin, might constitute a better test of judicial administration. In any event, the records of the Provincial Court for the royal period show continued pressure from a bar, capable and learned by colonial standards, to conform to and improve upon accepted procedures.[59]

Scattered through the records of the Provincial Court and the county courts are various rules of court or "rules and orders," largely concerned with civil causes. The county courts were specifically authorized by a succession of provincial acts to promulgate such rules, but there was little uniformity in the number, substance, or date of these rules from county to county.[60] Those of the Provincial Court were promulgated in more piecemeal fashion over an extended period of time. No authority for such rules of the Provincial Court appears in any act of Assembly and presumably promulgation was the exercise of an inherent power.[61]

There was no body of decisional law in the colony in the accepted sense. During the period 1675-1715, however, there was a substantial volume of rulings by the Provincial Court on demurrers, motions in arrest of judgment, writs of error, and appeals from the county courts. Some of the rulings involved substantive rules of law; most involved procedural points. It would be surprising if the Provincial Court bar made no attempt to preserve some of these rulings in common place or precedent books. But it must be admitted that there is little evidence of any citation of Provincial Court precedents or overt adherence to *stare decisis* in the rulings of the court. The few authorities relied upon by counsel consisted of English cases and commentators, acts of Parliament, acts of Assembly, and maxims (some in Latin). In a great number of cases, propositions of law were confidently advanced by attorneys without citation of authority. It may be that such propositions were assumed to constitute part of the corpus of law familiar to the court, or perhaps supporting authorities were supplied in oral argument.[62] The great emphasis upon procedural error indicates, however, that the administration of justice in Maryland had attained by this period a higher level than some commentators on the colonial scene would be prepared to admit.

During the early proprietary period, some proclamations were issued by the governor pursuant to the power granted by commission to make "wholesome, reasonable and profitable" ordinances, edicts, and proclamations. Most of the proclamations were made in connection with settlement of the Province or served as a substitute for legislation. In the period of royal rule, the governors frequently resorted to the use of proclamations to complement or supplement existing laws. Some of these proclamations contemplated punishment under existing laws or gave a new interpretation to such laws. Still others seemingly created new offenses and proceeded on the theory that disobedience would constitute contempt.[63] For the most part these proclamations made little reference to jurisdiction. It is doubtful, however, whether in practice they added significantly to the jurisdiction of either the Provincial Court or county courts. In a few isolated instances, royal proclamations issued in England were put into effect in the Province.[64] A few scattered cases show that the Governor and Council resorted to conciliar orders to implement existing laws, including the ordering of court procedures.[65]

While it is true that law and authority in Maryland during the period under consideration presented a complex and, in some respects, uncertain picture, some evaluation of the constituent elements is possible. The charter and the later royal commissions were significant for providing the constitutional framework in which all the other elements operated. Probably the most important of such other elements consisted of the acts of the Assembly. In matters of public law peculiar to the conditions of the Province, only acts of the Assembly were significant. Next in importance rank acts of Parliament and the common law of England — the laws and customs of England. In certain private law fields the common law of England was the influential factor. Local acts, the common law, and acts of Parliament, all exerted influence in the areas of probate, administration, and real property. In civil procedure several elements were fused — English common law, acts of Parliament, local laws, and judicial practice. On the criminal side, acts of the Assembly were largely confined to establishing punishments for minor offenses. The substantive law for serious crimes and criminal law administration, on the other hand, were almost entirely governed by the laws and customs of England. The judicial commission served as an auxiliary device in establishing jurisdiction and imposing rules of judicature. The role of local custom and usage is difficult to assess from the surviving records; seemingly decisional law was not a material factor. Proclamations and conciliar orders played a rather minor role. The dominant characteristic of law and authority thus viewed was its complexity. Courts and lawyers operating in colonial Maryland, therefore, can scarcely be chided for failing to attain the levels of Westminster Hall.

COLONIAL AMERICA

FOOTNOTES

1. For counsel and assistance in the preparation of this essay I am indebted to Julius Goebel, Jr., Professor Emeritus, Columbia University School of Law; Dorothy Burne Goebel, Professor Emeritus, Department of History, Hunter College; Dr. Morris L. Radoff, Archivist and Records Administrator, Hall of Records, Annapolis, Md.; Gust Skordas, Assistant Archivist, Hall of Records; Lois Green Carr, formerly Junior Archivist, Hall of Records; and my wife Edith S. Smith. In the following notes the *Archives of Maryland* (Baltimore, 1883-date) are cited as *MA;* the *Maryland Historical Magazine* (Baltimore, 1906-date) as *MHM; Court Records of Prince Georges County, Maryland: 1696-1699* (Amer. Legal Records — Vol. 9, ed. Joseph H. Smith and Philip A. Crowl, Washington, 1964) as *PGCC;* and the manuscript *Provincial Court Judgment Books* at the Hall of Records, Annapolis, Maryland, by liber designations derived from clerical initials, such as WC, DS No. A, TL No. 1, etc. The designation Md. H.R. indicates other manuscript court records at the Hall of Records in Annapolis.
2. Whether the laws and institutions of Virginia should be considered a source of Maryland law and authority requires a more extended comparison than any now available.
3. The Latin original and an English translation by Thomas Bacon appear in *The Federal and State Constitutions, Colonial Charters, and Other Organic Laws of the States, Territories, and Colonies now or Heretofore Forming the United States of America*, ed. Francis N. Thorpe (Washington, 1909) III, 1669-1686. See also the textual criticism of John L. Bozman, *History of Maryland*, (Baltimore, 1837) II, 11. As late as 1678 the House of Delegates complained that the charter was available only in translation. 7 *MA* 12, 15. For proprietary commissions to the lieutenant general (governor) reflecting charter powers see 3 *ibid.* 49, 108, 151, 201, 323, 391, 439, 542; 15 *ibid.* 1, 105; 17 *ibid.* 247, 426. Proprietary instructions to the same officer are at 3 *ibid.* 324, 329, 335; 5 *ibid.* 63; 15 *ibid.* 9. Commissions to the provincial Council are at 3 *ibid.* 114, 159, 211; 15 *ibid.* 6, 109; 17 *ibid.* 252, 430. For conditions of plantation see 3 *ibid.* 47, 99, 223, 231, 233; 5 *ibid.* 54, 63; 17 *ibid.* 142, 239; John Kilty, *The Land-Holder's Assistant and Land-Office Guide* (Baltimore, 1808) c. III.
4. Passing references are at 1 *MA* 389-390; 2 *ibid.* 355-356; 5 *ibid.* 147.
5. On *Quia Emptores* see William Kilty, *A Report of All Such English Statutes . . . .* (Annapolis, 1811) 146. For a proprietary attempt to introduce copyhold into the Province see 1 *MA* 330-331.
6. For judgment of escheat of goods and chattels upon *felo de se* see 66 *MA* 136-137; 68 *ibid.* 93.
7. The records of only one manorial court (St. Clement's Manor) have survived (53 *MA* 627-637); a court probably was held at St. Gabriel's Manor. The impression given in Harry W. Newman, *The Flowering of the Maryland Palatinate* (Washington, 1961), 104-106 of a wide-

spread system of manorial courts is not supported by the available evidence. Charles M. Andrews concludes more cautiously "that the holding of courts leet and baron was practiced on many of the manors at the beginning is likely enough." *The Colonial Period of American History*, (New Haven, 1936) II, 295. J. Hall Pleasants believes that very few of the 74 manors appearing in the Land Office records functioned with court leet and court baron. 53 *MA* lxii.

8. 51 *MA* 383 (1671), 567 (1668).
9. 1 *MA* 300; 3 *ibid.* 507; 5 *ibid.* 136-137, 139-140; 8 *ibid.* 120-122, 130-131, 149-150; 13 *ibid.* 162. For a statement of the rights claimed see the 1638/9 proposed Act for the Liberties of the People. 1 *ibid.* 41. As to Magna Carta see 1 *ibid.* 83, 122, 398, 429; 5 *ibid.* 354; 7 *ibid.* 153-154; 57 *ibid.* 75, 543-544, 571-574; William Kilty, *A Report of All Such English Statutes* . . . . 9-12, 139-141, 205-208.
10. For criticism of the clause as uncertain and not reserving an appeal to the King. 3 *MA* 18. For a 1650 proprietary explanation that the clause granted royal jurisdiction see 1 *ibid.* 263-264. The "Royall Rights Jurisdictions Authorities and preheminences" were recognized by act of Assembly "soe farre as they doe not in any sorte infringe or prejudice the Just and Lawfull Lybertyes or priviledges of the free-borne subjects of the Kingdome of England." 1 *ibid.* 300. For a complaint invoking the act see 5 *ibid.* 136-137. A 1661 act for a mint may have been based upon this clause. 1 *ibid.* 400, 414-415. See also the reservation of royal rights belonging to a court palatine in a 1638/9 proposed act. 1 *ibid.* 48.
11. 5 *MA* 344.
12. Governor Lionel Copley's commission and instructions are at 8 *MA* 263, 271; Governor Francis Nicholson's commission is at 20 *ibid.* 33; his instructions, at 23 *ibid.* 540. For Solicitor General Thomas Trevor's opinion as to proprietary rights after 1691 to fines and amercements and to *ferae naturae* see 8 *ibid.* 422-423; Assembly opinion thereon is at 13 *ibid.* 313-314.
13. As to the 1700 compilation see W. F. Dodd, "Maryland Compiled Laws of 1700," *MHM*, V (1910), 185; Lawrence C. Wroth, *A History of Printing in Colonial Maryland, 1686-1776*, (Baltimore, 1922), 22-26, 153.
14. These acts are scattered through volumes 1, 2, 7, 13, 19, 22, 24, 26, 27, 29, 30 and 38 of the *Archives of Maryland.*
15. For discussion of these actions in a representative period (1696-1699) see *PGCC*, lix-lxiii. County court commissions c. 1705 specifically conferred jurisdiction over popular actions and actions upon the statute. Prince Georges County Ct. Rec., Liber B, 380a, 410a (Md. H.R.).
16. But see the 1669 representation that vexatious informers were a public grievance. 2 *MA* 169.
17. Three 1642 acts respectively providing punishment for "certain greater capitall offences," "certain lesse capitall offences" and "some offences not capitall" are at 1 *MA* 158, 192-193. Later acts dealing

with serious offenses are at 1 *ibid.* 247, 248, 286, 287, 346, 350; 22 *ibid.* 568; 26 *ibid.* 340, 431, 514, 630; 27 *ibid.* 144, 146; 30 *ibid.* 298; 38 *ibid.* 122.

18. 1 *MA* 159, 193, 251, 286, 342-344, 375, 444, 455, 503; 2 *ibid.* 140, 273, 277, 398; 7 *ibid.* 201; 13 *ibid.* 439, 458, 477, 479, 487; 22 *ibid.* 477, 523, 553; 24 *ibid.* 98; 26 *ibid.* 231, 266, 321, 341; 27 *ibid.* 140; 29 *ibid.* 192, 329; 30 *ibid.* 233, 243, 304; 38 *ibid.* 19, 82, 119, 152.

19. 1 *MA* 159, 194, 288, 348, 487, 501; 2 *ibid.* 276, 305, 389; 13 *ibid.* 442, 449, 473; 19 *ibid.* 116; 22 *ibid.* 481, 544; 26 *ibid.* 262, 361; 30 *ibid.* 252, 323. As to town lands see 19 *ibid.* 257, 279; 26 *ibid.* 332; 30 *ibid.* 323.

20. For early acts "touching testamentary causes" and orphans' estates see 1 *MA* 108, 154, 188, 353, 354, 374, 493; 2 *ibid.* 325. For the earliest Commissary General commissions see 15 *ibid.* 24-25, 74-75; 17 *ibid.* 18, 129, 435. For the later acts see 7 *ibid.* 195; 13 *ibid.* 215, 430, 498; 19 *ibid.* 166, 209, 469; 22 *ibid.* 533; 24 *ibid.* 273; 26 *ibid.* 234; 38 *ibid.* 22, 41, 91. See also Edith E. MacQueen, "The Commissary in Colonial Maryland," *MHM*, XXV (1930), 190.

21. 1 *MA* 148-153, 184-187, 195. An act for the forms of proceeding in causes provided that the Provincial Court was to be guided by former precedents and usages of the court and, in defect thereof, by the forms of England in the same or like cases, except when specially provided by the law of the Province. 1 *ibid.* 150, 185-186.

22. 1 *MA* 232-233, 352, 361, 449, 485-486, 492-493, 496, 498, 502, 504; 2 *ibid.* 135, 142, 201, 206, 209, 218, 221-222, 289, 323, 395, 397, 411, 537, 562; 7 *ibid.* 70-71, 205, 323, 606; 13 *ibid.* 122, 444, 447, 449, 476, 481, 502, 514, 519, 521-522, 528, 530; 19 *ibid.* 237, 377, 470, 551; 22 *ibid.* 463-464, 466, 469, 500, 511-512, 528; 24 *ibid.* 201, 414; 26 *ibid.* 220, 283, 286, 298, 316, 324, 329, 346, 356, 358, 424; 27 *ibid.* 168, 174, 337, 364, 367, 481, 559, 577; 29 *ibid.* 191, 333, 336, 439; 30 *ibid.* 229, 235-243, 299, 302, 308, 317, 320; 38 *ibid.* 6, 22, 25, 56, 59, 93-94, 100, 101-103, 111, 143, 150, 154, 177.

23. Acts relating to attorneys are at 2 *MA* 132, 322, 409, 467; 13 *ibid.* 483; 22 *ibid.* 502; 26 *ibid.* 334, 348; 27 *ibid.* 360, 485; 29 *ibid.* 191; 30 *ibid.* 248; 38 *ibid.* 113, 160. Some acts relating to sheriffs are at 1 *ibid.* 448; 2 *ibid.* 132, 222, 322; 13 *ibid.* 471, 483, 484; 22 *ibid.* 465, 504; 26 *ibid.* 223; 30 *ibid.* 264; 38 *ibid.* 110, 127.

24. See Calvin's Case, 7 Co. Rep. 2a (1608) and the discussion in Joseph H. Smith, *Appeals to the Privy Council from the American Plantations* (New York, 1950), 464-476.

25. For representative acts extending the laws of England, or parts thereof, in particular areas see 1 *MA* 81, 97, 108, 151, 157, 158, 410, 487; 2 *ibid.* 130, 135, 139, 279, 398; 7 *ibid.* 60, 201; 13 *ibid.* 425, 537; 20 *ibid.* 422 (proclamation); 22 *ibid.* 568; 27 *ibid.* 335 (ordinance); 38 *ibid.* 103. For extension of the mortmain statutes before Henry VIII by conditions of plantation see 3 *ibid.* 227, 336. For some of the resort to or recognized divergence from the laws of England see 1

ibid. 107, 121, 348, 465, 501-502, 528; 2 *ibid.* 24, 54-55, 119, 249-250, 361, 391, 408, 425, 446, 563; 5 *ibid.* 138, 267, 556; 7 *ibid.* 72, 201-203, 354; 8 *ibid.* 34, 62; 13 *ibid.* 215, 257, 285, 297, 304, 361; 19 *ibid.* 8-9, 12, 16; 24 *ibid.* 239, 349-350; 25 *ibid.* 160-161; 26 *ibid.* 98-99, 109-110, 118; 27 *ibid.* 192, 220; 29 *ibid.* 253, 326-327. See also Provincial Court entries at 4 *ibid.* 38-39, 180, 249, 333; 10 *ibid.* 219, 256-257; 41 *ibid.* 368; 49 *ibid.* 213; 65 *ibid.* 32, 158, 229; 66 *ibid.* 423.

26. 1 *MA* 147 (An Act for Rule of Judicature), 184, 210, 448 (An Act Concerning Proceedings at Law), 487, 504; 13 *ibid.* 39, 43, 99, 103-104, 483; 19 *ibid.* 426; 22 *ibid.* 558-562; 24 *ibid.* 4-5, 104-107.
27. William Kilty, *A Report of All Such English Statutes . . .*, 139-187, 205-248.
28. 41 *MA* 10-11 (3 Jac. I, c. 7), 558 (Magna Carta c. 29 and Statute of Marlborough, 52 Hen. III); 51 *ibid.* 279-280 (27 Eliz. I, c. 8), 305 (several English statutes); WC, 188-191 (31 Eliz. I, c. 5), 499-503 (31 Eliz. I, c. 5; 21 Jac. I, c. 4), 681-690 (16 and 17 Car. II, c. 8); DS No. A, 4 (43 Eliz. I, c. 6), 10-12 (8 Eliz. I, c. 2), 297-299, 301-306 (29 Car. II, c. 3), 412-414 (23 Hen. VI, c. 10), 565-566 (5 and 6 Edw. VI, c. 16); SS, 13, 16-24 (Magna Carta, c. 29), 55-59 (16 and 17 Car. II, c. 8), 62-69 (statute against usury); TL No. 1, 552-553 (Magna Carta); I, No. 1, 399-402 (21 Jac. I, c. 16); VD No. 1, 234-239 (21 Jac. IO, c. 16), 297-300 (29 Car. I, c. 3).
29. In 1674 a proposal was made to list the laws of England applicable in criminal cases. 2 *MA* 347-349, 368-370, 372, 374-375. Agitation in 1704-06 resulted in a limited declaration. 26 *ibid.* 37, 122, 540-541, 545-546, 597-599, 601, 630. See also the later discussion at 29 *ibid.* 159, 365-367, 410-411, 419.
30. 1 *MA* 9 (*cf.* the lost act of 1634/5 which apparently applied the laws of England to serious offenses), 47 (proposed act), 147, 184, 210 (no reference to laws of England), 448, 487, 504; 13 *ibid.* 483.
31. The courts held by charter at St. Mary's and at Annapolis appear to have been courts of record. 51 *MA* 383, 567; Elihu S. Riley, *The Ancient City: A History of Annapolis, in Maryland* (Annapolis, 1887), 87. *Cf.* 19 *MA* 498; 27 *ibid.* 358.
32. For reliance on the rules of the Court of Chancery in England see 51 *MA* 8, 52, 290, 294, 487. For rules and orders promulgated see 51 *ibid.* 8, 15, 52, 419, 501; Chancery Record, Liber PC, 1671-1712, 321, 355, 379, 422, 427, 434, 451, 465, 470, 523, 677 (Land Office, Annapolis, Md.).
33. 49 *MA* 538-545; 57 *ibid.* 62-65, 74-75.
34. 1 *MA* 18, 23; 2 *ibid.* 540; 7 *ibid.* 104, 473; 22 *ibid.* 556; 26 *ibid.* 512, 513; 27 *ibid.* 139.
35. Julius Goebel, Jr., "King's Law and Local Custom in Seventeenth Century New England," *Columbia Law Rev.*, XXXI (1931), 416; George L. Haskins, *Law and Authority in Early Massachusetts*, (New York, 1960), 76-78, 167-174, 218-219.
36. The few commissions to administer justice within a hundred in Mary-

land were not patterned after the hundred court in England. 3 *MA* 70-71, 89-90. See also the proposed act making Kent a hundred and establishing a court therein. 1 *ibid.* 55-57.

37. The county courts were directed by acts in 1678 (7 *MA* 70) and later years to procure copies of Dalton's *Justice of the Peace* (*The Country Justice*) and Keble's *Abridgement of the Statutes* (*Statutes at Large*).
38. For reference to the custom of London see 66 *MA* 423.
39. Both St. Mary's and Annapolis had limited by-law powers. See references *supra*, note 31. For promulgation of by-laws for St. Mary's by the Council see 17 *MA* 418-423.
40. For pleadings see 65 *MA* 309, 333, 576; 66 *ibid.* 326; TG, 138; DS No. A, 18, 72, 82, 478-479; SS, 49-52, 52-55; DS No. C, 81-83; VD No. 1, 217-219.
41. See the reference to judgment by the custom or law merchant of England in the court of admiralty, proposed in 1638/9. 1 *MA* 46-47.
42. 1 *MA* 10, 398; 2 *ibid.* 42, 178; 7 *ibid.* 61, 114-115, 135-136, 138-139, 414-415; 13 *ibid.* 102, 156, 159, 176, 364-366, 417; 27 *ibid.* 535-536; 29 *ibid.* 170-172, 177, 243-244.
43. Two early Acts for Rule of Judicature in civil causes referred to "the law or most Generall usage of the province since its plantacion or former presidents of the same or the like nature." 1 *MA* 184. A similar reference appeared in two Acts Touching Causes Testamentary. 1 *ibid.* 155, 189. By a 1647/8 act, causes in the county courts were to be judged according to the laudable customs of the province, equity and good conscience. 1 *ibid.* 232. Lord Baltimore in 1678 stated as to the Province: "And where the necessity and exigencyes of the Provynce Doe not enforce them to make any Particular Lawes They use no other Lawe than the Lawe of England." 5 *ibid.* 264-265. The phrase "any law, custom or usage to the contrary notwithstanding", or some similar phrase, appears in many acts of Assembly. Whether this language, copied from the stock language used in acts of Parliament, constituted recognition of the role of custom is difficult to determine. At times custom may have been equated with the common law of England received in the Province.
44. 1 *MA* 53, 97, 409, 453; 2 *ibid.* 402-403, 525; 4 *ibid.* 361, 447, 464, 470-471, 539; 41 *ibid.* 417, 493-494; 57 *ibid.* 586; 66 *ibid.* 50, 203-204; 68 *ibid.* 107-108.
45. 4 *MA* 414-415; 10 *ibid.* 23, 108-109, 128-130; 41 *ibid.* 438; 49 *ibid.* 27, 32, 40, 129, 130, 388, 419, 424, 427. For servants "by custom of the country" see Eugene L. McCormac, *White Servitude in Maryland, 1634-1820*, Johns Hopkins Univ. Studies in Historical and Political Science, Series XXII, Nos. 3-4, 1904, c. IV.
46. *PGCC*, lxxxvii. See also the alleged custom at 24 *MA* 315.
47. 23 *MA* 88; 22 *ibid.* 40, 115. See also the reference to custom in the protest against the disbarment of James Crawford. *PGCC*, xxix-xxxi.
48. For the controversy over the assizes see 27 *MA* 4, 11-14, 17, 50-51, 58, 63, 68-69, 73-76, 88, 113-114, 183, 227, 235-236, 239, 279,

281-282, 285-287, 397-398, 447; 25 *ibid.* 216-217, 220, 226, 236; 29 *ibid.* 223.

49. 3 *MA* 59, 60-61, 62-63, 70-71, 80-81, 89-90, 216-217, 237-240, 257-258. See also the justice of the peace powers in commissions to Council members. 3 *ibid.* 159, 327, 439-441.

50. 3 *MA* 422, 534, 553; 5 *ibid.* 52; 15 *ibid.* 65, 216, 224, 256, 316, 323, 346, 395-398; 41 *ibid.* 87; 51 *ibid.* 74, 78, 81, 348, 353, 365; *PGCC*, 1, 186, 519; Prince Georges County Ct. Rec., Liber B., 379a, 380a, 409a, 410a (Md. H.R.). For two periods c. 1679-81 and c. 1705-15 two commissions were used in each county — a commission of the peace (criminal jurisdiction) and a commission of oyer and terminer or for the trial of causes (civil jurisdiction only or civil and criminal jurisdiction); a greater number of justices were usually named in the commission of the peace. At times councilors, commissioned as justices of the peace, sat on the county courts. Early oaths of a commissioner required judgment by the precedents and customs of the Province and acts of Assembly. 3 *MA* 423; 41 *ibid.* 89. Compare later oaths at 3 *ibid.* 553 (no standard) and *PGCC*, xxv (laws of England and acts of Assembly).

51. 15 *MA* 8-9, 110-111, 129-130, 357-358; 17 *ibid.* 250, 431-432; 66 *ibid.* 141-142; WC, 635-636.

52. DS No. C, 10-11, 38-40, 49-50, 323; TL No. 1, 1-2, 120-122; HW No. 3, 131; WT No. 3, 1-3, 612-614; WT No. 4, 165-168; TB No. 2, 65; PL No. 1, 233.

53. HW No. 3, 263 (1697 commission of oyer and terminer, to hear and determine according to the laws, orders and customs of England and of the Province); 20 *MA* 583, 589-592; 23 *ibid.* 376.

54. Chancery Court Record, Liber PC, 1671-1712, 294-295, 320-321 (Land Office, Annapolis, Md.).

55. 15 *MA* 24-25, 74-75; 17 *ibid.* 129. *Cf.* 17 *ibid.* 435. The contempt power granted was that of the Court of Chancery, 17 *ibid.* 18.

56. 20 *MA* 91-97, 172, 225, 238, 478-481; 23 *ibid.* 274, 321-322, 345, 368-369, 389-390; 25 *ibid.* 12, 61-67.

57. For the sheriff see 3 *MA* 61; *PGCC*, 2-3; for the coroner see 2 *MA* 130-131; 3 *ibid.* 91; 13 *ibid.* 515; for the constable see 1 *ibid.* 410-412; 3 *ibid.* 59-60, 70, 89; 13 *ibid.* 515-516; 26 *ibid.* 343-344; 30 *ibid.* 274.

58. 41 *MA* 91. The tithingman (1 *ibid.* 54-55) had no lasting significance.

59. DS No. C, 148-152, 173-176, 176-180, 287-291, 304-307, 356-361; TL No. 1, 28-32, 100-105, 222-225, 516-518, 520-523, 546-548, 713; TL No. 2, 121-122, 128-130, 130-132, 140-142; HW No. 3, 88-93, 159-160, 232-234; IL. 123-124, 124-125; WT No. 3, 502-505, 556-564, 565-572, 573-579, 784-791, 792-799, 799-808, 808-815; WT No. 4, 116-119; TL No. 3, 87-90, 108-110, 113-115, 116-119, 120-124, 234-241, 350-352, 607-609, 635-642, 642-648, 648-654, 654-659, 659-662, 662-665; TB No. 2, 23-25, 25-28; PL No. 1, 57-60, 60-67, 71-

75; PL No. 2, 1-3, 3-7, 7-11, 11-17, 107-112, 180-184, 226-229, 245-248; PL No. 3, 493-496, 497-508, 508-512, 652-656, 656-658, 674-678, 678-683; VD No. 1, 224-226, 254-256, 259-265, 265-272, 363, 366, 379-382. See also the cases starting with DS No. C in note 62 *infra*.

60. For the acts see 7 *MA* 70; 13 *ibid.* 521; 22 *ibid.* 463-464; 26 *ibid.* 283-285. For some county court rules see Charles County Ct. Rec., Liber S., No. 1, 61-64; Baltimore County Ct. Proc., Liber G, No. 1, 287, 417, 551-559; Kent County Ct. Proc., Liber I, 580-582 (all Md. H.R.); *PGCC*, 42, 105, 113, 350, 542, 615.
61. 66 *MA* 49; WC 68, 632, 636, 739, 762, 764, 768, 899; DS No. A, 225, 288, 450; TL No. 1, 700-701, 702; TL No. 2, 4-5; HW No. 3, 134; WT No. 3, 257-258, 629; TL No. 3, 264, 583; TB No. 2, 194; PL No. 1, 90, 234-235; PL No. 2, 23, 122-123, 129, 248, 348. For reliance upon court rules by a litigant see 67 *MA* 421; DS No. A, 152-154.
62. 66 *MA* 347-350, 425-426; 67 *ibid.* 68-70, 346-350, 352-354; 68 *ibid.* 5-6; WC 37-40, 152-154, 168-169, 171-175, 175-191, 191-195, 232-235, 261-267, 269-273, 322-325, 496-499, 499-503, 506-509, 510-514, 585-588, 624-628, 681-690, 731-732, 850-852, 863-869; DS No. A, 10-12, 17-18, 24-25, 33-36, 56-57, 72-74, 85-87, 248-249, 258-260, 297-299, 301-306, 407-410, 467-470, 565-567; SS 13-16, 16-24, 24-39, 55-59, 62-69; DS No. C, 111-119a, 125-132, 153-156, 162-164, 164-169, 169-172, 370-375, 380-385, 389-393; TL No. 1, 37-44, 210-213, 213-217, 228-232, 238-242, 243-246, 523-526, 531-538, 548-549, 551-552, 552-553, 553-554; TL No. 2, 135-137, 137-140, 150-158, 180-181; HW No. 3, 76-79, 235-238; IL, 104-106, 122-123; WT No. 3, 43-44, 399-406, 535-541; TL No. 3, 105-108, 669-673; TB No. 2, 11-23; PL No. 3, 462-465, 668-674; IO No. 1, 399-402; VD No. 1, 234-239, 297-300. See also Joseph H. Smith, "The Provincial Court and the Laws of Maryland: 1675-1715" in *Essays in Legal History in Honor of Felix Frankfurter* (New York, in press). For some description of law practice in Maryland in the early eighteenth century see Land, *The Dulanys of Maryland* (Baltimore, 1955), 6-22; *Proceedings of the Maryland Court of Appeals, 1695-1729* (Amer. Legal Records — Vol. 1, ed. Carroll T. Bond, Washington, 1933), xviii-xxix.
63. 15 *MA* 39, 65, 100, 127, 131, 136, 140, 154-157, 159-161, 177, 193, 194, 201, 211, 215-216, 228, 235-236, 391; 17 *ibid.* 114, 142, 178-180, 219, 239, 261, 269, 403, 404, 424; *PGCC*, xlviii-xlix.
64. 20 *MA* 339; 23 *ibid.* 444; 25 *ibid.* 300-301; 27 *ibid.* 350 (last two intended for plantations).
65. 15 *MA* 127, 380; 20 *ibid.* 314, 510, 517-518, 536, 582; 23 *ibid.* 120-121; *PGCC*, xlix.

LAW AND AUTHORITY IN COLONIAL VIRGINIA

WILCOMB E. WASHBURN

Smithsonian Institution

ON MAY 17, 1959, a tablet was erected at Jamestown by a committee of the Virginia State Bar Association to commemorate the advent of the common law in Virginia. The plaque reads:

> THE COMMON LAW
>
> Here the Common Law of England was established on this continent with the arrival of the first settlers on May 13, 1607. The first charter granted by James I to the Virginia Company in 1606 declared that the inhabitants of the colony '. . . shall have and enjoy all liberties, franchises and immunities . . . as if they had been abiding and borne within this our realme of Englande. . . .' Since Magna Carta the Common Law has been the cornerstone of individual liberties, even as against the Crown. Summarized later in the Bill of Rights its principles have inspired the development of our system of freedom under law, which is at once our dearest possession and proudest achievement.[1]

One of the purposes of this essay is to show that such a summary statement is more confusing than enlightening and reflects the assumptions and heritage of a later age rather than the experience of an earlier age.

The charter of 1606 bespoke an intention to adopt English legal practices in the colonies, but it did not proclaim a fully elaborated theory of colonial liberties. In the opinion of Charles M. Andrews, the words:

> 'liberties, franchises and immunities' are to be taken literally, as meaning just what they were understood to mean in England at that time. They have nothing to do with civil liberty, self-government, or democracy; they were strictly legal, tenurial, and financial in their application.[2]

The extremely narrow construction of Andrews may, like the broad interpretation of the Virginia Bar, be questioned. It is possible to consider the phrase in the Virginia charter as a shorthand way of expressing the hope and intention that the legal rights and obligations of individual Englishmen — as they had emerged historically and haphazardly from the legal culture of England to that time — could *in general* be applied to the Englishmen who chose to remove to the new colonies. How such rights might be applied specifically was another matter. As Sir William Blackstone put it, in commenting upon the claim that all English laws accompany colonists planting in an uninhabited country, "this must be understood with very many and very great restrictions."[3]

The meaning of the words in the charter, in sum, were to be determined specifically by the subsequent pragmatic experiences of the colonists. The words did not represent pre-existing principles that could automatically be applied in a new country — even though the colony was to be formally incorporated into the general legal framework of the mother country. Nor can the assertion by the newly independent State of Virginia, on July 3, 1776, of Virginia's inheritance of the English common law prior to the settlement of the colony, be considered more than a later formal statement of the general proposition that English law should normally be expected to follow an English colonist.[4]

What did come to Virginia were traditional English legal customs and practices. Law regarded as practices rather than as principles can justly be considered to have been imported into the colonies. Were Englishmen to ignore or repudiate their upbringing and traditional forms for no reason? If the law is a cultural growth designed to place tradition, environment, and challenges into a valid relationship, it cannot be shed like a cloak as fancy chooses. The spate of handbooks for justices of the peace and sheriffs which were imported to the colonies from England were as logical a cultural "import" as language itself.[5] As Henry St. George Tucker put it, "what was more natural than a tacit acquiescence by every individual in the authority of the laws to which they had always been accustomed?" "We can scarcely presume," wrote the Virginia jurist, "that any but enthusiasts would adopt a jurisprudence entirely foreign to their habits instead of the institutions of their fathers." With perhaps a wry smile, Tucker added at this point, in a footnote citing Thomas Hutchinson's history, "The people of Massachusetts adopted the laws of Moses."[6]

It is equally clear, however, that the New World environment altered, replaced, or rendered superfluous many of the legal forms sanctioned by the tradition that the colonists had brought with them. The changes, as well as the survivals, should be acknowledged and described, though it is beyond the scope of this essay to do so. What should be kept in mind is that many of the "principles" upheld by later generations were not necessarily inherent in these earlier practices, but were interpretations from them, selectively adduced in support of still newer practices.

The later interpreters of seventeenth-century law have labored under a double handicap. Not only are their attitudes attuned to a philosophical rather than an historical study of "the law," but the lack of a proper historical record makes the approach to seventeenth-century colonial law extremely difficult. George Chalmers, perhaps more qualified than any of the early writers to look at the law from the double vision of a lawyer and an historian, noted that:

> Many years of agitation and revolution have elapsed, since it occurred to me, that the commentaries on the Laws of England were barren on such legal topics as relate to our Colonies, Fisheries and Commerce. The commentator was, probably, unable to obtain materials; as the appeals from our foreign dominions lay to the King in his Council, and not to the King in his Bench. There have been scarcely any reports of cases, which were decided on such appeals, and were accessible to research, but, if such appeals had lain to the King in his Bench, then there would have been many reports laid before the public, whence the commentator on the laws of England might have drawn, with an inquisitive spirit and a liberal hand."[7]

Indeed, it was in the course of Chalmers' research in the books of the Board of Trade, and other depositories, for his *Political Annals of the Present United Colonies* (London, 1780), that "I was thus induced to take copies of such law opinions as appeared in the course of my researches."[8] Buried in government archives the opinions were useless to the administrators, lawyers, and judges. It was Chalmers' great service to transmute these opinions from historical to legal uses — though by today's standards his effort was modest, and unfortunately was limited primarily to the eighteenth century.

The truth of Chalmers' observation is apparent in the legal record of the seventeenth century. The principal reports and histories of the law are almost barren of colonial references. Sir Edward Coke's *Institutes of the Laws of England* never got beyond such exceptional jurisdictions as the County Palatine of Durham, the Cinque-Ports, the Isles of Jersey and Guernsey, Scotland, and Ireland. Coke's *Reports* are similarly barren of colonial references. The inability of administrators to agree on how to apply Coke to the legal problems raised by Bacon's Rebellion provides a powerful proof of the practical significance of this omission.[9]

Similarly, Sir Matthew Hale (1609-1676), Lord Chief Justice of England in the reign of Charles II, in his *History of the Common Law*, wrote as though the colonies did not exist for him. And in truth they probably did not, though they bulked large in the thoughts and action of his master, Charles. Hale dealt briefly with Ireland, Jersey, Guernsey, and Sark, but the only reference to what we would consider colonies is in the notes of his eighteenth-century editor, Charles Runnington, who commented:

> As to our colonies, or plantations, the student may consult the first volume of Mr. Justice Blackstone's *Commentaries*, from page 106 to page 109 from whence he may derive sufficient information.[10]

The utter silence about colonial law in the works of the principal exponents of English law of the seventeenth century is a more serious problem than has been realized. If the colonies formed a unity with the mother country in theory and in fact, such a relationship was ignored by the legal writers who created the corpus of legal references of the seventeenth century. I believe that ignorance of colonial conditions rather than the assumed unity was the reason it was ignored. The silence of the legal writers is a remarkable demonstration of the cultural gulf that was unthinkingly created between the two bodies of English subjects. Certainly Virginia might have warranted a comment that would have given it the prominence, in legal texts, of Sark or the Isle of Man, to say nothing of Ireland. But, for the most part, the study of English law in the seventeenth century ignored the legal culture of the colonies.

Essential to the thinking of the mother country from the first project to establish settlements in the New World down to the final break with the colonies was the assumption that they could be incorporated "within the Realm" in terms of individual rights if not in terms of imperial policy. Once Englishmen were granted the right to depart the realm — but to maintain their rights as though they had not departed the realm — the main purpose of colonial policy should have been to maintain a bond that would have achieved that objective. Whether the objective was to be achieved by royal government, by proprietary government, by charter government, or by shifting policies of the moment, the fundamental purpose ought to have been to annihilate geography as a factor in thinking about the rights of an Englishman. The difficulty of finding a meaningful phrase for this unity (other than "British Empire" which is a later expression and which has a different meaning) reflects the difficulty of mentally making the leap across oceans without altering the basis of government.

It may well be that it is impossible for a unitary democracy to spread its arms across an ocean and remain a democracy. Indeed, some ancient theorists thought that a voice's carry was the proper range of a democracy. Greek democracy could not spread to Sicily and both remain a democracy and maintain its mainland Greek connection. An empire held by compulsion can, of course, extend as far as the compulsion is effective. A body of citizens united in a democratic community making their own laws, however, can extend only so far as the democratic dialogue and representative linkages can function efficiently. Virginia gallantly attempted to maintain its democratic nature — through representative institutions and royal leadership — in the seventeenth century. It was a losing fight, because of the failure satisfactorily to establish and maintain the dialogue.

Chalmers, in his *Political Annals*, which is a legal argument as much as it is a political history, put it this way:

> When we throw our eyes over the globe, it must appear that it is not the perceptible boundaries of nature, a mountain or desert, a river or an ocean, which forms a state. For it is an incorporeal thing, a body politic, composed of aggregates of men; who, uniting for mutual advantage, are fellow-subjects of the same sovereign, who are subjected to the same laws. And our country, therefore, is the nation of which we are members, and not the town, the county, or the province, where we first saw the light. When a wilderness is subsequently peopled, and a colony is planted, however separated and however distant from the principal establishment, it becomes a part of

> the ancient dominions, and equally composes the common country of the same people.[11]

A fine idea. But neither Chalmers' own theory that Parliament always remained the fount of authority despite the arbitrary actions of the Stuart kings, nor the contrary assumption that the colonies were merely personal dependencies of the Crown, could bridge the real gap between the assumed equality — as Englishmen — of residents of the colony and of the mother country, and the actual inequality that existed. Both Parliament and King failed to concentrate their efforts on preventing a separation. The eyes of both were more often on their prerogatives. The colonies fell between their two interests.

An incident that is at once representative of the problem — as well as of the failure to solve the problem — of the colonial relationship to the mother country was the decision to declare vacant the seat of Sir George Somers in the House of Commons on his accepting service as admiral of the fleet that sailed for Virginia in May, 1609 carrying 500 new settlers.[12] We lack detailed records of the debate, but we do know that Sir George Moore, reporting for the Committee on privileges, on February 14, 1609/10 recommended that Somers not be removed. Moore cited the precedent of James Ley, first Earl of Marlborough, Member of Parliament for Westbury during the period 1604-1605, when he was also Chief Justice in Ireland, and Commissioner of the Great Seal at Dublin. Sir Edwin Sandys argued also that Somers' case did not come under any of the traditional causes for removal. Among these causes was appointment as an ambassador, but Sandys pointed out that "That, foreign; this, home." Despite these efforts the House seems to have considered Mr. Nicholas Fuller's reasoning that "The end of parliaments, to have men present, that do represent" to be of greater force. It was voted to remove Somers and to call for a new election.[13]

A more perceptive Commons might have foreseen the consequences of an act which, while reasonable by the customary logic of parliamentary procedure, undermined the attempt to project the more vital legal concepts of "England" and "English rights" beyond the seas without essential loss of their meaning. Few historians have noted the monumental significance of this early parliamentary decision.

Virginia's early years were turbulent and unsatisfactory not only because of the initial difficulties of founding a colony in a remote area, but because of the failure to create more than a quasi-military, quasi-feudal sub-culture authorized under the aegis of the commercial company that gave it being. This is not to say that Captain John Smith's military discipline and Sir Thomas Dale's laws were not necessary in this early phase. They were, simply because English society could not at one fell swoop be transferred intact to a hostile shore in which the greed, hatred, and desire that would have been controlled in England by judicial restraints — or the lack of objects of those desires or hatreds — were unchecked.

Twentieth-century libertarian historians condemn the introduction of military discipline into the Virginia colony. Thomas J. Wertenbaker writes that

> The Divine, Moral and Martial Laws, as they were called undoubtedly brought about good order in the colony, and aided in the establishment of prosperity, but they were ill suited for the government of free-born Englishmen. They were in open violation of the rights guaranteed to the settlers in their charters, and caused bitter discontent and resentment.[14]

What the twentieth-century historian overlooks here is that the rights of the individual seventeenth-century Englishman were circumscribed by his membership in larger social units — whether those units were the armed services, the church, or joint-stock companies. These institutions possessed their own legal rights. In determining whether individual or social rights took precedence in a conflict, the seventeenth century usually placed a higher value on the rights of the larger organism than the twentieth century is wont to do. Such an attitude was particularly true in those colonies where the problems of distance, Indians, disease, and lack of supervision forced experimentation in government and occasionally the imposition of martial law. Despite the problems that faced the early Virginia governors, a unity was maintained and the English character of the colony safeguarded. This was the principal problem — legal and practical — to be faced in Virginia in the seventeenth century. The seventeenth-century administrator may be pardoned if he failed to anticipate the twentieth-century historian, armed with different assumptions, principles, and facts.

The primacy of the relationship to the mother country was carefully observed by succeeding Virginia governors. Some — Sir John Harvey is an example — governed roughly "by the book." Sir William Berkeley, on the other hand, governed caressingly and by example. The problem of the early years was to make the colonists willing to stay and to create an English settlement. Under the Company this required almost a military organization and, sometimes, martial law.

It soon became apparent that greater participation by the settlers in their government might simplify the task, and forge the bond more effectively. The allowance of an "assembly", begun under the Company and continued when royal government was instituted in 1625, was an expedient designed for this purpose.[15] Thus Governor John Harvey, on May 31, 1630, could write to Sir Robert Heath, the Attorney General,

> At the Assemblie it was generallie concluded to build a forte at Pointe Comforte, Capeable of 16 peeces of Ordnance, most of which I hope will be mounted before Christemas next. By which you may perceave, that the people are nowe more then ever resolved to make this, theire Countrye, seinge at their owne Charges, they have undertaken soe greate a work as is this fortification.[16]

There is a certain irony in the phrase that "the people are resolved to make this their country" since it foreshadows the separation that was to follow. But, in its context, Harvey's remarks illustrate the concern of the English government at the time to get Englishmen in Virginia to stay. It was in this context that a representative assembly was not only allowed but encouraged. The primary motive for allowing it was not a concern for law, but a concern for the healthy existence of the colony. Where the administrators in the mother country failed was by not following up their interest in establishing the basic legal forms of the colony with a genuine concern for maintaining their proper coordination with the law of England.

It so happened that the hopes for a fort capable of controlling entrance into the James River were to be dashed because of the ineffectiveness of the artillery of that day to span the width of the channel. Yet as the scheme seemed appealing to the administrators in England, and as their attempts to control activities in the colony grew, renewed orders were given to build such a fort at Point Comfort. It was typical of Governor Sir William Berkeley that, though he knew that the fort would not serve its intended purpose, he nevertheless, because of his belief in the supremacy of the principle of loyalty and obedience to the King, worked mightily to see that it was built. This was no easy matter when he had, in the Assembly, to deal with planters less highly motivated towards the principle of loyalty than he.[17]

The loyalty of Virginia during the Parliamentary period, following the execution of Charles I on January 30, 1649, indicates the extent to which this fundamental emotional commitment underlay Virginia society. As soon as news of the deed arrived, the Virginia Assembly of October 1649 passed an act declaring that if any person in the colony should defend "the late traiterous proceedings . . . under any notion of law and justice" by words or speeches, such person was to be adjudged an accessory *post factum* to the death of the King. Anyone who expressed doubt, by words and speeches, as to the inherent right of Charles II to succeed his father as King of England and Virginia was likewise to be adjudged guilty of high treason.

Berkeley's speech to the Virginia Assembly of March 1651, called to consider the Parliamentary threat to the colony, similarly rejected the "ridiculous" reasoning of the Parliamentary forces: "For if you looke into it, the strength of their argument runs onely thus: we have laid violent hands on your land-lord, possessed his manner house where you used to pay your rents, therefore now tender your respects to the same house you once reverenced . . . ." Berkeley went on to point out the practical benefits of Virginia's traditional society:

> What is it can be hoped for in a change, which we have not already? Is it liberty? The sun looks not on a people more free then we are from all oppression. Is it wealth? Hundreds of examples shew us that industry and thrift in a short time may bring us to as high a degree of it, as the country and our conditions are yet capable of: Is it securety to enjoy this wealth when gotten? With out blushing I

> will speak it, I am confident theare lives not that person can accuse me of attempting the least act against any mans property.[18]

At the conclusion of his speech, the Assembly rejected the restrictive Parliamentary act of October 3, 1650, as illegal and resolved to continue in allegiance to Charles II.

Both Virginia and New England in the early stages of the seventeenth century were founded on a policy in which the individual strived to serve a higher entity. In the case of Massachusetts, it was God. In the case of Virginia, the King. Self-seeking was not, of course, unknown, and "convenient" reasoning that what was good for an individual was good for God or King was similarly not unknown. But one would misconstrue the history of the two colonies in the early years if one assumed that Smith or Berkeley, or Bradford or Winthrop, were not governed by motives which were principally unselfish and which lay beyond the individual's private goals.

The goals of the Puritan colony required no necessary connection with the mother country; indeed, they almost required separation. The goals of the Virginia colony required just such a connection with the mother country, the lack of which would spell death to the philosophic concept underlying it. The administrative practice of the two colonies flowed logically from their basic assumptions of purpose. Massachusetts tried to recognize no administrative source of authority higher than its own governors. The Virginia colony gloried in its dependence upon His Sacred Majesty — even though the King's will was too often obscured by the workings of a Kafka-esque "Castle" administration in which decisions sometimes seemed to emerge without reason from sources deep within the power structure.

The English government's attempt to deal with the crisis of Bacon's Rebellion revealed a striking ignorance and incompetence in safeguarding the crucial tie of loyalty between the mother country and its colonies. The link that Governor Berkeley had for so long tenderly nursed was torn to shreds. Like the one-hoss shay, the structure collapsed under stress, and a formal relationship replaced a vital one.[19]

It is instructive to note that the hierarchy of the Church of

England was responsible for similar blunders in the religious administration of the colonies because of its ignorance of religious conditions and systems in the colonies. As Carl Bridenbaugh has put it: "No High-Church official ever crossed to investigate the situation in America; only one person, an unknown and inconsequential layman, was ever authorized to do so. The Church of England must, therefore, share with the English political system, Parliament, and the Crown the responsibility for the loss of the colonies".[20]

With the breakdown of unity between king and subject in Virginia, which had been precariously maintained by Governor Berkeley in the years preceding Bacon's Rebellion, the battle lines were rapidly drawn. Philip Ludwell, Robert Beverley, and other loyalist supporters of Berkeley championed what commentators usually call the "rights of the people" against the royal governors following Berkeley. Their attitude marks the dissolution of the ties that formerly bound the society into a royalist body politic looking to England for leadership, and the creation of a new orientation of interests centered on Virginia and the economic welfare of the individual planters.[21]

The conflict between the lower house (in the case of Virginia with substantial support of the Council) and the King's representative in the late seventeenth century was played out before a backdrop of loyalty to the Crown, but the stakes were essentially based on individual interests. The royal panoply served to dignify the proceedings and divert critical attention while not affecting the play of basic interests. The Virginians' relationship to the Crown was increasingly formal rather than emotional, and their true interests self-centered. This was the "revolution in the minds of the people" that John Adams talked about. The eventual shedding of the outworn form was only a matter of time. When the break occurred it required a justification, and the political arguments of the pre-Revolutionary period supplied them — but these arguments were in a sense an attempt to explain what had happened, not why it must happen.

While the eighteenth century saw the enactment of the physical revolutions of our time, the seventeenth century saw the philosophic shifts that made them inevitable. The nature of that philosophic revolution is disputed, but it was, in more ways than many of us wish to recognize, a revolution of "possessive individualism", as Professor C. B. MacPherson has called it in his significant study, *The Political Theory of Possessive Individualism: Hobbes to Locke.* From the time of that revolution whose influence made itself felt in various ways, the logical consequences of a love of self as the higher law (rather than God or King) sets the background for governors who, whether rapacious or kindly, ignorant or wise, made their policy relate increasingly to assumptions that the individual good was the higher law of the colony. One does not have to interpret Macpherson's use of the term "Market relations" in defining the basic assumptions of possessive individualism — "that man is free and human by virtue of his sole proprietorship of his own person, and that human society is essentially a series of market relations" — in a narrowly economic sense to appreciate his point that it was the interest of the individual, rather than that of society, that has formed the substructure of English democratic theory since Hobbes and Locke.[22]

One has only to look at the historical record to find the philosophic assumptions of the pre-possessive age and the post-possessive age in governors and officials of the seventeenth century. Lord Culpeper and Lord Howard of Effingham in the late 1670's and 1680's represent a real concern for self combined with a merely formal loyalty to the Crown. How different are their assumptions and personalities from those of their predecessors such as Berkeley! The evolution to a philosophy of possessive individualism is evident also in the shift from a headright system of land grants to a "treasury right" system of land acquisition. The ancient headright system, by which land allotted to individuals was tied in a fixed ratio to the number of persons paying their way, or brought at the expense of another, to the colony, had been subject to abuse, of course. But it had remained as a significant brake on unregulated expansion and on individual aggrandizement. Under the administration of Sir Edmond Andros (1692-1698), however, the practice of selling "rights" to land began.[23] Andros could see no harm in granting large tracts to individuals in exchange for money.

The practice was incorporated into law in the early eighteenth century, and defended by successive governors.[24]

By the end of the seventeenth century, Virginia's economic system had radically changed. Slavery was replacing indentured servitude as the dominant system of labor and large plantations were slowly beginning to exert their influence over small farms as the most significant form of landholding.[25] The enhanced interest in property values was represented and defended by a vigorous House of Burgesses and a powerful Council. Working together in their own individual (and, in their conception, Virginia's) interest, they succeeded in reducing successive governors to submission, acquiescence, anger, or despair.[26] Since the Assembly's quest for power met only feeble resistance on the part of the royal representative, there was no need at first to challenge the formal authority of the King. The Virginia gentry were more concerned with the substance than the form, while the English administrators were content to accept the form even if the substance was weak. Eventually the disparity grew too great to reconcile peaceably, but, in the words of Professor Jack P. Greene, "Perhaps the most striking characteristic of Virginia politics between 1689 and 1763 was its tranquility."[27] A sign of the factual, if not formal, breaking of the earlier intimate bond to the mother country is the fact that from 1704 until 1768 the Virginia governorship was a sinecure, and the lieutenant governor actually administered the colony.[28]

Another illustration of the shift from a feudal, or king-centered community, to an individual-centered community is to be found in the Indian relations of the period of Bacon's Rebellion. The attempt of Governor Sir William Berkeley to sustain a single community, including tributary Indians, subject to the law and justice of the King, collapsed under the assault of Bacon and his rebels. Since both Berkeley and Bacon were trained at the Inns of Court, and since they expressed their legal assumptions with some fullness, the issue was clearly drawn. Briefly stated, the assumption of Bacon was that the Indians were outside the law, and could be preyed upon by any individual so inclined. Berkeley held that they were the King's subjects and must be protected so long as the principles of justice and loyalty controlled that relationship. The difference of opinion was settled in the history of the resulting clash rather than in the logic of "the law." Though Bacon was vanquished in that clash, Berkeley proved unable to uphold the concept of royal justice for Indian subjects as well as for English subjects. Indeed, the loyalty of the English community could scarcely be maintained except by the sacrifice of the rights of the Indian community. That this solution had a powerful historical logic, if not a legal logic, is evident from the similar solutions found to the "Indian problem" in the eighteenth and nineteenth centuries.[29]

To summarize: the really significant legal evolution in the seventeenth century was one altering the fundamental assumptions underlying colonial life. While the legal bond of loyalty to the king as representative of a larger social organism was maintained until the Revolution, the life of the "law" gradually evaporated and left merely a form. The vital new controlling spirit — which saw the state existing to further the ends of the individual — would not acquire the necessary legal structure to clothe itself until the Revolution, but it did exert a growing influence upon Virginia society.

Interpretations of the seventeenth-century legal culture of Virginia have been hampered not only by the lack of a satisfactory legal record of cases and actions pertaining to the colony and to its status as an English colony, but by the failure of historians to perceive the underlying shift from the values controlling law in a semi-feudal society to those supporting a semi-individualistic society. But perhaps the most difficult stumbling block the twentieth-century historian has to overcome is the individualistic bias of his own era. This is not the place to argue the merits of an individualistic society versus that of a traditional society. It should be pointed out, however, that it is possible to question the values of individualism even in the context of its very assumptions. An increase in freedom for some can result in a loss of freedom for others, even within the same legal community, while excessive freedom to individuals within one community can conceivably result in the destruction of other legal communities, or, indeed, of the home community itself.

Yet, because of the strong commitment of legal historians to individual liberties, there is a tendency to judge seventeenth-century law in terms of its approximation to the values of twentieth-century individualistic society.[30] At the same time there is an uncritical willingness to equate a legal concept in England and in America, whatever the practical differences stemming from that concept on each side of the Atlantic. Thus, the jury system in the racially homogeneous, physically compact English scene cannot historically be equated with the jury system as it operated in the racially heterogeneous, physically scattered Virginia settlements.[31]

An insistence on bringing twentieth-century value judgments to the study of Virginia's colonial legal institutions has frequently rendered the history of the latter little more than an exercise in liberal apologetics. Similarly, the assumption of the automatic equivalence of legal "principles" such as the jury system, in the mother country and the colony, has led to false conclusions about the legal culture of the colony. The problem for the historian of seventeenth-century English colonial legal culture is to abandon all values, assumptions, and principles about the law until the compilation and study of a vastly greater number of specific cases warrants such analysis. As Richard B. Morris put it in a pioneering study, "No general rule can be formulated .... The extent to which the common law was adopted in the colonies must be actually determined in each specific situation."[32]

Unfortunately we know precious little about the various cases that arose in Virginia courts, particularly about those that concerned the relationship between the colony and the mother country. A salient example is the case of Lt. Governor Herbert Jeffreys against Colonel Philip Ludwell in 1677-1678 for scandalously accusing the governor of breaking the laws of the country.[33] Space does not allow the inclusion of the evidence here, but the important point is that the case was never reported in a manner that might have placed it in the corpus of English common law had it occurred in England and been reported upon by legal writers there. Though significant issues were involved, and persuasive arguments made (including a futile attempt to plead truth as a defense), the case was merely an incident in the conduct of colonial administration and as such was dealt with primarily by the King and his executive officers, and soon forgotten. Knowledge of such cases did not flow normally into the standard channels of communication by which the English common law was made known to lawyers, judges, administrators, students and others in the kingdom.

While trying to follow English law as best they could, the colonies had constantly to be guided by other considerations peculiar to their condition, such as the lack of trained lawyers, the lack of demand for specialized courts, and the like. Thus, Robert Beverley, writing about the General Court, asserted that

> They us'd to come to the merits of the cause, as soon as they could without Injustice, never admitting such impertinences of Form and Nicety, as were not absolutely necessary: . . . . By this method all fair Actions were prosecuted with little Attendance, all just Debts were recover'd with the least expense of Money and Time; and all the tricking, and foppery of the Law happily avoided.[34]

In both directions, therefore, the links between Virginia jurisprudence and the English common law tradition were subject to significant modifications and qualifications. The concept of "the common law" as a principle operative in the legal culture of seventeenth-century Virginia, far from being an aid to understanding, is a stumbling block to our comprehension of that culture, and should be abandoned. The historian should collect the long concealed cases and publish them. Only then will the interminable and essentially fruitless theoretical arguments about the origin of colonial law become meaningful.

LAW AND AUTHORITY

FOOTNOTES

1. Virginia State Bar. Committee commemorating the advent of common law in Jamestown, 1607. Report. 2 vols., typescript and printed verifax copy, in Virginia Historical Society, Richmond. Mss. 3.V8197a.
2. Charles McLean Andrews, *The Colonial Period of American History*, Vol. 1, *The Settlements* (New Haven, 1934, reprinted 1954), 86n.
3. St. George Tucker, ed., *Blackstone's Commentaries: with Notes of Reference, to the Constitution and Laws, of the Federal Government of the United States; and of the Commonwealth of Virginia*, 5 vols. (Philadelphia, 1803), I (Book I), 108. Tucker, in his Appendix "Of the Unwritten or Common Law of England; and its Introduction into, and authority within the United American States," urged that "In examining this question, we must, therefore, abandon the ground of strict, legal, technical construction; since upon that ground the colonies must either have been swallowed in the vortex of anarchy, or have expired under the *peine forte et dure* of submission to rigid, and impracticable rules." (I, Appendix, 386). Tucker was the father of Henry St. George Tucker cited in footnote 6.
4. The statute reads: "*Be it ordained by the representatives of the people now met in General Convention*, That the common law of *England*, all statutes or acts of Parliament made in and of the common law prior to the fourth year of the reign of King *James* the first, and which are of a general nature, not local to that kingdom, together with the several acts of the General Assembly of this colony now in force, so far as the same may consist with the several ordinances, declarations, and resolutions of the General Convention, shall be the rule of decision, and shall be considered as in full force, until the same shall be altered by the legislative power of this colony." The act is printed in *The Revised Code of the Laws of Virginia*, edited by Benjamin Watkins Leigh, 2 vols. (Richmond, 1819), I, 135. This act was modified by the act of Dec. 27, 1792, *ibid.*, I, 136-7. For a discussion of the later adoption of English common law in American state statutes, see William Wirt Blume and Elizabeth Gaspar Brown, "Territorial Courts and Law: Unifying Factors in the Development of American Legal Institutions," *Michigan Law Review*, Vol. 61, (1962-63), 39-106, 467-538.
5. Consider, for example, Act XX of the laws of the Virginia Assembly of 1666, which states that "Whereas for the better conformity of the proceedings of the courts of this country to the lawes of England, it appears necessary for their better direction therein, all the former statutes at large and those made since the beginning of the raigne of his sacred majestie that now is and a few other approved books of law should be purchased, *It is therefore . . . enacted accordingly* that all the aforesaid statute books, and Daltons justice of the peace, and office of a sherriffee, and Swinburnes book of Wills and Testaments may be sent for by the auditor for the use of the generall courts and assembly, to be kept at James Citty, and paid for out of the two shillings per hogshead; and that the like bookes be sent for by some of the commissioners of the

severall county courts for the use of the respective Counties, and paid for out of the county levy." William W. Hening, *The Statutes at Large . . . A Collection of All the Laws of Virginia (Richmond*, [etc.], 1819-1823), II, 246.

6. Henry St. George Tucker, *Commentaries on the Laws of Virginia, Comprising the Substance of a Course of Lectures Delivered to the Winchester Law School*, 2 vols. (Winchester, 1831), I, 6-7. Philip Alexander Bruce, *Institutional History of Virginia in the Seventeenth Century*, 2 vols. (New York, 1910), I, 463, states: "In making a settlement in the New World, the English emigrants carried with them their system of laws as well as their social customs and their religious doctrines; and time was to prove that this system was to undergo, after transplantation, as slight modification as the forms of their church government and the framework of their social life."
7. George Chalmers, *Opinions of Eminent Lawyers on Various Points on English Jurisprudence, Chiefly Concerning the Colonies, Fisheries and Commerce of Great Britain: Collected and Digested, from the Originals in the Board of Trade, and Other Depositories* (Burlington, Vermont, 1858), I. The work was first published in London in 1814. The Burlington edition is the first American edition.
8. *Ibid.*, 1-2.
9. Wilcomb E. Washburn, *The Governor and the Rebel: A History of Bacon's Rebellion in Virginia* (Chapel Hill, 1958), 111-2, 144-5.
10. Sir Matthew Hale, *The History of the Common Law.* The 4th edition, edited by Charles Runnington, Esq. Barrister at Law (London, 1779), 194 n. The brief compass of Blackstone's discussion of the colonies is a measure of the problem as it still existed in the eighteenth century.
11. George Chalmers, *Political Annals of the Present United Colonies, from their Settlement to the Peace of* 1763: *Compiled Chiefly from Records, and Authorized often by the Insertion of State-Papers.* Book I. (London, 1780), 676.
12. Richard L. Morton, *Colonial Virginia*, 2 vols. (Chapel Hill, 1960), I, 21.
13. Leo Francis Stock, ed. *Proceedings and Debates of the British Parliaments respecting North America*, Vol. I, 1542-1688 (Washington, 1924), 19.
14. Thomas Jefferson Wertenbaker, *Virginia under the Stuarts* (Princeton, 1914, reprinted 1958), 23.
15. Wesley Frank Craven, *The Southern Colonies in the Seventeenth Century, 1607-1689* (Baton Rouge, 1949), 127.
16. Virginia State Library, Richmond. Virginia Mss. A. L. S.
17. Letters to the Earl of Clarendon from Thomas Ludwell, July 18, 1666, and from Sir William Berkeley, July 20, 1666, calendared in Survey Report No. X 53, Colonial Records Project, Virginia 350th Anniversary Celebration Corporation.
18. Wilcomb E. Washburn, *Virginia under Charles I and Cromwell, 1625-1660*, Jamestown 350th Anniversary Historical Booklet (Williamsburg, 1957), 42-47.

19. Wilcomb E. Washburn, "The Effect of Bacon's Rebellion on Government in England and Virginia," U. S. National Museum, Bulletin 225, *Contributions from the Museum of History and Technology*, Paper 17 (Washington: Smithsonian Institution, 1962), 137-151.
20. Carl Bridenbaugh, *Mitre and Sceptre: Transatlantic Faiths, Ideas, Personalities, and Politics, 1689-1775* (New York, 1962), 337-8. The uncertain and complicated question of the colonial jurisdiction of the Bishops of London is perceptively analyzed by J. H. Bennett, "English Bishops and Imperial Jurisdiction, 1660-1725," *Historical Magazine of the Protestant Episcopal Church*, Vol. XXXII, (Sept. 1963), 175-188. Bennett's article includes "Comments" by Anthony H. Forbes.
21. Washburn, *The Governor and the Rebel*, 150-152.
22. C. B. MacPherson, *The Political Theory of Possessive Individualism: Hobbes to Locke* (Oxford, 1962), 270.
23. Morton, *Colonial Virginia*, I, 362. The headright system was not abolished, however.
24. *Ibid.*, II, 539-40.
25. Thomas Jefferson Wertenbaker, *The Planters of Colonial Virginia* (Princeton, 1922, and New York, 1959), especially Chap. viii.
26. Jack P. Greene, *The Quest for Power: The Lower Houses of Assembly in the Southern Royal Colonies*, 1689-1776 (Chapel Hill, 1963), 26.
27. *Ibid.*, 29.
28. *Ibid.*, 130.
29. Washburn, *The Governor and the Rebel*, *passim*.
30. George Lee Haskins, *Law and Authority in Early Massachusetts: A Study in Tradition and Design* (New York: Macmillan, 1960), occasionally refers to the "improvement upon English practices" of various provisions of Massachusetts law (198, 202, 203). I would suggest that these provisions, *for the historian*, represent changes rather than improvements.
31. St. George Tucker, in his edition of Blackstone's *Commentaries*, *op. cit.*, included an appendix on "Trial by Jury in Virginia" which is a scathing indictment of the system. After discussing the practice of making up juries with loiterers around the court who want their expenses paid, Tucker wrote: "Whether to this cause is to be ascribed the number of acquittals against positive evidence, (more especially in cases of homicide and malicious mayhem,) which an attentive observer might enumerate, the author of these pages cannot pretend to decide, but from the multiplicity of such acquittals, the inference to be drawn is, that there must be an infinite degree of perjury in the witnesses, or of unpardonable disregard to their duty in the jurors." Tucker sadly added: "The expence of a better system is the only reason that I have ever heard alleged in favour of the present: . . . ." Vol. IV, Appendix, 66-67).
32. Richard B. Morris, *Studies in the History of American Law with Special Reference to the Seventeenth and Eighteenth Centuries* (New York, 1930), 12.

33. The case is discussed briefly in Washburn, *The Governor and the Rebel*, 233-234.
34. Robert Beverley, *The History and Present State of Virginia*, edited by Louis B. Wright (Chapel Hill, 1947), Book Four, Chap. VI, 255.

THE LOCUS OF AUTHORITY IN COLONIAL MASSACHUSETTS

CLIFFORD K. SHIPTON

American Antiquarian Society

WE OF THE western world generally agree that the purpose of life is the realization of a set of values which in their political form we call democracy, by which we mean that they rest authority in the people. The course of the evolution of these principles is clearly marked from the Magna Carta, through the Massachusetts Civil Code of 1648, to the Bill of Rights in the Federal Constitution. The century and a half during which the Colony and Province of Massachusetts Bay were trying to adjust law and authority in order to realize these principles are critical ones in this long period of their evolution. But what went on in these years has been quite generally misunderstood by historians, particularly by those who have not realized that in the period and the group with which we are concerned, religious and civil life were an integrated whole. Religious values were not segregated out and discriminated against as they are today when members of the Massachusetts legislature demand of anyone who would testify on social problems, "Do you take your stand on moral grounds," and deny him a hearing if he pleads guilty. The Puritan's preoccupation with moral values made him keenly aware that he should keep an eye out for the fallen sparrow, and should temper the law to the shorn lamb, or to the debtor. This is why Massachusetts passed the first statute forbidding cruelty to animals, and, for their day, the most liberal laws for the protection of debtors. With the concern for the physical well-being of the individual went a certain amount of respect for his opinions.

The last generation of writers on colonial New England were cynical of the Puritan professions, and saw the Bay Colony as a self-centered autocracy devoted to the perpetuation of a particular theological orthodoxy. According to this interpretation, the significance of the evolution of law, authority, and democracy in Massachusetts was in the liberation of the colony from a theocracy by the extension of the franchise. One would have thought that this thesis had been entirely disproved by the research of this generation, but the recent publication of Emery Battis' excellent biography of Anne Hutchinson contains the following utterly irrelevant conclusion to describe the situation in the Bay Colony after Mrs. Hutchinson's exile: "the established church was the sole repository of religious truth, with full scope to determine who had erred against that truth in matters of doctrine and morals."[1] Nonsense. There never was an established church in Massachusetts, there was no agreed-upon body of dogma, and serious moral deviation was punished by the state, not by the church.

In spite of the integration of civil and religious life in the seventeenth century, the government of Massachusetts never was a theocracy in any normal sense of the term. There was no unitary church, and many of the normal functions of the established churches in Europe were here transferred to the state. This was true at the local level as well. For most of the settlers, the accustomed instrument of local government had been the oligarchic Church of England parish; in New England its functions passed to the town, and were exercised by the inhabitants in open town meeting. Today, the established churches in England, Scandinavia, and the Latin countries exercise authority in what were purely civil fields in colonial Massachusetts. The Bay Colony never had an established church which could have exercised these civil powers; it had only individual and independent churches. The law required that every town maintain a minister and a schoolmaster, both of its own selection; but beyond that point the Colony and Province exercised no authority. Taxation of non-members of the church by the town to support the ministers was defended on the same ground as taxation of childless people to support the schools. Many towns were cited by the General Court for failing to maintain a school, but I cannot recollect a case in which a town was taken to task for failing to maintain a minister, though many did for years on end. The town, acting with the concurrence of an ecclesiastical council of its own choosing, formed the local church, which possessed no funds or property, and was independent of all other churches and of any outside authority. The town did not legally participate in the call of subsequent ministers until 1692, but inasmuch as the minister's contract was with the town, he was never called by the church without previous assurance of the concurrence of the town. Since all inhabitants, regardless of denominational preference, participated in these transactions, the minister's theological views had to be acceptable to the majority. Quakers, Baptists, and Presbyterians were vocal in these town and parish meetings, with the result that the minister's theological difficulties were usually with the civil body rather than with the church.

Unlike the Scottish presbyteries, the Massachusetts associations of ministers exercised no authority over the individual churches or their members. Their powers, like those of the occasional synods, were purely advisory. Their consent was not required for either the ordination or the dismissal of a minister, these functions being exercised by ad hoc councils chosen jointly by town and church with an eye to getting their own decisions ratified quietly. Ordaining councils heard any opponents of a call, and never proceeded to settle a minister who was opposed by a majority or even a large minority of the inhabitants of a town, knowing that he would be denied adequate financial support. Technically, the consent of such a council, chosen jointly by the disputants, was necessary for the dismissal of a minister. But even where the minister was clearly in the right, all that the council could do to protect him was to arbitrate the best possible terms of separation for him; for the town could refuse to pay the settlement and could go on calling other councils until it obtained a decision which it considered suitable. Where there was recourse to the courts, and it was frequent, the decision was almost always on the terms of the financial contract; rarely was cognizance taken of theological questions which might have been the reason for the dismissal.

It has been argued, however, that although there was no legal authority for a theocracy in Massachusetts, one existed because of the influence of the clergy. This is amply disproved by the legislative history of the Colony, and by the contrasts between the suggestions of the synods and the subsequent legislation by the General Court. The tradition that a Black Regiment of the clergy led the American Revolution in New England has little substance. Many individual Congregational ministers were neutral or Tory, and ministerial associations usually avoided even expressions of opinion on political matters. Robert E. Brown in his *Middle-Class Democracy and the Revolution in Massachusetts 1691-1780* exaggerates the political influence of the clergy, as when he mistakenly makes the Reverend Charles Chauncy a member of the upper house of legislature.[2] Brown was unaware of the existence of an absolutely fundamental principle of separation of church and state in Massachusetts, which forbade the election of clergymen to the General Court in Colony or Province time. So clearly understood was this principle that the clergy were not to participate in government that when the Province asked a missionary to the Eastern Indians to negotiate a treaty, a wise old Roman Catholic chief pointed out to the minister the fact that his profession disqualified him from any such participation in government.[3]

The clergyman was excluded from office in the civil government in the Bay Colony, but the meanest inhabitant was invited to participate in the legislative process. From the first, Massachusetts law provided that "Every man whether inhabitant of Forreiner, free or not free" had the right "to come to any publique Court, Council or Town Meeting" and there either by speech or writing to initiate and advocate action. The radical nature of this system is apparent when one realizes that through most of the world today legislation can be introduced only by the executive or by the ministry.

The great majority of the early settlers in the Bay Colony had held their English property not in what we would call fee simple, but by some type of feudal tenure or grant, and all of them had lived under local governments which were self-perpetuating oligarchies. In the Southern colonies, the English practice of local government by a self-perpetuating oligarchy of vestrymen remained. In New England, a few of the first town meetings had oligarchic tendencies, but within a decade the legislative and executive processes had passed into the hands of the body of inhabitants. In Massachusetts, the settler owned his land in fee simple, voted the taxes upon it in town meeting, and disposed of it at will. Liberty 12 of the Massachusetts Code of 1648 had guaranteed to everyone the right of a voice in town meeting, and, as Thomas Hutchinson later put it, "anything in the semblance of a man" was permitted to vote in spite of property qualifications established by law. In consequence, all of the functions of the English parish vestries, borough councils, and similar local bodies, passed into the hands of the body of inhabitants, who thus had control of most of the matters which affected their daily lives. The only cases I have found where votes have been challenged on the ground of voting by unqualified individuals have occurred when the minority has included the church members and more substantial people, while the majority has consisted of Baptists, Quakers, and small farmers, some of whom pretty obviously could not have met the property qualifications established by law. In no case which I have seen did the court which heard the appeal base its decision on the legal qualifications of the voters. So far as one can determine from the colonial record, the situation in town meeting was then precisely what it is today, when the chairman of the finance committee tries in vain to get the moderator to exclude unqualified persons from voting. The colonial statutes in regard to voting qualifications had little to do with actual practice, and give no substantial evidence as to the degree of democracy prevailing. Far better evidence, but quite impossible to evaluate, are such pictures as Governor Winthrop laboring in the fields with his servants, and Governor Endicott taking his turn in the saw pit.

One of the best criteria of the degree of democracy in any state is the amount of protection afforded by its laws to the individual; protection against the state itself, against other individuals, and against economic adversity. In this regard, the Massachusetts Code of 1648 was centuries ahead of the greater part of the world. The compilers, whetting their consciences to discover the will of God, selecting wisely, innovating when necessary, drew a document which is a milestone in the history of individual liberty. Their successors, a century and a half later, put forth the essence of these principles at the price of Massachusetts' ratification of the Federal Constitution, and they became the substance of the Bill of Rights.

Guarantees of freedom of the person and of property of the type afforded by the Massachusetts Code of 1648 are, we of western tradition believe, essential to a life worth living. Even more important, however, is freedom of the mind. It is the attitude toward this freedom which is the critical difference between the East and West today. Indeed, it has been a problem in every civilized society. To the Massachusetts Puritans of 1630, the whole good of man, which was the end of society, required freedom for every man to live according to his conscience. What, then, was the actual place of this most crucial freedom, the freedom of the mind, in the legal system and in the society, of the Colony and Province of Massachusetts Bay? This is a point on which historians are still confused, and which even Perry Miller and George L. Haskins did not think through. The statement of the Cambridge Platform of 1640 is this:

> Idolatry, Blasphemy, Heresy, venting corrupt & pernicious opinions, that destroy the foundations, open contempt of the word preached, prophanation of the Lords day, disturbing the peaceable administration of the worship & holy things of God, the like, are to be restrayned & punished by civil authority.

Today every state will use the civil authority against those who disturb "the peaceable administration & Exercise of the worship" of God, or of the doctrines of Karl Marx; and every state has certain ground rules beyond which lie blasphemy and heresy, or intolerable indecency. Becoming a citizen of a state has always involved joining in a compact and accepting the local ground rules. North Americans who today live in other parts of the world may not like the local ground rules, but they must recognize the fact that the world respects the right of every state to make its own rules and to enforce them against those who have accepted its citizenship.

The Massachusetts Code of 1648 states explicitly that all who settle in the colony are assumed "totally to submit to this government." Massachusetts authorities, like those of any other state, used the civil power against individuals who "vented corrupt and vicious opinions" which tended to "destroy the foundations" of the City upon a Hill. Liberty of mind was limited to matters of "faith and conscience." This was the reason, however mistaken as a matter of policy, for the civil action taken against Roger Williams, Anne Hutchinson, and the Quakers. These Antinomians held that authority was vested in the conscience of the individual, not in the state, the church, nor in the consensus of the people. While accepting this principle, the Bay authorities believed that the venting of the views which Mrs. Hutchinson held was a danger sufficient to require the disarming of her followers. Note that the authorities did not claim jurisdiction over the beliefs of the Antinomians, but only over the promulgation of them.

The Bay government never sought out intellectual deviates. The great majority of Antinomians, Baptists, and Quakers in the Bay Colony lived in good relations with their neighbors who adhered to the majority view, and even Cotton Mather welcomed such dissenters at the Communion Table of his church. By contrast, the Book of Common Prayer of the Church of England forbade such unconfirmed persons to approach the Communion Table, and Blackstone declared that by the laws of the kingdom, all dissenters were criminals.

The New England respect for freedom of conscience eventually carried over into the political field. In the American Revoultion, New England Tories suffered less than the losing side in perhaps any other civil war. There were no purges, no executions, and no lynchings. The right of Tories to their opinion was respected so long as they were not a menace to the state. Our yearning for freedom of the mind is not satisfied with mere tolerance; we insist that our beliefs must be accorded the dignity of reasonable truth. When the suggestions of the Cambridge Synod were incorporated into the legal code as adopted by the Colony in the same year, they were qualified by a provision that "No human power [is] Lord over the Faith and Conscience of men, and therefore may not constrain them to believe or profess against their Consciences." That this was fundamental to the thinking of New England Puritans is indicated by the corresponding clause in the New Haven laws of 1656, asserting that "no Creature be Lord, or have any power over the faith and consciences of men, nor constreyn them to believe or profess, against their consciences."

After this doctrine had been tried in the fires of controversy with the New Haven Quakers for a century, William Livingston in

The Independent Reflector for August 2, 1753, rephrased the Puritan principle thus: "The civil Power hath no jurisdiction over the [religious] Sentiments or Opinions of the subject, till such Opinions break out into Actions prejudicial to the Community, and then it is not the Opinion but the Action that is the Object of our Punishment." It has been recently asserted that this principle of freedom of thought was first expressed as state policy in the Virginia statutes of January 16, 1786, but it may well be that this is another case where the Virginians were deliberately drawing on Puritan documents.[4]

What were the heresies which could not be vented without danger to the Bay community? In 1646 the General Court enumerated a number of theological errors the promulgation of which should be punished by banishment. All of these, it pointed out, were recognized as dangerous errors in most contemporary societies; the Puritans were not peculiar in dreading them. Neither the General Court, nor any ecclesiastical body in Massachusetts attempted to define heresy in any way other than by pointing out European consensus. Since there was no theological code in the Bay Colony, it is not surprising that there was no civil trial for heresy in Colony or Province. Of the literally hundreds of ecclesiastical councils before which ministers were charged with, among other things, theological deviations, there was only one which was clearly a heresy trial, and in that the foolish young defendant was out of bounds by most standards.[5]

Modern historians are fond of using the word "orthodoxy" in connection with the Puritans, although the latter rarely employed the word themselves. Haskins uses the term "Puritan Orthodoxy" without defining it, and other historians use it with the terms "Baptist Orthodoxy" and "Quaker Orthodoxy" as if these were clearly stated theological positions. If by "Puritan Orthodoxy" you mean loyalty to the community, the term has cohesion, but once you try to prod its theological implications, you are in trouble. The fact is that orthodoxy was incompatible with the Puritan faith in reason. Orthodoxy is static. The Reverend John Robinson's parting words to the Pilgrims leaving Leyden included an admonition not to close their minds, as the Lutherans and Calvinists had done, to the progress of the knowledge of the nature of God. The minority in the Westminster Assembly of Divines took this same attitude, and they represented the Independent element which provided the leadership for the settlement of Massachusetts. Oliver Cromwell was probably the only head of state ever to beseech his followers to believe that they might be mistaken. The Puritans, recognizing that they were the children of an intellectual reformation resulting from individual examination of orthodoxy, thought of themselves as in a current sweeping toward a better knowledge of God, a knowledge to be reached by learning and study, not by the unpredictable personal revelations of the Antinomians.

To map the theological beliefs of a few Puritan theologians and to call the result "Puritan Orthodoxy" is to ignore one of the chief tenets of that community. The favorite Biblical text of the New England ministers was that which enjoins us to call no man father; and the improvement which they made of it was to point out that they, the clergy, had no authority to enjoin upon laymen any particular interpretation of doctrine. Even some of the most conservative of the Massachusetts ministers, themselves completely Calvinistic in doctrine, told the members of their congregations that the layman's chief duty toward God was to arrive at an understanding of Him by an examination of the validity of every tenet of Christian doctrine. The Calvinistic and Lutheran churches of Europe required that their members accept certain theological dogmas, but in Massachusetts the primary requirement for church membership was an individual experience of God's Grace, described by the individual in his own words.

This emphasis on freedom of the mind was then unique, and today is far from universal. Most of the early settlers of Massachusetts had been members of Church of England parishes, which were by definition agencies of an external power which dictated doctrine and practice, and discouraged criticism of it. Today the Roman Catholic Church denies liberty of conscience in matters of orthodoxy and morals, and the Protestant Episcopal Church requires its members to accept its doctrines and discipline. The colonial New England churches, like the Church of England, required the consent of the individual members to their moral discipline, but each offender was heard by his peers in open church meeting, instead of being tried by the clergy according to a fixed external standard. Instead of an established Congregational Church with power to enforce conformity in doctrine and morals, we have only individual churches which could punish what they determined to be heresy or sin only by denying the sinners fellowship until they repented. Actually, they rarely excommunicated anyone for heresy. The General Court submitted the Platform of 1648 to the local churches for their approval, but no ratification was called for, for it would not have been binding. The General Court printed the result of the Boston Synod of 1662, and "commended" it "unto the churches and people." In 1680 it ordered the Savoy Confession printed "for the benefit of the churches," but its use was optional. In 1708 Connecticut "commended" the Saybrook Platform to the churches.

Puritan orthodoxy, then, was a consensus of the views of the whole community, most members of which did not feel that they were authorized to cast stones at any man who held other theological opinions. Let's see how this worked out in practice. The one significant employment of the term "orthodoxy" in Massachusetts law was that requiring every town to maintain a learned and orthodox minister. Under this law, a few towns or parishes called Baptist ministers and used the power of civil taxation to support them, but there never was a case, so far as I can find, in which the town's choice of a minister was challenged in the courts on the basis of his orthodoxy.

After a town had chosen a minister, a group of neighboring churches was invited to send lay and clerical delegates to ordain him. In eighteenth-century ordinations there were frequently minority protests to the effect that the candidate was not sound on certain points of Calvinistic theology, but in few if any cases was a candidate rejected on primarily theological grounds. The council sometimes advised a candidate to decline a call because his theological views would cause trouble in that particular town, but I cannot remember the record of a case in which he was denied ordination because the council disagreed with his theology. The general custom was for the council to ask the candidate to state his religious convictions in his own words, although there were some ministers who would never permit a council of which they were members to require any theological statements. If the candidate said that he agreed with the Westminster Assembly of Divines, his orthodoxy was questioned no further; but candidates were never required to subscribe to the Westminster Catechism, or to accept any creed, or any other prearranged theological formulation. The minister who delivered the charge to the candidate commonly took the opportunity to disclaim any authority over his beliefs, or teachings.

The candidate would accept the covenant of the church over which he was ordained, but this document usually contained no theology, being a general statement of pious intent which any good man of the present generation could accept. Among the Massachusetts churches, the confession of faith was a late and limited development. When, in the Calvinistic reaction of the eighteenth century, some of the churches adopted detailed theological covenants, they also, commonly, adopted simple and untheological "forms of admission" so that people with "tender consciences" would not be excluded from communion. Some of these churches thus had a kind of theological "Half Way Covenant" which permitted Arminians and Unitarians to be members of Calvinistic town churches. In any case, the covenant or confession of faith was not dictated by any external authority, but was arrived at by mutual consent of its members and was subject to frequent revision. No Puritan church used any of the creeds in its services, much less required the acceptance of them as proof of orthodoxy. The creeds were, the ministers said, worthy of respect as the beliefs of pious men, but they were formulated by men, and therefore no other man could be required to accept them. Ministers who were Calvinists held to their beliefs because to them they seemed logically sound, not because they were received from authority. Revelation was confined strictly to the Bible, and if a colleague could find no proof of the Trinity in it, this personal idiosyncracy did not disqualify him as a minister in good standing.

Since there was no Congregational Church, but only individual churches, each with a doctrine arrived at by a consensus of the opinions of the inhabitants of town or parish, there could be no Congregational orthodoxy except of the vaguest and most general sort. There was no clear-cut theological difference between Congregationalists, Baptists, and Episcopalians. So far as the Baptists were concerned, the Congregationalists admitted that they were right as to baptism. The dread which the early Puritans had of Baptist Antinomianism had proved unfounded, and their chief criticism of that denomination was the lack of college-educated clergy among them. The Baptists tended to attack the Congregational ministers as not being sound Calvinists, but some of their own ministers were overt Arminians. The Baptist churches were congregational in polity, each with its own consensus of theological beliefs, so a Baptist orthodoxy would be as hard to find as a Congregational one.

The Puritans made the Thirty-Nine Articles the shibboleth which divided Dissenter from Anglican, but their objection was not to the theological content of the Articles but the fact that they were a limitation on freedom of conscience. The liberal bishops were as Arminian as Charles Chauncy could wish, while the American converts to the Church of England tended to be as Calvinistic as any New-Light whose noisy conduct they deplored. The American converts to Anglicanism to a large degree represented a reaction against the democratic theological polity of the Congregationalists. One of the reasons for the founding of King's College was to have an institution in which the students were not, as at Harvard and Yale, encouraged to get intellectual exercise by playing battledore and shuttlecock with the axioms of Christian dogma. Thus the difference between Anglican and Congregationalist was not in theology, but in the locus of authority.

Massachusetts in her first century and a half was an ideal proving ground for the principles on which our democratic way of life rests. Fortunate choice of settlers, happy isolation which afforded freedom to experiment, a basic philosophical faith in the reason of the common man, and freedom from the shackles of orthodoxy, make this a critical period in the growth of the democratic doctrine which we today regard as fundamental. The critical moment of the American Revolution came in the first decade of settlement, when the individual settlers took into their own hands and managed, through democratic town and church machinery, all of the matters of property, civil government, and religion which could be handled at that level. They made what was perhaps the most remarkable effort in the history of civilization to establish a society in which authority rested, in so far as possible, on the conscience of the individual. The rest of the colonial period in New England is the story of the adjustments in law and authority which that revolution made necessary.

FOOTNOTES

1. Emery Battis, *Saints and Sectaries*, (Chapel Hill, 1962), 289.
2. Robert E. Brown, *Middle-Class Democracy and the Revolution in Massachusetts*, 1691-1780, (Ithaca, 1955), 369.
3. *Sibley's Harvard Graduates*, XII, 46.
4. William Livingston and others, *The Independent Reflector*, ed., Milton M. Klein (Cambridge, Mass., 1963), 311 fn2.
5. *Sibley's Harvard Graduates*, VIII, 221-223.

THE MIRROR OF PURITAN AUTHORITY

Darrett B. Rutman

University of Minnesota

"PURITANISM" is a time-honored word in American history. On the highest level of scholarship it signifies a concept dear to historians who have made a life's work defining the New England "mind" and its role in the evolution of a peculiar American "mind." On the lowest level it is one of many catch-words and slogans which serve to half-educate our youth, a capsule description to distinguish the New England colonies from those to the south and explain the course of New England's institutional and political development. On either level, the historians' "Puritanism" would seem to be their own creation, a stereotype which, as any intimate view of a "Puritan" community will show, has little to do with reality in New England.

The stereotype has arisen as the result of a tendency among historians of early New England, and particularly the intellectual historians who have dominated the field in the last generation, to limit themselves to the study of the writings of the articulate few, on the assumption that the public professions of the ministers and magistrates constitute a true mirror of the New England mind.[1] The historian seeking to understand a New England concept of authority, for example, has familiarized himself with the literature of England and Europe relative to the nature of man in society. He has scanned the works of such lay leaders of early New England as John Winthrop, noting his "little speech" on liberty of July 1645 and his earlier "A Modell of Christian Charity": "God Almightie in his most holy and wise providence hath soe disposed of the Condicion of mankinde, as in all times some must be rich some poore, some highe and eminent in power and dignitie; others meane and in subjeccion." He has thumbed through the ministerial writings to find Thomas Hooker: "However it is true, [that] the rule bindes such to the duties of their places and relations, yet it is certain, it requires that they should *first freely ingage* themselves in such covenants, and *then* be carefull to fullfill such duties." Or perhaps he has dipped into the pages of John Cotton: "It is evident by the light of nature, that all civill Relations are founded in Covenant. For, to passe by naturall Relations between Parents and Children, and Violent Relations, between Conquerors and Captives; there is no other way given whereby a people . . . can be united or combined into one visible body, to stand by mutuall Relations, fellow-members of the same body, but onely by mutuall Covenant; as appeareth between husband and wife in the family, Magistrates and subjects in the Commonwealth, fellow Citizens in the same Citie."[2]

On occasion, the historian has turned also to the law, noting that it is replete with examples of the intrusion of authority into every aspect of New England life: "Taking into consideration the great neglect of many parents and masters in training up their children in learning, and labor, and other implyments which may be proffitable to the common wealth," it is ordered that the selectmen of every town "shall henceforth stand charged with the care of the redresse of this evill"; "forasmuch as in these countryes, where the churches of Christ are seated, the prosperity of the civil state is much advanced and blessed of God" and the ministers' preaching of the word "is of generall and common behoofe to all sorts of people, as being the ordinary meanes to subdue the harts of hearers not onely to the faith, and obedience to the Lord Jesus, but also to civill obedience, and allegiance unto magistracy" it is ordered that "every person shall duely resort and attend" to church services; it is ordered that "hereafter, noe dwelling howse shalbe builte above halfe a myle from the meeteing howse."[3]

From such sources modern historians have drawn a picture of a highly cohesive and ordered social structure in which authority was omnipresent — the authority of the father in the family, of the minister in the church, of the magistrate in town and commonwealth. Both the cohesiveness of society and the authority were God-ordained, for man from the moment of Adam's fall was a degenerate being who required the oversight of his fellows in order to avoid the worst of sins. ("*In multitude of counsellers is safetie*," Cotton was fond of saying.)[4] Within the family, the father's authority was a natural concomitant to parenthood. But for the rest, man chose for himself. He submitted himself to the oversight of a congregation and through it a presbytery of ministers and elders, and to the civil authority of a king or prince or magistrate. Having submitted, however, he was bound by a godly duty to "faithe patience, obedience." Thus the ministers wrote that the congregations were obliged to "yeeld obedience to their Overseers, in whatsoever they see and hear by them commanded to them from the Lord"; the magistrates that "we have our authority from God, in way of an ordinance, such as hath the image of God eminently stamped upon it, the contempt and violation whereof hath been vindicated with examples of divine vengeance."[5] To further the interests of the community as a whole, the individual's personal aspirations were to be sublimated. "Goe forth, everyman that goeth, with a publicke spirit, looking not on your owne things onely, but also on the things of others," Cotton commanded the settlers who sailed with Winthrop in 1630. And Winthrop echoed him: "Wee must be knitt together in this worke as one man." Magistrates and ministers, too, were committed to the welfare of the entire community. The ministry was to guide the community in the way of God's truth. The civil authorities were to preserve the community in its liberty to do "that only which is good, just, and honest." The "ultimate and supreme" goal of both was that "the common Good of the Society, State or Kingdom" be preserved and "*God in all things . . . glorified.*"[6]

The current view of New England Puritanism, of which this view of New England authority is but a part, rests upon two major implicit assumptions. The first is that there is such a thing as "Puritanism" — a term impossible perhaps to define, but capable nevertheless of being described — and that the acme of Puritan ideals is to be found in New England during the years 1630-1650. After that date, it is asserted, degeneration set in and there was a gradual falling away from the Puritan ideal. George L. Haskins, the outstanding writer on law and authority in early Massachusetts, reflects this assumption when he writes that "the initial decades of the Bay Colony's existence were the formative years" when, "under the pervasive influence of Puritan doctrine," government, law, ecclesiastical polity, and social structure were fully shaped; "the early social and political structure was to endure for several decades, but it gradually crumbled as primitive zeals began to wane and the religious aspects of life were subordinated to commercial interests."[7]

Haskins owes an unacknowledged debt to Cotton Mather and other New England Jeremiahs, for the notion of Puritan quintessence and decline goes back to Mather's day. Sitting down to pen his *Magnalia Christi Americana* at the end of the seventeenth century, Mather was convinced that the years in which he was living were degenerate ones, that the years preceding his — the founding years — had constituted a golden age of which he was one of the few pure survivors. By telling the story of the past and its leaders he hoped to call his own time to the dutiful obedience to God's will (in both religious and social matters) which had previously prevailed. Mather's motive was succinctly set forth in the introduction to his sketches of the lives of the early ministers: "Reader, behold these *examples;* admire and follow what thou dost behold *exemplary* in them. They are offered unto the publick, with the intention . . . that *patterns* may have upon us the force which *precepts* have not."[8]

This first assumption, though old, has proved of great pragmatic value to the modern historian. Having established that the first decades of New England were the acme of Puritanism, the historian can then turn around and describe Puritanism in terms of what he has found in New England during those early years. Hence, he can avoid the problem of defining Puritanism, a task which Samuel Eliot Morison once found distasteful but necessary.[9] The historian can also evade the issue of separating those facets of New England thought and character which were uniquely Puritan from those which merely reflected the way of life in England. Moreover, by accepting Mather's progression from golden age to degeneration, the historian can conceptualize Puritanism by drawing upon a vast quantity of material without worrying whether his sources are being used out of context as regards time, place, or persons.[10] If Puritanism can "best be described as that point of view, that philosophy of life, that code of values, which was carried to New England by the first settlers in the early seventeenth century" and became "one of the continuous factors in American life and thought," as a leading anthology by Perry Miller and Thomas H. Johnson asserts, then certainly (the historian reasons) one can postulate a unique and unchanging Puritan ideal of society in terms of the letters and tracts emanating from New England during the first two decades of settlement, and, with increasing caution in view of the degeneration, from the whole of the seventeenth century[11] The same anthology contains selections from Winthrop's 1630 "Modell of Christian Charity" through John Wise's 1717 *Vindication of the Government of New-England Churches* to exemplify a Puritan theory of state and society, and concludes that:

> the most obvious lesson of the selections printed herein is that . . . the theorists of New England thought of society as a unit, bound together by inviolable ties; they thought of it not as an aggregation of individuals but as an organism, functioning for a definite purpose, with all parts subordinate to the whole, all members contributing a definite share, every person occupying a particular status . . . . The society of early New England was decidedly 'regimented.' Puritans did not think the state was merely an umpire, standing on the side lines of a contest, limited to checking egregious fouls, but otherwise allowing men free play according to their abilities and the breaks of the game . . . . The state to them was an active instrument of leadership, discipline, and, wherever necessary, of coercion . . . . The commanders were not to trim their policies by the desires of the people, but to drive ahead upon the predetermined course . . . . There was no questioning that men who would not serve the purposes of the society should be whipped into line. The objectives were clear and unmistakable; any one's disinclination to dedicate himself to them was obviously so much recalcitrancy and depravity.[12]

The second major assumption is that one is free to ignore the "if" in Winthrop's "little speech" on liberty: "If you stand for your natural corrupt liberties, and will do what is good in your own eyes, you will not endure the least weight of authority, but will murmur, and oppose, and be always striving to shake off that yoke."[13] Winthrop, had of course, no call to speak of those who "stand" for natural liberties unless there were individuals who took such a point of view. Similarly, one assumes oneself free to ignore the nature of the law — that law reflects not merely the assumptions of society, but the antithesis of those assumptions. The law calling upon town selectmen to insure the proper upbringing of children when their parents were neglecting to educate them to serve the community indicates not only that children were expected to receive such an education, but implies strongly that some children were *not* being prepared in the prescribed manner.[14] The law requiring settlers to build their houses within a half-mile of the agencies of social control — church and magistrates — not only echoes the ideal of a cohesive society, but the fact that some persons were perfectly willing to break with the ideal and scatter across the rich New England countryside. One indication that the law (and the ideal it reflected) was being disregarded is a 1639 letter written by the Plymouth congregation to Boston's First Church "concerning the holding of Farmes of which there is noe lesse frequent use with your selves then with us . . . by means of [which] a mans famylie is Divided so in busie tymes they cannot (except upon the Lord's day) all of them joyne with him in famylie duties." The repeal of the Massachusetts law in 1640 on the grounds that it was unenforceable is still further substantiation.[15]

The assumption is not without its rationalization. If the historian accepts as a matter of faith that, as Richard Schlatter writes, "it was the Puritan leaders who shaped the culture of New England, whatever the rank and file may have wanted" — an extension of the notion of a Puritan oligarchy from the political to the social milieu — then it is easy to explain away those who disregarded the law or who stood for "natural corrupt liberties."[16] Once again, Mather has provided the modern historian with a ready-made answer. To him incidents of social and religious dissent were merely the "continual *temptation* of the devil" which were, at least in the early years, overcome by the pure in heart.[17]

That an ideal arrangement of society was visualized by some of the first comers to New England and that they contemplated realizing the ideal in the New World is patently obvious. One need only glance at Winthrop's "Modell of Christian Charity" to see it.[18] But was the ideal uniquely Puritan? The thought that men, like the diverse parts of nature, ideally stood in ordered symmetry is to be found in Shakespeare's *Troilus and Cressida*:

The heavens themselves, the planets and this centre,
Observe degree, priority and place.

. . . . O, when degree is shaked,
Which is the ladder of all high designs,
The enterprise is sick! How could communities . . .
Prerogative of age, crowns, sceptres, laurels,
But by degree, stand in authentic place?[19]

The notion of men entering society by compact or covenant and thereby binding themselves to authority was a pervading theme in Western thought, although particularly relevant for the religious polemicists of the sixteenth and seventeenth centuries. One finds it, for example, in the *Vindiciae Contra Tyrannos* of the French Protestants and in Richard Hooker's *Ecclesiastical Polity.* In Hooker's work, too, is found the idea of the divine nature of authority once established by man: "God creating mankind did endue it naturally with full power to guide itselv, in what kind of societies soever it should choose to live," yet those on whom power "is bestowed even at men's discretion, they likewise do hold it by divine right" for "albeit God do neither appoint the thing nor assign the person; nevertheless when men have established both, who doth doubt that sundry duties and offices depending thereupon are prescribed in the word of God"; therefore, "we by the law of God stand bound meekly to acknowledge them for God's lieutenants."[20]

More importantly, was the ideal — so often expressed by the articulate few and commented upon by the intellectual historians — ever a reality in New England? Certainly conditions in America were not conducive to it. The very ideal contained a flaw, for while in England the social and religious covenant was an abstract principle to be toyed with by logicians, in New England it was, in town and church, transformed into practice. How does one convince the generality that the forms and personnel of authority are within its province, but that once established they are in God's domain and are to be honored as such? What spokesman for New England orthodoxy could surpass Ireland's Cuchulinn in battling the waves of the sea? Moreover, the transition from old to New England constituted a break in the social fabric familiar to the individual. In an English borough or village the individual located himself according to well-established social and political relationships, but these were no more. Family ties in New England during the early years were relatively few. Ties to the traditional elements of authority — vestrymen, churchwardens, manor stewards, borough councillors, justices-of-the-peace — had disappeared, to be created anew in the New England town, it is true, but such new relationships lacked the sanctity of long familiarity. And even when new ties existed, there was little stability in the New Englander's place in the social and political order. What mattered the regular assertion that God had ordained some to ride and some to walk when those who walked one day could, by virtue of the absence of traditional leaders, the presence of New World opportunities, and the application of their own diligence, ride another?

Such musings give a hint of the answer as to whether the ideal was ever a reality in New England. For more than a hint, however, one must turn to the New Englander's own habitat, his town. For many historians such research necessitates a shift to an entirely different set of sources. It means leaving behind published sermons, tracts, and laws and turning instead to town and church records. It calls for an end to the relatively comfortable perusal of the writings of a few and undertaking the drudgery of culling local records to identify the persons in a given town — their backgrounds, landholdings, economic activities, social and economic affiliations, and politics. Research of such nature is time-consuming, but the rewards are rich.

One such study is that of Sudbury, Massachusetts, undertaken by Sumner Chilton Powell.[21] Sudbury was a small interior town devoted to the raising of cattle. It was not directly affected by the turn to trade and commerce in the 1640s as were some other communities. Moreover, its population was relatively homogeneous during the period with which Powell dealt. One might expect, therefore, that all the generalizations respecting Puritan attitudes would be reflected in the activities of Sudbury's people. But Powell's story is far from that. The founders were acquisitive English yeomen, little touched by any formal Puritan movement in England. During the town's first years, its people were devoted to building and cultivating the land, using the "open-field" or common agricultural method which most of them had known in England. In the early 1650s, however, they felt the pinch of too little land and solicited the General Court for an additional tract.

The subsequent enlargement opened Pandora's box. One segment of the town demanded a shift to closed agriculture — large tracts individually operated — and a division by which "every man shall enjoy a like quantity of land"; another resisted. This issue became entangled with a second, the desire of some to build a new meeting house. Matters were complicated still further by a third issue, the desire of the older settlers to limit the number of cattle allowed on the town meadow. The heated debates that followed involved every person in the town, including minister Edmund Brown. Town meetings became "exciting and well-attended"; tempers flared. In the end, the town split, one faction moving away to found Marlborough, Massachusetts.[22]

The debates divided the town into warring factions, Peter Noyes and Edmund Goodnow representing the first settlers and heads of families, John Ruddock and John How leading the younger men of the town, and minister Brown acting largely in his own interest. At one point Goodnow declared that, "be it right or wrong, we will have [our way] . . . if we can have it no other way, we will have it by club law." At another point, How threatened secession by the young men: "If you oppresse the poore, they will cry out; and if you persecute us in one city, wee must fly to another." Pastor Brown called a meeting "to see to the constraining of youth from the profanation of the Lord's day in time of public service" and turned the session into a political harangue; subsequently the minister appeared at a town meeting to cry out he would "put it to a Vote, before I would be nosed by them." Townsmen refused to attend Sabbath lectures and services for fear of being "ensnared" by their political opponents. One party visited the minister "to desire him not to meddle" and Ruddock bluntly told his pastor that, "setting aside your office, I regard you no more than another man." The Reverend Mr. Brown ultimately attempted to have the dispute submitted to a council of elders drawn from neighboring churches, but the various factions refused on the grounds that "it was a civil difference."[23] Where in this debate is there any indication that the New Englanders "thought of society as a unit, bound together by inviolable ties . . . all parts subordinate to the whole . . . every person occupying a particular status"?

In Boston, too, much the same story is to be found: actions quite contrary to attitudes so often generalized upon. In 1634, the generality — again, a relatively homogeneous populace — challenged the town's leadership by demanding an immediate division of all available land on an equal basis.[24] The response of the leadership was to some extent based on attitudes made classic by historians. Winthrop, thinking in terms of the community, argued against the allocation of more land than an individual could use, partly out of his desire "to prevent the neglect of trades, and other more necessary employments" and "partly that there might be place to receive such as should come after." To him, it would be "very prejudicial" if newcomers "should be forced to go far off for land, while others had much, and could make no use of it, more than to please their eye with it." But the townsmen would have none of it. Land was too much a way to personal gain.

The issue reached a climax in December when a committee of seven was elected to divide the town lands. Winthrop "and other of the chief men" failed of election. The townsmen feared "that the richer men would give the poorer sort no great proportions of land" and chose "one of the elders and a deacon, and the rest of the inferior sort." All the advocates of an ordered society were brought to bear to overturn the election. Winthrop spoke of his grief "that Boston should be the first who should shake off their magistrates," and the Reverend Mr. Cotton of "the Lord's order among the Israelites" by which "all such businesses" were "committed to the elders." "It had been nearer the rule," Cotton argued, "to have chosen some of each sort." The generality gave way for the moment and agreed to a new election. Subsequently a more proper committee was chosen "to devide and dispose" of the land "leaving such portions in Common for the use of newe Commers, and the further benefitt of the towne, as in theire best discretions they shall thinke fitt."[25]

The battle, however, was by no means over. The pursuit of individual gain continued to prompt political activity. The prevailing economic view (and one not uniquely Puritan) was that all phases of the economy were subject to government regulation.[26] Town governments in Massachusetts had the authority to regulate land distribution, land usage, and the laying out of streets; in Boston, the town government established embryonic building codes and licensed inns and wharves. Given this actual exercise of power over the various avenues of opportunity, it was to one's advantage to participate in public affairs.

Land, for a time, continued to be the principal issue. The town had a limited area into which it could expand. By the second decade it had become difficult to find plots for newcomers or additional acreage for older settlers. In 1641, popular pressure forced the selectmen to review the larger grants made in the 1630s, but this action served little purpose. Even where surveys indicated that a Winthrop, Oliver or Cotton held more land than had been allocated, the selectmen took no remedial action.[27] During the following year, the selectmen — in order to obtain more room on Boston's tiny peninsula for house lots — resurrected an earlier order denying the inhabitants permanent possession of their lots in the Boston fields. The result was an angry town meeting in which the order was repealed "for peace sake, and for avoyding of confusion in the Towne."[28]

Boston's turn to trade in the 1640s brought about a change. Opportunities for personal aggrandizement in land were gradually replaced by the better chances for advancement in commerce and allied crafts such as coopering, leatherworking, and shipbuilding. For the artisan, participation in local government was equally as important as it had been for those persons interested in land. The leatherworker or butcher, subject to the selectmen under local regulations regarding the cleanliness of his establishment, or even his very right to carry on his trade within the town, of necessity participated in the town meetings to elect the men who could, in a moment, curtail or end his business activities. The retailer, subject to the inspection of clerks of the market operating under commonwealth law, was quick to make known his choice for such officials. Almost everyone engaged in any kind of economic activity — the laws limiting the electorate notwithstanding — sought to vote for the deputies to the General Court and the Assistants inasmuch as these men wrote the commonwealth ordinances governing economic activity.[29]

On the inter-town level in Massachusetts, too, the desire for personal aggrandizement played havoc with the ideal of an orderly and cohesive society. Town rivalries arose; boundary disputes raged interminably between communities, the prize being a rich meadow or copse.[30] Craftsmen in one town were jealous of those in another. Shoemakers outside Boston, for example, objected to shoemakers within that town organizing a company and seeking exclusive privileges regarding shoes sold in the Boston market. Do not allow "our Brethren of Boston" to "have power put into their hands to hinder a free trade," they wrote to the General Court. "Keeping out Country shoomakers from Coming into the Market," they continued, "wil weaken the hands of the Country shoomakers from using their trade, or occasion them to Remove to boston which wilbe hurtful to Other townes."[31] Merchants and tradesmen in the northern towns — Ipswich, Salem, Newbury — bitterly resented the fact that "Boston, being the chiefest place of resort of Shipping, carries away all the Trade." They reacted in a series of political moves aimed at reducing Boston's central position in the commonwealth. An effort was made to move the seat of government from Boston; an attempt got underway to change the basis of representation in the House of Deputies to Boston's disadvantage; and an alliance was formed between northern towns and country towns to create a bloc within the House to oppose those towns immediately around Boston harbor.[32]

The political activity in and among the towns suggests that the people of Massachusetts Bay, and one can extrapolate to include the other New England colonies, were not acting within the concept of authority and cohesive, ordered society which modern historians have so carefully delineated and pronounced to be characteristic of Puritanism and Puritan New England. Society was not something to which the people of the Bay commonwealth invariably subordinated their own interests. Indeed, the abstract concept of "society" seems to have held little meaning for a generality intent upon individual pursuits. Nor was authority a pervasive thing, obliging the individual through family, church, and state to sublimate his personal aspirations to the interests of the community as a whole. The "state" in Sudbury — in the form of either town or commonwealth government — could provide no other solution to the town's disputes than to permit the community to divide. The church—the Reverend Mr. Brown personally and the elders of the neighboring churches invited in by Brown—was unable to interpose its authority to settle matters. Family fidelity failed to check the personal aspirations of the "landless young sons" who followed Ruddock and How.[33]

The people of Massachusetts, it would appear, were coming to view the elements of authority as being divided rather than united. In particular, they viewed the church and state as distinct entities with well-defined (and to a large extent mutually exclusive) areas of operation. In Sudbury, for example, Pastor Brown's intervention in a civil affair led to his being asked not to "meddle." In Boston, the calling of the Synod of 1646-48 by the commonwealth government roused strong opposition from those who lashed out against the interjection of "civil authority" in church business.[34] The conflict so begun would eventuate in a full scale assault upon the imposition of ministerial authority within the church and of synodical authority among churches — further evidence that the historians' concept of authority and cohesiveness bears little resemblance to New England reality. The historians might cite as evidence of the concept the Cambridge *Platform* which emanated from the Synod and pronounced ministerial and synodical authority to be part of the New England Way, but the deathbed utterances of the Reverend John Wilson are more to the point. Wilson cited as "those sins amongst us, which provoked the displeasure of God" the rising up of the people "*against their Ministers . . . when indeed they do but Rule for Christ*," and "*the making light of, and not subjecting to the Authority of* Synods, *without which the Churches cannot long subsist.*"[35]

The same dichotomy between church and state which one finds in the towns may be seen on the commonwealth level. The historians have noted all too often those laws passed by civil authorities to further the views of the church and those cases where the ministry advised the magistrates on civil matters. But they have paid far too little attention to the arduous efforts made to define the respective spheres of church and state. As John Cotton wrote in 1640, "the government of the Church is as the Kingdome of Christ is, not of this world, but spirituall and heavenly . . . . The power of the keyes is far distant from the power of the sword." To him church and state in Massachusetts were involved in the same task, "the Establishment of pure Religion, in doctrine, worship, and [church] government, according to the word of God: As also the reformation of all corruptions in any of these." Hence the ministers, in whose care the word of God was placed, could logically press for "sweet and wholsom" laws and "civil punishments upon the willfull opposers and disturbers" of the church. But for the things of this world — "the disposing of mens goods or lands, lives or liberties, tributes, customes, worldly honors, and inheritances" — "in these the Church submitteth, and refereth it self to the civill state."[36]

For the most part, too, historians in the past few years have tended to overlook those cases where there was a clash between magistrates and ministers. In 1639, the General Court decided that too frequent and overly long church meetings were detrimental to the community and asked the elders "to consider about the length and frequency of church assemblies." The ministers promptly denounced the magistrates. The request "cast a blemish upon the elders," they said, one "which would remain to posterity, that they should need to be regulated by the civil magistrates."[37] The over-anxious intervention of an elder in a matter before the Assistants in 1643, on the other hand, drove one magistrate to exasperation. "Do you think to come with your eldership here to carry matters?" he shouted. On another occasion, when the elders of Essex County went beyond the bounds that Winthrop considered proper in espousing the cause of the northern towns against Boston — for when town argued with town the elders tended to identify with their communities — the governor lashed out. They "had done no good offices in this matter, through their misapprehensions both of the intentions of the magistrates, and also of the matters themselves, being affairs of state, which did not belong to their calling."[38]

In the division of authority that was taking place, it would seem that the church was freely conceded the power of opening and closing the doors of heaven. To whatever extent the individual sought heaven, he honored the authority of the church in moral and theological matters. But the keys to personal aggrandizement in this world were lodged with the state, and the generality was coming to look upon the state in a peculiarly modern way. In one sense the state was the servant of the individual, obligated to foster his welfare and prosperity. At the same time, it was to protect him from the aspirations of others — acting, so to speak, as an umpire for society, exercising authority in such a way as to avoid collisions between members of the community who were following their individual yet concentric orbits. One can perceive such a view of society, however obliquely, in the political theory of the later New Englanders. For indeed, their writings on this matter are not all of a piece. There is a subtle difference between a Winthrop or Cotton for whom the goal of society was the pleasing of God; a Samuel Willard to whom a happy, contented people was most pleasing to God; and a John Wise to whom "the Happiness of the People, is the End of its [the state's] Being; or main Business to be attended and done."[39]

The view of society discernible in the New England community is quite different from that expounded by intellectual historians who have turned to the writings of the articulate few — and little else — as their mirror of New England's mind. Are we to discard their mirror and the "Puritan" concepts which they have seen in it? The purpose of intellectual history is to delineate the ideological framework within which a people acted. If the actions of the people under consideration do not fall within the framework created, it follows that the framework is invalid. It is not that simple, of course. In the case of New England, the intellectual framework erected over the past years has been firmly based upon the writings of the leading laymen and clergy in the society. We must accept such works as a valid expression of their ideals, even though their ideals might not apply to the people as a whole.

But what are we to describe as "Puritan," the ideals of the articulate few which, relative to society and authority, were neither unique nor pervasive, or the actuality of the man in the street — more accurately, the man in the village lane — which does not fit the ideals? The very fact that such a question can be asked would seem to imply that the description of New England in terms of Puritanism, or of Puritanism in terms of New England, is erroneous. Certainly, the concept of a Puritan golden age, followed by decline, disappears. Mather's degeneration is, in large part, nothing more than the insistence by the generality upon a relationship between the individual and society rather different from that held to by the leaders. And the golden age, as Mather himself admitted, was marked by continual controversies which "made neighbours that should have been like *sheep*, to 'bite and devour one another' " and inspired "unaccountable *party-making*," a symptom of that different relationship.[40]

The historian must, of course, address himself to the problem of New England's intellectuals. Isolated from reality as they were, they clung for almost half a century to ideals which grew more outdated with the passing of each day, and then gradually and subtly accomodated their ideals to the realities of the situation facing them. But their accomodation and the forces in society that caused them to make changes represent a much more important aspect of history than the mere description of "Puritanism." And the historian must dispense with the easy generalization that such leaders "shaped" New England's culture regardless of what "the rank and file may have wanted." He must seek instead to understand the rank and file, their motivations, aspirations, and achievements. For in the last analysis which is more vital, an ideological "Puritanism" divorced from reality which has received so much attention over the years, or the reality which has received so little attention but which was in essence laying down the basis for two-and-a-half centuries of American history ahead?

COLONIAL AMERICA

FOOTNOTES

1. One takes "judicial notice" of the late Perry Miller's influence in molding our view of New England. See his *The New England Mind: From Colony to Province* (Cambridge, Mass., 1953), x: "As far as possible I have again employed the premise of my general title, that 'mind' means what was said and done publicly. Therefore I have made sparing use of diaries or private papers."
2. James Kendall Hosmer, ed., *Winthrop's Journal "History of New England"*: 1630-1649, 2 vols. (New York, 1908), II, 237; "A Modell of Christian Charity [1630]," Massachusetts Historical Society, *The Winthrop Papers*, 5 vols. (Boston, 1929-47), II, 282; Thomas Hooker, *A Survey of the Summe of Church Discipline* . . . (London, 1648), pt. I, 69; J[ohn] Cotton, *The Way of the Churches of Christ in New-England* . . . (London, 1645), 4.
3. Nathaniel B. Shurtleff, ed., *Records of the Governor and Company of the Massachusetts Bay in New England*, 5 vols. (Boston, 1853-54), II, 6, 177-178; I, 157, 181.
4. Cotton, *Way of the Churches of Christ*, 45, and his *The Keyes of the Kingdom of Heaven*. . . (London, 1644), 55.
5. Winthrop, "Modell of Christian Charity," 283; Cotton, *Keyes of the Kingdom*, 37; Hosmer, ed., *Winthrop's Journal*, II, 238.
6. John Cotton, *Gods Promise to His Plantation* . . . (London, 1630), 20; Winthrop, "Modell of Christian Charity," 294; Hosmer, ed., *Winthrop's Journal*, II, 239; John Barnard, *The Throne Established by Righteousness*. . . (Boston, 1734), quoted in Perry Miller and Thomas H. Johnson, comps., *The Puritans*, 2 vols. (New York, 1963), I, 275.
7. George L. Haskins, *Law and Authority in Early Massachusetts: A Study in Tradition and Design* (New York, 1960), ix-x.
8. *Magnalia Christi Americana; or, The Ecclesiastical History of New-England* . . . 2 vols. (Hartford, 1853), I, 233.
9. Samuel E. Morison, *Builders of the Bay Colony* (Boston and New York, 1930), 54.
10. Miller, *From Colony to Province*, *x*: "[I] have, on matters of larger concern, taken my illustrations indifferently from whichever writer seemed most to the point."
11. *The Puritans*, I, 1.
12. *Ibid.*, 183.
13. Hosmer, ed., *Winthrop's Journal*, II, 239.
14. A major point in Bernard Bailyn's *Education in the Forming of American Society: Needs and Opportunities for Study* (Chapel Hill, 1960).
15. John Reyner and William Brewster "in the name and with the consent of the rest" of the Plymouth Church to the "reverende brethren the church of Christ in Boston to the Elders there," August 5, 1639, Cotton Papers, Prince Collection, Boston Public Library, Boston, Massachusetts; Shurtleff, ed., *Records of the Governor and Company of the Massachusetts Bay*, I, 291.
16. Richard Schlatter, "The Puritan Strain," John Higham ed., *The Re-*

construction of American History, (New York, 1963), 26. The notion of a political oligarchy has been under sharp attack by, among others, B. Katherine Brown. See her "Puritan Democracy: A Case Study," *Mississippi Valley Historical Review*, L (1963), 377-396.

17. *Magnalia Christi Americana*, II, 490.
18. Darrett B. Rutman, *Winthrop's Boston: Portrait of a Puritan Town, 1630-1649* (Chapel Hill, 1965), chap. I analyzes the ideal in terms of Winthrop's "Modell": *idem*, "God's Bridge Falling Down: 'Another Approach' to New England Puritanism Assayed," *William and Mary Quarterly*, 3d Ser., XIX (1962), 408-421 briefly traces its fate.
19. Act I, scene iii.
20. Sir Ernest Barker, *Church, State and Education* (Ann Arbor, 1957), 87-88; Richard Hooker, *Of the Laws of Ecclesiastical Polity*, Bk. VIII [1648], chap. ii, pars. 5-6, 9.
21. *Puritan Village: The Formation of a New England Town* (Middletown, Conn., 1963). Powell is evidence of the hold that "Puritanism" as a historian's concept has, for his own evidence against the validity of the concept is forced into the conceptual framework.
22. *Ibid.*, 119.
23. *Ibid.*, 124ff.
24. Rutman, "God's Bridge Falling Down," 410-412. The conclusions following are largely drawn from the author's *Winthrop's Boston.*
25. Hosmer, ed., *Winthrop's Journal*, I, 143-144; "Boston Town Records [1634-1660/61]," City of Boston, *A Report of the Record Commissioners*, II, (Boston, 1877), 3.
26. E. A. J. Johnson, *American Economic Thought in the Seventeenth Century* (London, 1932), 17-18 *et passim.*
27. "Boston Town Records," 26, 59, 60, 61.
28. *Ibid.*, 65.
29. E.g. in *ca.* 1655 a committee of the General Court protested that everyone, including "scotch servants, Irish negers and persons under one and twenty years," was voting for deputies to the General Court in contravention of the law, Dan[iel] Gookin and others to the General Court, Manuscript Photostats, Box 7, Mass. Hist. Soc. Library, Boston. The statement, although extreme, is by no means unique.
30. Shurtleff, ed., *Records of the Governor and Company of the Massachusetts Bay*, and John Noble and John F. Cronin, eds., *Records of the Court of Assistants of the Colony of the Massachusetts Bay: 1630-1692*, 3 vols. (Boston, 1901-28), II, are replete with such disputes.
31. Gowen Anderson and others to the General Court, 1648, Massachusetts Archives, State House, Boston.
32. J. Franklin Jameson, ed., *Johnson's Wonder-Working Providence: 1628-1651* (New York, 1910), 96. Lawrence Shaw Mayo, *John Endecott: A Biography* (Cambridge, Mass., 1936), 470ff alludes to the existence of an "Essex Clique" in Massachusetts politics; the clique can be further identified by a close analysis of the officers and committeemen of the House of Deputies as found in Shurtleff, ed., *Records of the Governor and Company of the Massachusetts Bay*, III.

33. Powell, *Puritan Village*, 137.
34. Hosmer, ed., *Winthrop's Journal*, II, 278ff.
35. Quoted in Rutman, "God's Bridge Falling Down," 416.
36. *Way of the Churches of Christ*, 19, 50; *Keyes of the Kingdom*, 50; *A Briefe Exposition of the Whole Book of Canticles . . .* (London, 1642), 251.
37. Hosmer, ed., *Winthrop's Journal*, I, 326. Note, too, Thomas Shepard's comment: "The Magistrate [must] kisse the Churches feet" and "meddle not beyond his bounds," "The Autobiography of Thomas Shepard," Colonial Society of Massachusetts, *Publications*, XXVII [1932], 397.
38. Hosmer, ed., *Winthrop's Journal*, II, 117, 190.
39. Willard, *The Character of a Good Ruler. . .* (Boston, 1694), in Miller and Johnson, comps., *The Puritans*, I, 254; Wise, *Vindication of the Government of New-England Churches* (Boston, 1717), 46.
40. *Magnalia Christi Americana*, II, 490.

THE JUDICIARY AND PUBLIC OPINION IN REVOLUTIONARY MASSACHUSETTS

JOHN D. CUSHING

Massachusetts Historical Society

ON THE EVE of the American Revolution, the Massachusetts judicial system consisted of an hierarchy of county courts at the top of which stood a single Superior Court of Judicature.[1] This was a circuit court whose five justices held sessions in nearly every county in the Province at least one each year, sometimes twice. The judges were thus relatively free from parochial interests and, endowed with a certain urbanity, were often regarded as the very personification of government, the only tangible sign of royal authority that many communities ever saw. In normal times, therefore, the judges enjoyed great prestige and their advent in shire towns, accompanied by a retinue of servants, attorneys, clerks, and litigants, and surrounded by pomp and ceremony, provided an occasion of nearly holiday proportions.[2]

But there were times when the bench was not held in such esteem. For example, when an act of Parliament or of the provincial government happened to be unpopular, it mattered not that the judges had little, if anything, to do with its origins, or even whether they approved of it. The Superior Court had to go out on circuit and face a people, many of whom regarded the bench as "government" and a convenient place to lodge complaints and grievances.[3] Complaints might take the form of protests or even abuse, and as a result the judges sometimes found their positions uncomfortable, even untenable. Exactly what the bench did when confronted with such situations has yet to be fully chronicled. The official papers of the court shed practically no light on the subject and among the private papers of the judges the only substantial evidence indicating that the court ever took cognizance of its plight, or that of the administration, is to be found in the charges delivered to the grand juries of the several counties.

Traditionally, a charge to the grand jury was composed of several distinct parts. First, the chief justice usually explained to the jurors the nature and necessity of their duties. Secondly, it was customary to recite a list of indictable crimes together with an explanation or example of each, and if a person accused of a particular offence was scheduled to appear at that session, the court might dwell at some length on that crime. Finally, it was not unusual for the presiding justice to seize the opportunity to deliver a lecture upon some appropriate subject, usually moral philosophy, or even upon some timely political topic. Major deviations from this, the usual format, attract immediate attention.

Charges to the grand jury were traditionally intended as juridical instruments, but a survey of those surviving from the Revolutionary period reveals that some of them were more political than juridical in content.[4] Furthermore, it appears that those charges with the heaviest political orientation were delivered at times when the Province was embroiled in great turmoil, and when the authority of the government, including the judiciary, was under attack. On the basis of such evidence it is reasonable to conclude that the court frequently used the charge to the grand jury as an instrument to defend its own integrity and to support the authority of the provincial government. If there is no conclusive evidence to indicate that this technique was ever deliberately conceived and adopted as a matter of policy, there are numerous examples available to demonstrate that the Superior Court often seized such opportunities to assume an active extra-judicial role during the Revolutionary War era.

One such example occurred in May of 1770, two months after the Boston Massacre had brought the wrath of a large segment of the public down upon the provincial government. The Suffolk County Grand Jury had returned criminal indictments against some of the British soldiers, the alleged perpetrators of the incident, but the court postponed the actual hearings with the hope that the popular temper might abate in the interim and thus allow the soldiers to receive a fair trial. For their pains the judges were rewarded with endless calumnies and insults, interspersed with demands for summary justice.[5] Similarly, the case of one Ebenezer

Richardson, a former royal customs employee accused of murdering a boy when he fired into a mob demonstrating before his house, brought noisy disorders and demands for summary justice from spectators in the courtroom. The jury, apparently swayed by public passions, found the defendant guilty of murder rather than manslaughter, thus forcing the court to find a technicality in order to postpone sentencing.[6] That the judges did postpone the sentence was a tribute to their courage for, as they must have anticipated, they immediately became the object of more abuse than ever. Clearly a disquieting situation existed and all accounts indicate that the court stood in considerable awe of the mob.[7]

One of the few surviving documents attesting that the judges took any measures to stem this rising tide of public sentiment is a charge delivered to the grand jury at the Barnstable session of the Superior Court on May 10, 1770.[8] The address opened on a familiar note with what was ostensibly an explanation of the right to a trial by jury. But instead of pursuing this topic to a logical conclusion, the courts directed extensive attention to the merits of the British constitution as a whole and particularly to the historic role of Parliament in preserving *all* of the rights contained in Magna Carta. Having thus established Parliament as the author and guardian of the constitution, the passage concluded blandly: "But how it can be said that that authority [Parliament] which had power to enact had no power to repeal or alter may be justly questioned." With this conclusion, however contrived the logic, it appears quite beyond question that the court was defending the *status quo* and answering the extremists who were both stigmatizing their government as "tyrannical," and increasingly contesting the right of Parliament to legislate in any manner for the empire.

This introduction was followed by the usual list of indictable crimes.[9] Eleven specific offenses were mentioned and normally the presiding justice would have gone on to explain or define each. But such was not the case. Instead, only treason, murder, and riot were singled out for special attention. In view of the times it is not unreasonable to assume that the concentration on these three crimes to the exclusion of all others was inspired by the recent disorders in Boston.

In examining this section of the charge, attention is first drawn to repeated emphasis upon the beneficence of the English system, the safeguards provided in the reign of Edward III[10] for all persons accused of treason, and the further improvements brought about by the Treasons Act of 1696. In its zeal to illustrate these points, the court cited an extreme example, the notorious conduct of Chief Justice George Jeffries at the treason trial of Algernon Sidney.[11] This case was cited apparently for the sole purpose of illustrating that Englishmen, including Americans, need never again fear such gross perversions of justice. While a man might be hanged for treason, he would be assured of a fair trial first. But the most striking feature of this paragraph is the unusually extensive attention devoted to a crime that had not appeared on a Massachusetts docket during the tenure of the oldest member of the bench.[12]

The charge went on to treat both murder and riot in similar fashion. In explaining homicide, the usual distinctions between murder and manslaughter were explored in a rather lengthy passage that appears to have been superfluous since the Barnstable docket reveals that no man was accused of homicide at that term. It is to be kept in mind, however, that the dispute between the court and jury in the trial of Ebenezer Richardson centered upon a misunderstanding, wilful or otherwise, of these distinctions and that the outcome of the pending "massacre trials" would also probably depend to no small degree upon an adequate understanding of those distinctions. Was this passage designed to educate the public in some of the niceties of criminal law? Unless the presiding justice had some such end in mind, it is difficult to explain why he spent so much time on the subject at that particular session.

Perhaps the most outstanding and pointed passage in the entire charge was the straightforward and blunt treatment of riot:

> A riot is where 3 or more people assemble together and do some act of a private nature with force and violence to the disturbance of the peace. Two cannot commit a riot. It must be three or more and if they assemble to redress grievances of a public nature and their intention is executed it is a leavying war against the King and is treason as L[ord] Cook [Sir Edward Coke] mentions in his third Institutes.[13] These riots have of late been more frequent than heretofore

> and as it is said divers murthers have been committed *this youl specially inquire into.*

This portion of the address was proclaimed from the relatively unassailable citadel of the common law, and for good reason. The chapter of the Province Laws known as "The Riot Act" was about to expire and the General Court had refused to renew it, much to the annoyance of the friends of orderly government.[14] The court, however, here pointed out, in effect, that the omission would be of small consequence, for the common law, upon which the riot act was based in the first place, never expired. Perhaps there were men present in the courtroom that rainy May morning who may have reflected soberly upon the stringency of the common law proviso that redressing public grievances by violence "is a leavying war against the King and is treason."[15] Since there were no presentments for riot at that session, this extensive passage also appears to have been as much admonitory as functional and addressed to a broader audience than the grand jury.

Taken as a whole, the charge thus far could reasonably have been considered a plea for support of law and order at a time when public authority was held in increasing contempt. Most notable was the effort made to weave into each paragraph salutary remarks on the nature of the English government and laws, but equally remarkable was the absence from the Barnstable court of anyone accused of murder, treason, or riot.[16] In short, it is evident that this portion of the charge was designed for political as well as juridical purposes, but the concluding lines of the address exhibit an even more pointed political orientation:

> And here I cannot but just hint at that gen[era]l uneasiness which has been and still subsists between America and the mother countrey to the great disadavantage of both. But I hope those difficulties will soon be removed . . . . I am satisfied no person of prudence and discretion will in the least countenance any unjustifiable measures for redress of their grievances. The people in general and I believe all in America are well attach't to King George 3d and the present royal family and I hope will always remain so and that this uneasiness will soon subside . . . .

The political subtleties in the first or supposedly juridical section of the charge were thus brought to a logical conclusion in a direct appeal to the better instincts of men of good sense. It was a reasonable appeal, devoid of any trace of the harsh threats or brute authority that might have been expected from a "despotick" government.

The immediate effect of this pronouncement upon those who heard it is impossible to evaluate; it can only be presented here as one attempt, probably among many made by the court, to win support for the *status quo.* But in the larger picture these tactics obviously did little, if anything, to establish a lasting reconciliation between the administration and the people.[17] Neither did they succeed in restoring the bench to public grace, for six months later when the verdicts in the "massacre trials" were returned ,the judges were accused of being prejudiced in favor of the defendants and were subjected to more abuse than ever. From this unenviable position, the court never fully recovered, and two years later events took an even more decided turn for the worse.

This time the controversy centered on the question of whether the Crown or the General Court of Massachusetts was to pay the salaries of the judges. The resolution of this issue, it was claimed in some quarters, would determine whether the judiciary would be responsible to the people or become an instrument in the hands of a designing Parliament.[18] The issue brought the judges under close public scrutiny, and when most of them finally agreed to accept the salary grant from the Crown, the Superior Court became, in effect, a nullity. Instead of serving as a symbol of royal authority, it came to be regarded as the personification of royal tyranny. The court's position deteriorated rapidly and it soon became impossible to muster the judicial quorum required to open court.

A day of reckoning had to come, however, and it arrived when the new revolutionary government of Massachusetts, anxious to establish its authority throughout the state, began to rebuild the shattered judicial structure. Every effort was made to create a new Superior Court of Judicature that could command the respect of the people, and to this end great care was exercised in selecting the new judges. But even with a carefully chosen panel ready to resume the old circuit, there was considerable fear that the public might not be favorably disposed toward the new tribunal. For over two years the high bench had been an anathema to the people and an increasing number of men found the absence of an effective judiciary to their advantage. Now, it was of vital importance that the new court be accepted by the public, for at stake was not only the question of establishing justice, but the much more critical problem of whether the people would accept peaceably the authority of the new goverment. Therefore, it was with no little anxiety that attention was turned to Ipswich, in Essex County, where, on June 18, 1776, William Cushing, the senior associate justice, opened court with a scant quorum on the bench.[19]

There was no disturbance in the courtroom as the justices exhibited their new commissions and began the charge to the grand jury. This carefully worded document had been composed by John Adams, officially adopted by the Council and House of Representatives, and designed, according to Adams, as "an appeal to the conservative principles of the people."[20] Now it was put to the test.

The address opened with an explanation of the social compact and its violation by Great Britain. This portion of the charge was a reasoned justification of the American Revolution as well as an explanation of the necessity for vacating all royal offices. It was also a justification of the assumption of power by the representatives of the people and the formation of a government characterized as "More immediately in all its branches under the influence and control of the people and, therefore, more free and happy than was enjoyed by their ancestors." With this elaborate introduction, a dissertation upon the powers and duties of that government might reasonably have been expected. Instead, the remainder of the address was devoted to a single phase of the subject, the establishment of a judiciary, its powers, and its relationship to the people:

> As an army has become necessary for our defense, and in all free states the civil must provide for the control of the military power, the major part of the council have appointed magistrates and courts of justice . . . whose happiness is so connected with that of the people, that it is difficult to suppose they can abuse their trust. The business of it is to see those laws enforced, which are necessary for the preservation of peace, virtue, and good order. And the Great and General Court expects and requires that all necessary support and assistance be given, and all proper obedience yielded to them; and will deem every person who shall fail in his duty in this respect toward them, a disturber of the peace of this colony and deserving of exemplary punishment.

Clearly these blunt words served notice that a new government was in office, that it had asserted its authority by establishing a judiciary, and that all men were required by law to lend it their support. The message was punctuated with a concluding paragraph that considered in general terms most categories of indictable crimes, called upon all civil officers to bring offenders to "condign punishment," and to "use their utmost endeavors to have the resolves of Congress and as laws of this colony duly carried into execution."[21]

This "appeal to the conservative principles of the people" was a straightforward plea for support for both the new judiciary and the authority that had created it. It was an effort to assure the people of the merits of self-government and, at the same time, it was a threat to all opponents of the new regime. As the author admitted, it was designed to influence the people toward a desired end. In this respect it is important here as one of the few charges that can be documented as a deliberate effort to use the judiciary as an emissary of government.

Once again, it is difficult to evaluate the effect this address may have had on those who heard it. But, whatever its influence, the judges appear to have at least considered the approach useful, perhaps necessary, for it was employed with increasing frequency in the years to come. When the people groaned under the burden of supporting an army and fighting a war, the Superior Court would plead the necessity of new and heavier taxes. When the tides of war appeared to be running against the American cause, the judges repeatedly attempted to bolster public morale with timely charges to the grand jury. If complaints concerning inflation were broadcast, it was the court that tried to explain the evil and to promise better times with the return of peace. If a rash of crimes suddenly appeared on the docket in a particular county, the plea was for law and order, and respect for authority. Sometimes a charge was obviously prepared with an eye to its effect on the people of a particular locality. At other times the address was more general in nature and was used in county after county until some turn of events called for the preparation of a new one.[22]

As months passed into years these addresses tended to become more political than juridical, until the traditional list of indictable crimes became almost incidental to a carefully reasoned political dissertation. Basic to all of these charges was the emphasis upon the powers of duly constituted authority and the necessity for obedience to law. The addresses also explained and interpreted the natural rights of Englishmen, the right and duty to oppose tyranny, and the need to overthrow governments subversive of the constitution. They invariably stressed the duty of every man to support the new government and to fulfill his obligations under the social compact. The penalty for failure in this respect was portrayed in the darkest terms as the failure of free government and a return to the yoke of despotism.

When considering matters of such scope, the chief justice usually employed authoritarian terminology befitting his status, but when specific political topics came under discussion the approach was sometimes more subtle, even oblique. Here the core of the issue might first be singled out, placed within a convenient frame of reference, and then treated to an application of logic designed to lead listeners to a desired conclusion. Among the illustrations of this approach are several charges delivered in 1780 in an obvious effort to win support for the new state constitution. At least one of these was delivered while the state constitutional convention was still at work and appears to have been intended to prepare the public for the instrument that would soon be sent to the towns for approval.[23]

The address began with a few positive remarks on the merits of the British constitution. The people were reminded that while it was not perfect it had served them well and was not to be abandoned hastily or rashly. The forthcoming state constitution was characterized as an improvement, but the people were warned not to anticipate radical departures from the past, nor to expect a greater degree of perfection than could reasonably be hoped for in any frame of government. The chief justice carefully abstained from extolling the virtues of any particular provision of the forthcoming document. Instead, he turned, ostensibly, to an analysis of the criteria of good government and a discussion of what a constitution ought to do for a people. It would appear to be more than coincidence that those subjects to which he devoted most attention were also the very topics debated at greatest length by the convention. Thus was the public forewarned of some of the features of the new frame of government. More important, notice was also served that, far from being a unique innovation, the new constitution would be designed to promote one of the original purposes of the Revolution: to secure and safeguard for Americans the rights of Englishmen.

When the constitution was finally completed and sent to the towns, the Superior Court, riding the spring circuit, repeatedly spoke in its favor. Now specific topics were discussed, such as the need for a strong executive, a militia, and a system of courts, tenure for the judiciary, and the tax-supported church provided by the controversial Article III of the Declaration of Rights. But the court appears to have been less concerned with these specifics than with educating the public in the nature of the proposed constitution, repeatedly stressing that it was not intended to be an abrogation of the old system but a continuation of it that would "secure and perpetuate the same to the latest posterity." This approach, coupled with the invariable emphasis upon the role of the people in creating and implementing the new instrument, was at once an answer to those malcontents and innovators who sought a sharp break with the past, as well as assurance that the new order was not to be entirely in the hands of a new ruling elite.[24]

The efficacy of the court's endeavors in this matter is somewhat clearer than its efforts in other areas. First, the judges were a veritable clearing house for information on the subject. They had attended the convention and been privy to its debates. They also traversed the circuit listening to views and exchanging opinions with men in every part of the state. The court, therefore, more than any other organ of government or any other group of men, was acquainted with public opinion on the subject and in an advantageous position to adjust its pronouncements accordingly.

The public, on the other hand, had fewer and far less satisfactory sources of information. Newspapers of the day devoted ample space to foreign affairs, the war, and even to trivia, but practically none to the constitution. No newspaper printed the full text, nor did pamphleteers or public figures take pen in hand or speak out either for or against it. Delegates to the convention doubtless reported their views to their communities, but the convention was very poorly attended. When the document finally reached the towns, some town meetings debated each article at length, but others gave only cursory attention to the whole.[25] In short, sources of reliable information on the subject were few, and their influence at best was divisive; whereas the charges to the grand juries had the advantage of being uniform and, above all, positive. Therefore, since the constitution was ratified on the basis of a most questionable majority, and there appears to be little doubt that such was the case, it is almost certain that the role of the court was important in securing this ratification.

Having thus helped to create the new frame of government, the bench in the years to follow sometimes found it necessary to speak out in defense of some of its provisions. Perhaps the greatest effort was evoked six years later when the Shays's Rebellion threatened to undermine the constitution and overturn the government. The controversy centered, at least in part, on the judiciary, just as it had in the pre-war dispute about the judges' salaries. Therefore, the bench found itself once more in a precarious and potentially dangerous position. Again, the challenge was met, not with hangings, brute authority, nor partisan administration of justice, but with pointed charges to the grand juries. As each session of the court opened, the chief justice, standing squarely on the constitution, delivered a searing denunciation of the insurgent cause. A typical example is the address delivered at Salem in November of 1786, shortly after many inhabitants of the Commonwealth were outraged by the temporary suspension of the right to writs of *habeas corpus*.[26]

The chief justice began with the usual list of indictable crimes and, just as his father had done at Barnstable sixteen years earlier, placed heavy stress upon riots, routs and unlawful assemblies, crimes of which no man stood accused at that session. Riot was defined as "an unlawful act of a private nature." If it was also an attempt to regulate "weighty affairs of state," to suspend the laws, stop the courts, and obstruct justice, then it was declared to be high treason, "a treasonable attempt to wrest the powers of government from the hands of those in whom the constitution and the body of the people have placed them; an attempt to subvert the government; to bring on general anarchy . . . ; to set all property afloat; to bury all public and private security together." The consequence of this trend, it was confidently predicted, would be the subjugation of the Commonwealth to some foreign power or the equally distasteful prospect of a despotic military government at home.

The emotional opening paragraph was typical of the remainder of this lengthy attack on the county conventions which, according to the court, were at the root of the rebellion. Nearly 3,500 words were poured forth, first denouncing the conventions as unconstitutional, subversive of the legislative process, and a breach of the social compact; then a treatment of the demands made by some of the conventions. Pleading the rights of private property, denouncing the economic anarchy advocated by many of the insurgents, and hinting darkly at the horrors of civil war, the chief justice stigmatized the instigators of the troubles as

> artful and designing [men] . . . involved in debt . . . with a view, perhaps, by multiplying grievances, and raising artful insinuations against our representatives . . . to raise themselves into power and importance, to oust the present representatives, and substitute themselves in their places; and perhaps, to introduce a paper currency; by one bold stroke to extricate themselves from debt . . . . A paper currency, that engine of fraud and destruction of all common honesty . . . .

And so the address continued, lashing out at every demand made by the disaffected elements in the state. The weapons employed were ridicule, reason, and emotion; ridicule of the alterations in government proposed by the county conventions, reasoned explanations of constitutional methods of redressing grievances, and the repeated use of emotion-laden phrases apparently designed to instill fear in the hearts of honest men and also, perhaps, men whose allegiance might be wavering:

> For let every man depend upon it, that if the present government and constitution fall . . . all private right and private property will fall with them, and lie wholly at the mercy of the most idle vicious and disorderly set of men in the country. For numbers of the insurgents

> and some of their leaders, have, in fact, fully declared their design to abolish all publick and private debts, and have a general division of property among them.

While this was an emotional misrepresentation, or misunderstanding, of the facts, it was also a strong appeal for support of the *status quo*, an attempt to discredit the "plotted mischief" and "the spirit of lying and falsehood" that allegedly emanated from the councils of the malcontents. Nor did the chief justice attempt to conceal his purpose. Far from it, he stated clearly that his remarks were intended to inform the peaceable residents of Essex County of the threats posed by the insurrection to their peace, property, and prosperity. The publication of this charge in both the Boston and Salem newspapers also indicates that it probably was intended to be a strong pronouncement in support of the efforts by both government and private individuals to nip in the bud the rebellious spirit that threatened to spread throughout the entire state.

In county after county the public was treated to similar emotional denunciations of the insurgents and their objectives. Even after hostilities were officially at an end and a general amnesty proclaimed, courtroom audiences were harangued with the evils of the insurrection, the purpose then being apparently to impress upon the public that new and heavier taxes would be necessary to pay the costs of suppressing the rebellion.[27] These and similar charges delivered during the two year uprising offer outstanding examples of the effort made by the bench to wield its authority over the public mind. Many other causes, however, were also argued in similar fashion, usually with more detachment, but always with vigor and discernable purpose. Whenever a controversial issue arose wherein the nature of government, the constitution, or the laws was involved, the high bench usually had something to say on the subject.

Despite the availability of illustrations, there still remains the question whether the deliberate use of charges to the grand jury to achieve desired political ends was ever consciously and officially devised by any branch of government. To date practically no evidence in the affirmative has come to light. A second and more important question, concerning the results of these efforts, the influence of the addresses upon those who heard them, must also remain unanswered and likely unanswerable. It can only be said that the Superior Court of Judicature and its successor, the Supreme Judicial Court, had frequent opportunity to address relatively large numbers of people. Present in courtrooms were members of the grand jury, members of the bar, litigants, witnesses, petit jurors, and always many spectators to whom the opening of court was a welcome diversion from the humdrum of everyday existence.[28] Moreover, the voice of the bench was sometimes projected afar by the publication of some of its pronouncements in the press. But exactly how each man reacted to what he heard or read doubtless varied directly with his personal attitude toward authority, his opinion of the judges, and all the nebulae that have influenced the minds of men in all ages. Unfortunately, few people recorded their reactions in letters or diaries for the edification of posterity.

But putting aside imponderables, all evidence indicates that the judiciary was in a more advantageous position than any other branch of government to bring influence directly to bear upon an appreciable number of people. The governor was confined to the indirect expedients of issuing proclamations, addressing the legislature or, perhaps, attempting to influence directly a few individuals. The General Court enacted legislation that was not necessarily always popular, but it was impossible for that body to justify its actions to the people. In contrast, the political nature of the charges to the grand jury, shifting in emphasis with the rise and wane of major issues, indicates at least that the judges were aware of the opportunity at their command. They used it often.

The technique employed was neither novel nor unique. It was an ancient and well-established practice that was adapted to the pressing needs of the times. Nor can it be said that the judges made improper use of the charges to the grand juries, for regardless of the crisis of the day, the basic message was usually a plea for support of legally constituted authority. The last royal Superior Court passed into history with just such a plea. Its influence in the final crisis appears to have been inadequate, utterly incapable of dissuading the majority public opinion.[29] Its successor, adopting a more positive approach, made continuous efforts to justify to the people the overthrow of the old order and the establishment of a new authority. Once this end was attained, the chief effort was then directed toward stabilizing the political situation, supporting a government sufficiently strong and free from inroads upon its authority to pursue the war effort effectively, and maintaining an orderly civil society. If the technique was a success it is probably attributable to the repeated emphasis laid upon the popular origins of the new regime, the common benefits to be derived from its success, and the widespread disaster that would attend its failure. Authoritarian pronouncements and harsh invectives were usually reserved for use before trial juries hearing criminal causes.

In conclusion, it may be said that the role of the Superior Court in helping shape the course of Massachusetts history during the Revolutionary years, while incapable of exact measurement, was at least positive. All evidence attests that the judges considered their efforts important, perhaps vital, for in the course of carrying the law into every county in the Province and Commonwealth they rarely lost the opportunity to attempt to induce respect for all lawfully constituted authority.

FOOTNOTES

1. A useful summary of the Massachusetts court structure may be found in *The Charters and General Laws of the Colony and Province of Massachusetts Bay . . .* eds. Nathan Dane, William Prescott, and Joseph Story (Boston: 1814), 217 - 221, 239 - 240, 299 - 301. More detailed data are available in the appropriate sections of *The Acts and Resolves, Public and Private of the Province of The Massachusetts Bay. . . .* 21 vols. (Boston: 1869-1922), hereinafter cited as *Acts & Resolves.*
2. The presence of large numbers of people in the shire towns at "term time" is fully attested by the dockets of the court. But the ranks of the litigants were also swollen by countrymen who swarmed to the county seat seeking diversion, the opportunity to transact business, or both.
3. Chief Justice Thomas Hutchinson once announced to a grand jury and the usual crowd of spectators, "We . . . who are to execute the Law, are not to enquire into the Reason and Policy of it, or whether it is Constitutional or not . . . . We . . . are to enquire what is Law, and see that the Laws are inforced." Josiah Quincy, Junior, *Reports of Cases Argued and Adjudged in the Superior Court of Judicature of the Province of Massachusetts Bay Between 1761 and 1772*, ed. Samuel M. Quincy (Boston: 1865), hereinafter cited as *Quincy's Reports*, 307.
4. For examples of grand jury charges primarily juridical in nature see *Quincy's Reports*, 215 and 232. For examples of charges with a heavy personal or political content see *ibid.*, 175, 218, 241, 302. See also *The Diary and Autobiography of John Adams*, ed. Lyman H. Butterfield, 4 vols. (Cambridge, 1961), I, 281; hereinafter cited as *Diary and Autobiography of John Adams.*
5. When the judges decided to postpone the trials an irate committee, headed by Samuel Adams, waited upon them and demanded that the hearings take place immediately. The court, accused of being under the control of the British military, was in reality far more cowed by the popular temper and submitted to the demands made by the citizens committee. The trials were finally postponed only because one of the judges suffered an accident and could not continue on the circuit. See Thomas Hutchinson, *The History of the Colony and Province of Massachusetts Bay*, ed. Lawrence Shaw Mayo, 3 vols. (Cambridge, 1936), III, 200-205, hereinafter cited as Hutchinson, *History of Massachusetts*; Superior Court of Judicature, "Suffolk Minute Book," under March and August, 1770. The Minute Books, or dockets, as well as the records and papers of the court are in the Clerk's office at the Suffolk County Court House.
6. Hutchinson, *History of Massachusetts*, III, 206; *The Boston News-letter*, March 1, 1770; *The Boston Gazette*, February 26, and March 5, 1770; Robert Treat Paine, "Minutes & Trials of Law Cases," Suffolk session, April 1770, in the Massachusetts Historical Society.
7. The severe treatment of the judges, meted out by many elements of society, is attested, among other things, by a number of sermons

preached and published at the time. See, e.g., John Lathrop, *Innocent Blood Crying to God From the Streets of Boston* (London: Printed, Boston: Re-printed, 1771), and John Browne, *A Discourse Delivered on the Day of the Annual Provincial Thanksgiving, December 6, 1770* (Boston: 1771). The Lathrop sermon, with its incendiary title, was delivered in Boston on the Sunday following the massacre. Significantly, it was published a year later. Browne, preaching shortly after the "massacre trials," attacked the court for its lenient treatment of the soldiers. Neither he nor many other critics wasted epithets on the jurors who returned the verdicts.

8. The charge in mention was delivered in the absence of Chief Justice Benjamin Lynde by the senior associate justice, John Cushing III. The MSS is in the "Cushing Papers" at the Massachusetts Historical Society. See also the MSS diaries of Judge Lynde at the Massachusetts Historical Society, and Superior Court of Judicature, "Barnstable Minute Book," May 10, 1770.
9. The list of offenses usually tried before the Court of General Sessions of the Peace appears to have been read also, but it is not included within the text of this charge. The Barnstable jury was told that it might take cognizance of such matters if the standing jury attending the Sessions had been negligent; "But yor special business is to present to this court all persons who are guilty [*sic*] of high crimes and misdemeanors, such as high treason, murder, felonies of all sorts, perjury, forgeries, burglary, robbery, counterfeiting . . . , riots, routs, high handed assaults and trespasses, and all other high crimes and misdemeanors . . . . " See charge in mention.
10. 25 Edward III, c. 2. See also, William Blackstone, *Commentaries on the Laws of England*, 4 vols. (Philadelphia: 1774), IV, 76; hereinafter cited as *Blackstone*.
11. Algernon Sidney, an opponent of the extension of Stuart power, was brought to trial in 1686 on three charges of treason: conspiring to levy war against the King, seeking Scottish aid for a rebellion, and uttering a seditious libel. Only one witness testified for the Crown on the first charge. The second was not proved. The seditious libel was an answer prepared by Sidney to a publication by Robert Filmer, an opponent of the social compact theory. Lord Jeffries ruled, in effect, that the three charges were components of one act of treason and that the seditious manuscript was tantamount to the required second witness, although neither seditious intent nor publication were proved. See T. B. Howell, *A Complete Collection of State Trials and Proceedings for High Treason and Other Crimes*, 21 vols. (London, 1816), IX, 817 ff; and Cushing's version in the charge under discussion.
12. In charging the Essex County Grand Jury in November of 1766, Chief Justice Thomas Hutchinson hinted darkly that there were certain persons who might well be charged with treasonous offenses but that he preferred not to elaborate on the matter. See notes taken by John Adams at that session, "Adams Papers," in the Massachusetts Historical Society.

13. Sir Edward Coke, *The Third Part of the Institutes of the Laws of England; Concerning High Treason and Other Pleas of the Crown, and Criminal Causes* (London: 1644), III, 176; hereinafter cited as *Institutes*.

14. The Riot Act was omitted from the list of acts renewed by the General Court in 1770. *Acts & Resolves*, V. 39ff; *Journal of the . . . House of Representatives of . . . Massachusetts Bay . . . 1769* (Boston: 1769), 189-194; Hutchinson, *History of Massachusetts*, III, 203-204.

15. Cushing appears to have been poorly informed on the prevailing views and laws on riot, or at least failed to explain them fully. By the time of Blackstone the common law stipulated that at least twelve participants must be involved before a riot could become a capital offense. The Massachusetts act of 1751, which was continued from time to time, took precedence over the common law definition but was derived from the English Riot Act. It defined riot as the unlawful action of twelve or more armed men, or more than thirty unarmed men, but the common law death penalty was replaced with lesser punishment. *Blackstone*, IV, 142ff; *Acts & Resolves*, III, 544ff, 561. Cf. *Institutes*, III, 176, and also *Acts & Resolves*, III, 997 defining riotous assemblies. For additional data, relating to traditional definitions of treason in Massachusetts, see *Quincy's Reports*, 175ff.

16. An examination of the Barnstable docket reveals that the only criminal business at the session was an indictment, in absentia, for assault. If the Crown sought other indictments but failed to obtain true bills there is no evidence to that effect in the docket or in the diary and law notes of Robert Treat Paine, acting Attorney General for that session.

17. If we are to credit John Adams' acid reaction to Thomas Hutchinson's use of charges to the grand jury in support of royal authority, it would seem likely that the effort did more harm than good. *Diary and Autobiography of John Adams*, I, 281.

18. Varying accounts of this episode may be found in Peter Oliver, "The Origins and Progress of the American Rebellion in the year 1776," in "Gay Transcripts," Massachusetts Historical Society; Hutchinson, *History of Massachusetts*, III, 389, 545ff; *The Boston Gazette*, January 25, 1773, and other contemporary newspapers; *Diary and Autobiography of John Adams*, I, 188; II, 65-70, 77-79; III, 297-302.

19. The court at Ipswich consisted of Cushing, the sole survivor from the old royal Superior Court, James Sullivan, and Jedidiah Foster. Chief Justice John Adams was absent, since he was representing Massachusetts at the Congress in Philadelphia. See John Winthrop to John Adams, June 1, 1776 in "Heath Papers," Massachusetts Historical Society; James Sullivan to John Adams, May 17, 1776, in "Adams Papers," Massachusetts Historical Society; Superior Court of Judicature, "Record," fols. 2-8.

20. The General Court also required that this document be read at the opening sessions of the inferior courts, at every town meeting, and that it be recommended to the attention of the clergy. "Massachusetts Archives," 131:281 in Massachusetts State Archives; *The Works of*

John Adams . . ., ed., Charles Francis Adams, 10 vols. (Boston, 1850-1856), I, 192-196.

21. Judge Foster, writing to his family on the evening of June 18, told them that Cushing "gave a speech . . . by way of an address to the Grand Jury which did honor to the Court and him in particular." It is not clear whether this was the document drawn by Adams, the concluding lines of which impart much of the flavor of a charge to the grand jury, or another address. For present purposes the distinction is immaterial. The important point is that the opportunity to deliver a political address was utilized.
22. Charge to the grand jury dated April-June 1783, docketed "Concord, Worcester, Northampton, Barnstable, Plymouth, Ipswich, York, & Falmouth," in "Cushing Papers," Massachusetts Historical Society.
23. Undated and undocketed charge to the grand jury, "Cushing Papers," Massachusetts Historical Society. The date is apparent from internal evidence.
24. Charge to the grand jury docketed "Middlesex Supr. Court, April Term, 1780;" charge to the grand jury docketed "Delivered at Middlesex, Plymouth, and Barnstable terms, 1780," both in "Cushing Papers," Massachusetts Historical Society.
25. Samuel Eliot Morison, "The Struggle Over the Adoption of the Constitution in Massachusetts, 1780," Massachusetts Historical Society, *Proceedings*, L (1917), 353-374.
26. *The American Herald*, November 27, 1786. This is not to imply that the court played no judicial rôle in suppressing the insurrection. The great variety and number of indictments and trials is another story.
27. *The American Herald*, May 28, 1787.
28. Both Chief Justice Hutchinson and Justice John Cushing stated that when charging the grand jury they spoke on certain matters of public concern because of the large numbers of people present in the court room at the time. See *Quincy's Reports*, 218, and the Barnstable charge of 1770 discussed above.
29. During its final months of active life the Court had no opportunity to address the grand jury because jurymen refused to serve under Chief Justice Oliver who openly avowed his intention of accepting his salary from the Crown. Had such a situation not prevailed, however, and had the courts continued to sit, it is most unlikely that any number of politically oriented charges could then have diverted the floodwaters of revolution.

LAW UNDER PRESSURE: BOSTON 1769-1771

HILLER B. ZOBEL*

Co-Editor, Legal Papers of John Adams

LAW is a noun sufficiently plastic to cover every phase of social self-control from legislative enactment to judicial decree. To talk of *the* law existing in pre-Revolutionary Massachusetts is therefore impossible without additional definition and refinement. This essay is designed to focus neither on the law of the legislature nor that of the executive, nor even on the law of the judiciary. There will be no treatment here of the common law's brooding omnipresence, its reception in Massachusetts, or even its adaptation to American conditions. Any reference to these must be wholly incidental, for the concern of this essay is simply the condition of Massachusetts justice in the years 1769-1771. And because legal justice then as now emerged only from an adversary system of courts, litigation, and trials, the question will be more usefully recast thus: What causes could be fairly tried in Massachusetts in 1769-1771? The answer will depend, naturally enough, on an overall look at the court system and on an examination in some detail of several significant, although not necessarily innately important, trials.

Massachusetts trials took place in a remarkably sophisticated judicial organization. Although we may properly note that the Massachusetts of 1770 was closer, chronologically, technologically, and philosophically to the Bay Colony than to today's Commonwealth, and although it is true that in the 1770's, a convicted forger could have had an ear cut off, and a convict who could not pay his fine could be "sold to any of His Majesty's liege subjects" for a period of years,[1] the court structure itself was strikingly modern. In addition to the one Superior Court of Judicature, Court of Assize and General Gaol Delivery, the direct ancestor of today's Supreme Judicial Court, each county had an Inferior Court of Common Pleas, a Court of General Sessions of the Peace, and a Court of Probate, with the Governor and Council sitting as a Supreme Court of Probate and Divorce. Also, justices of the peace within the counties each held one-man courts of minor jurisdiction — it was before one of these that John Adams got his first litigation experience. Finally, the royal Court of Vice-Admiralty and the occasionally-convened special Court of Admiralty dealt with revenue and maritime matters.

This roster of the Massachusetts courts has been described simply to emphasize that whatever causes civil or criminal might arise, a suitable and experienced judicial apparatus was available for their resolution. Moreover, as the publication of John Adams' Diary, Autobiography, and Legal Papers have re-emphasized, the Massachusetts bar numbered among its membership enough men trained in the law and seasoned in trial practice to assure the competent presentation of any case in any of the tribunals.

The bench, too, carried its share of learned lawyers, like Edmund Trowbridge, and sound, albeit untrained, judges, like Thomas Hutchinson and Peter Oliver. Hutchinson, who ceased sitting as Chief Justice after he became acting governor on Governor Bernard's departure in 1769, made up for his missing legal education by wide reading, common sense, and a cultivated ability to make the barristers do the work for him. "I never presumed to call myself a Lawyer," he wrote to John Sullivan. "The most I could pretend to was when I heard the Law laid on both sides to judge which was right."[2] Thus, whatever factors may have influenced the probabilities of fair trial in Massachusetts, lack of learned, able counsel and an intelligent bench were not among them.

As it is the underlying premise of this essay that the interaction and cumulation of consecutive and concurrent events itself determined whether or not trials were fair, it will be useful to adopt at this point a technique essential to historians as well as trial lawyers by setting forth a chronology to give us a general view of the ground we shall be covering somewhat out of order later on.

The lengthy battle between the Commissioner of Customs and John Hancock over the cargo of the *Liberty*, which provided the overture to this series of legal imbroglios, ended on March 3,

1769, when Advocate General Jonathan Sewall withdrew the information, or charge, against Hancock, thus terminating the prosecution.[3] On April 22, at sea off Cape Ann, Lieutenant Henry Panton of H.M.S. *Rose* was killed while attempting to press four seamen of the brig *Pitt Packet;* on June 14-17, after several procedural delays, Michael Corbet and the three sailors were tried and acquitted by a special Court of Admiralty. On July 24, a group of British soldiers of the Fourteenth Regiment rescued out of the hands of a Boston constable Private John Riley, convicted of breaking the peace. On August 21, Tory publisher John Mein began printing in his *Boston Chronicle* evidence that many supposedly non-importing merchants were secretly violating the non-importation agreement. On September 5, James Otis and John Robinson fought their brawl in the British Coffee House in Boston. On October 28 a mob chased John Mein up King Street, into the Guard House, and, eventually, out of Boston forever.

In mid-December of 1769, the British soldiers were tried and convicted for the Riley riot. On February 22, 1770, a mob of schoolboys and their elders surrounded the house of Ebenezer Richardson and pelted the windows with stones; Richardson fired a musket at them, killing an eleven-year-old boy. On March 1, John Hancock received powers of attorney from two of John Mein's London creditors; that same day, John Adams wrote out the necessary writs, and the deputy sheriff seized Mein's books and printing equipment. On March 5, the Boston Massacre took place when eight soldiers of the Twenty-Ninth Regiment under Captain Thomas Preston fired on a mob and killed five men.

On October 24, Captain Preston's trial started, lasting until October 29 when he was acquitted. The trial of his men lasted from November 27 to December 5: six were acquitted, two were found guilty of manslaughter only. On December 12, the four civilians accused of complicity in the Massacre were tried and acquitted. In mid-January 1771, the actions against Mein went to trial in the Suffolk Inferior Court; he lost both, but appealed. On July 25, the trial of Otis' action against Robinson began, with the jury returning a £2000 verdict on July 27. On November 29,

Mein's cases were re-tried in the Suffolk Superior Court, and again he lost.

Although these cases will be taken up in order of their appearance, it will be helpful to keep in mind this sketchy chronology. The point to remember, of course, is that not only did the matters relate to and interact upon one another, but that they were in many instances proceeding at the same time. Thus in the spring and summer of 1770, John Adams worked simultaneously on the Mein litigation, the Massacre defenses, and the prosecution of Otis' action. Then, as now, lawyers perforce divided their attentions and their energies.

Rex v. Corbet et al., the first case here considered, grew out of the refusal of Michael Corbet and three fellow Irishmen to obey the orders of Henry Panton, the lieutenant, or executive officer, of H. M. Frigate *Rose*, to come out and be inspected. Corbet and his friends, crewmen of the brig *Pitt Packet*, homeward bound from Cadiz, Spain, to Marblehead with a cargo of salt, had armed themselves respectively with fish gig, hatchet, harpoon, and musket, and had barricaded themselves in the brig's forepeak. Panton, aboard with a party of sailors and marines, either searching for contraband to seize or seamen to impress — the evidence was conflicting — tried at first to talk the men into coming out. That failing, he then had *Rose's* boarding party pull down the bulkhead. One thing led to another, and in the ensuing scuffle Corbet's harpoon severed Panton's jugular vein.[4]

It was clear that the four sailors ought to be tried for something: but for what; and by whom? The common law courts had no jurisdiction, because the crime (if crime it was) had been committed beyond the bounds of any county. English statutes provided for Admiralty jurisdiction of offenses perpetrated on the high seas. It was quite uncertain, however, whether a jury trial was guaranteed in such cases; some of the statutes said yes, others appeared to say no. Naturally, the defendants, represented by John Adams and James Otis, sought a jury, while the Crown advocates (as lawyers are called when they plead before an Admiralty court) opposed it. Otis, incidentally, was not everything an advocate should be. "His unhappy distemper," Adams recalled later, "was then in one of its unlucid intervals, and I could hardly persuade him to converse with me a few minutes on the subject; and he constantly and finally refused to appear publicly in the cause."[5]

The problem of an appropriate court was settled fairly soon. There existed for just such situations, a standing Commission for the Trial of Piracies, which established a court consisting of twelve members, including the Governors of Massachusetts and New Hampshire, and other high dignitaries.[6] But before hearing any evidence, the court had to determine the precise crime of which the sailors stood accused and the substantive law which would control their fate. As to the crime, a statute dating from Queen Anne's time apparently forbade impressing American seamen. If that were so, Panton's press gang was illegal, the lieutenant had no authority to seize the men (or even to attempt it), and the killing was arguably justifiable self-defense. The loyalists, according to "A Journal of the Times," were suggesting that Panton had been searching, not for seamen, but for smuggled goods. This contention would escape the thrust of the statute, but by emphasizing the revenue aspects of the case, would arouse even higher the passions already ignited by the lengthy *Liberty* battle.[7]

The question of substantive law was also crucial. If the common law applied, then the accused men would have to justify the homicide (that is, establish that the killing was committed in self-defense) or else stand convicted of manslaughter. But the statutes were quite opaque on the question of pleading benefit of clergy (the common-law lifesaver in manslaughter cases) in trials before the special Admiralty court. If, however, the trial, like ordinary Admiralty proceedings, was to be conducted according to the civil law, then the verdict must either be murder or acquittal; the concept of manslaughter was unknown to the civil law.

After assorted learned arguments, the case finally came on for trial in the new court house on June 14, 1769, before a large audience. According to John Adams: "No trial had drawn together such crowds of auditors from day to day; they were as numerous as those in the next year, at the [Boston Massacre] trials of Preston and the soldiers." The court quickly decided to proceed without a jury, although the substantive law issue remained open. After three days of testimony, Adams began his closing argument, urging the court that the killing was only justifiable homicide. At this point, the court, on Chief Justice Hutchinson's motion, retired, deliberated for four hours, and returned to pronounce its decree: justifiable homicide, and the prisoners to be set at large. As Thomas Hutchinson wrote later:

> It appeared that neither the lieutenant nor any of his superior officers were authorized to impress, by any warrant or special authority from the lords of the admiralty; and the court (the commanding officer of the king's ships being one of the commissioners) was unanimously of opinion that the prisoners had a good right to defend themselves, and, though the fact of killing was fully proved, that they ought to be acquitted of murder, with which they were charged, and that, at common law, the killing would not have amounted to manslaughter.[8]

Adams, on the other hand, attributed the decision to his "discovery" of the non-impressment statute, the knowledge of which he conveyed silently to Hutchinson by placing the appropriate volume of the Statutes at Large on the table before him, the vital pages turned down in dog-ears. Fearful lest the law become known, Hutchinson immediately recessed the court and prompted the acquittal. That, at least, was Adams' theory. There are, it would appear, several things wrong with this conceit. First, it does not sufficiently credit the strength of the testimony that Adams adduced at trial and the law he applied to it so effectively. Second, it implies, without much evidence, that the court would rather have maintained the legality of impressments (a practice which admittedly was considered a principal grievance at the time of the *Liberty* riot in June 1768) than to have done justice. Finally, Adams apparently forgot that ten months before Panton died, the entire applicable section of the old Act had appeared in the "Instructions of the Town of Boston to their representatives," written by Adams himself.[9]

As the summer of 1769 wore on, resentment at the presence of British troops intensified. The Riley Riot of July 14 and the reaction to it illustrate the point neatly. Riley, a private in the Fourteenth Regiment, had fought and beaten a Cambridge victualler named Jonathan Winship on July 13 and had been brought before Justice of the Peace Edmund Quincy, where he pleaded guilty and was fined five shillings and costs. Sentence was suspended for a day, but when the soldier returned on July 14, accompanied by a group of his barrack mates, he was either unable or unwilling to pay his fine. Justice Edmund Quincy thereupon wrote out a *mittimus*, directing Boston constable Peter Barbour to take Riley to jail — where presumably he would languish until his fine was paid. Riley's captain, meanwhile, had asked Lieutenant Alexander Ross, an acquaintance of Quincy's, to "compound" the affair if he could — in other words, to fix the ticket. Ross, arriving as Quincy was drawing up the *mittimus*, vainly tried to persuade the justice to lighten the sentence. At this Riley and his friends began to demur physically. Ross, who was subsequently to have a distinguished career, including service as aide-de-camp to Lord Cornwallis (whom he represented in the Yorktown surrender negotiations), was unable to control the men. With a round of curses and blows from drawn broad swords the soldiers hustled Riley out to freedom.[10]

The popular reaction to this show of force appears to have been strong. Barbour and his aid, Jeremiah Belknap, were called the next day before the House of Representatives, which appointed "a Committee to make further Enquiry into the Circumstances . . . and report to the House a State of the Facts," which was to be transmitted to Provincial Agent Denys De Berdt in London. In a procedure which was to be followed the next year, after the Massacre, depositions were taken on July 24 and printed later. The matter was even brought to the attention of John Wilkes in England.[11]

For reasons not yet known, Ross and five of the soldiers were not indicted until the November adjournment of the August 1769 Suffolk term of the Superior Court. The indictment, dated November 21, was drafted by Attorney-General Jonathan Sewall and signed by him, as well as by Thomas Brattle, foreman of the Grand Jury, and a future loyalist. It charged the defendants with assaulting Barbour, with rescuing Riley, with assaulting some civilians who attempted to aid Barbour, and with a breach of the peace. At the trial, which took place in mid-December 1769, the jury found Ross and four of the soldiers guilty. The men were fined £7 each; Ross' attorney moved for a new trial, which motion was heard at the eventful March 1770 session of the court. With Preston and Richardson to worry about, the court denied the motion and fined Ross £20.[12]

The Tory newspaper publisher, John Mein, had provoked radical ire as early as 1768, when he and John Gill, one of the printers of the *Boston Gazette*, had scuffled over an anti-Mein piece which the *Gazette* had printed. Mein's standing with the radical party fell even lower beginning August 21, 1769, when his *Boston Chronicle* began printing cargo manifests indicating that many non-importers, including John Hancock, were in fact importing British goods. The radicals were loud in their denials and, if human nature was then what it is now, probably looking for revenge. We know, and perhaps the radicals may have guessed, that Mein, whose business included the sale of books and stationery, as well as newspapers, was by this time heavily indebted to two London firms, Thomas Longman, the bookseller, and Wright & Gill (apparently no relation to John Gill), stationers. Mein subsequently attributed his legal difficulties to John Hancock's having written "letters to . . . Longman . . . importing that . . . Hancock would willingly accept of a power of attorney from . . . Longman . . . in order to seize or attach [Mein's] effects." Unfortunately, Longman's records, which descended to the successor firm of Longmans, Green & Co., Limited, were destroyed by a German bomb in World War II.[13]

The surviving documents, however, indicate that it was in fact a letter from Longman to Hancock of July 22, 1769 which initiated the appointment of Hancock, and that Hancock only responded to suggestions from London. Transatlantic slowness delayed Hancock's acceptance and his receipt of the actual appointment. Mein, meanwhile, having stood surety for William Brown, who had been accused of aiding John Robinson in the assault on Otis, had become, as a contemporary wrote, "so obnoxious to the People on account of his publishing the Manifests that he's obliged to go Arm'd. And tis but a few Nights since that two Persons who resembled him pretty much were attack'd in a narrow Alley with

Clubs." The climax occurred on October 28, in broad daylight on King Street. As Mein was walking up toward the Town House from his bookshop, a crowd first followed, then surrounded him. Drawing his pistol, he faced the mob and carefully backed his way toward the guard house on the present site of Number One State Street. Just as Mein turned to go up the steps, Thomas Marshall, the tailor who held a Lieutenant Colonel's rank in the militia, scraped Mein's back with a shovel, and Mein's pistol went off in the melee. Sam Adams and William Molineux, having promptly taken out a warrant for Mein's arrest (for firing the pistol), personally searched the guard house for him. In this, they were unsuccessful: Mein eventually escaped to a vessel in the harbor.[14]

From his temporary refuge, he asked acting Governor Hutchinson for military protection so that he might seek civil redress against those who had mobbed him. Hutchinson refused. "In Ireland perhaps," he said in explanation, "where the people have been long used to the military upon an apprehension only of violence from the populace such a measure might have been advisable. In the present state of the colonies I could not think so; and rather thought it advisable for him to forebear prosecuting his complaint for some time." Hutchinson, it might be noted, was not always reluctant to encourage loyalists with grievances to resort to civil remedies. For example, he advised merchants victimized by the non-importation combination, "the Body," to sue their oppressors. The response was strongly negative. The merchants told Hutchinson they would have "no chance with a Jury." Even if they did, once an action commenced "neither their Persons nor Property were safe while it was depending." Finally, even if they should "escape the injuries they faced and recover damages, their business would" fail "and nobody would dare to have any trade or dealing with them." Control of the jurors was firmly in partisan hands. William Molineux is supposed to have boasted that the radicals "would always be sure of Eleven jury men in Twelve."[15]

Mein, without effective civil remedies of any sort, thereupon returned to Britain. Soon after, Hancock, armed with powers of attorney and bookkeepers' affidavits, had John Adams fill out writs and, on March 1, 1770, seize Mein's books, type and presses. Despite delays, obstructions, and Hancock's apparent disinclination to compromise, Mein's friends, notably the cantankerous Tory Scot, James Murray, managed to lift the attachment on the printing equipment and "set the press a going again" under the direction of John Fleeming, Mein's partner.[16]

The lengthy technical convolutions of the suits against Mein need not delay us here. They went to trial in the Inferior Court in January 1771 and in the Superior Court, on appeal — which under the Massachusetts system was a trial *de novo* — in November 1771. At the Inferior Court, it appears, the court directed the jury to bring in a defendant's verdict in one or perhaps both of the actions, but each time the jury found for the plaintiff. The purely legal significance of the result is of interest really only to legal historians. But the juries' rejecting the court's direction in order to find against John Mein is essential to the theme of this essay. Whatever the initial impulse of the litigation, Hancock and Adams (whom Hancock refers to several times in the documents as "my lawyer") seem to have seized on the opportunity to stop Mein's press by attaching his printing equipment. It is conceivable, and perhaps arguable, that the juries sought to make the stoppage even more permanent, by finding against Mein, no matter what the evidence or the judges' view of the law.

The famous Otis-Robinson scrimmage of September 5, 1769 has received a full and careful treatment elsewhere. For the purposes of this essay, it will suffice to note that the incident provoked an instant adverse reaction in Boston; John Rowe reported "the Inhabitants greatly alarmed at the Usage Mr. Otis met with — tis generally thought he was very Rascally treated." William Brown of Salem, a secondary participant, was indeed almost mobbed when he was examined by the justices of the peace in Fanueil Hall before a crowd of two thousand spectators.[17]

Otis retained John Adams and Sampson Salter Blowers, as well as Samuel Fitch, who strangely enough represented Robinson in the criminal proceedings. Otis' lawyers commenced an action in his name at the January 1770 Suffolk Inferior Court, alleging damages in the amount of £3,000. After numerous continuances, the matter finally went to trial on July 25, 1771. Even the Adams Papers contain no minutes of the evidence. But from one deposition in the Suffolk Court Files, we can get a vivid picture of an embattled Otis "without a hat or Wigg with the blood flowing from his head . . . held by two or three persons" while Robinson hits him "in the face with his fist." And from the attending doctors' depositions, we can learn of the wound "above the forehead, over the right eye . . . a very little curved" "about an inch and half in length . . . near or quite down to the bone . . . made with a sharp instrument."[18]

Yet even this evidence, substantiating both the liability and the damages features of the case, does not accurately foreshadow the outcome of the case. Even the knowledge that Otis' behavior deteriorated in the months after the assault, does not explain the verdict. For the jury which tried the case and which, according to the eighteenth-century rules of evidence, was not permitted to hear testimony directly from the principals, returned a decision for Otis in the astounding amount of £2000, higher than any contemporary tort award and, in terms of twentieth-century purchasing power, an exceptionally substantial recovery. Even allowing for Robinson's unpopularity as a customs commissioner, and the strong feelings against him for having sailed to London eleven days after the Massacre with the loyalist version of the events in King Street, it is difficult to account for the verdict. Otis' medical bills totalled only 7 pounds 12 shillings; and his aberrant behavior clearly predated the assault. "From the best account I can get of the trial," Hutchinson wrote, "had Mr. Otis assaulted Mr. Robinson, in the same manner after receiving the like insult and abuse, the jury would not have given him [i. e. Robinson] a shilling."[19]

Strangely enough, both parties appealed the verdict; the plaintiff apparently because he sought even higher damages. In the August 1772 term of the Superior Court, however, Robinson through James Boutineau, his father-in-law and attorney, confessed his liability in writing, and literally begged Otis' pardon. Otis thereupon publicly remitted all but £112, 10 shillings, and 8 pence, covering costs, medical bills, and attorneys' fees. The legal aspects of the affair thus died forever.

As the non-importation agreement following the Townshend Acts tightened its grip on the Boston merchants, more and more storekeepers succumbed to the pressure. One of the few holdouts, Theophilus Lillie, "a very inoffensive man, except in the offense of importation," carried his resistance into print in January 1770:

> I cannot help saying, although I have never entered far into the mysteries of government, having applied myself to my shop and my business — that it always seemed strange to me that people who contend so much for civil and religious liberty should be so ready to deprive others of their natural liberty; that men who are guarding against being subject to laws [to] which they never gave their consent in person or by their representative should at the same time make laws, and in the most effectual manner execute them upon me and others . . . I own I had rather be a slave under one master (for I know who he is. I may perhaps be able to please him) than a slave to a hundred or more whom I don't know where to find, nor what they will expect of me.[20]

Lillie's shop was near the Boston house of a Woburn man named Ebenezer Richardson, who had customs affiliations and consequently an unpopular reputation. On February 22, 1770, a market day and school holiday, a crowd of boys set up a derogatory sign before Lillie's shop. Richardson, trying to remove the sign, only provoked the boys. They chased him into his home and began tossing rocks at the windows. Men joined the boys; insults and threats passed back and forth. Finally, Richardson aimed a gun through one of the demolished windows and "snapped" it at the crowd. This had no effect, so he fired a charge of bird shot, some pellets of which struck an eleven-year-old German boy, Christopher Seider.[21]

Now the crowd broke into the house in earnest, tore out Richardson and a companion, almost lynched them at a convenient signpost, and settled for dragging them through the streets to Fanueil Hall where, before a thousand people, four justices of the peace committed them to prison. "After the Examination, when the Sheriff was carrying them to Gaol, several attempts were made to get a rope around Richardson's neck." It should be noted that all this took place while the Seider boy still lived, for he did not die until that evening.[22]

The patriot press seized on the "barbarous Murder," to eulogize "the unfortunate boy," "inhumanly murdered," and to castigate the "infamous" killer and "his Abettors," meaning, of course, the customs commissioners. Seider's burial rites were a massive propaganda display. John Rowe, attending with John Adams, was "very sure two thousand people" were there. And Adams himself "never beheld such a funeral." Placards reminded the crowd of such Biblical sentiments as "Thou shall take no Satisfaction for the Life of a Murderer," and "Though Hand join in Hand, the Wicked shall not pass unpunished."[23]

Richardson's indictment awaited only the opening of the next term of the Superior Court, scheduled for March 13. His chances at trial would have been difficult under the most tranquil of circumstances. Between the Richardson Riot and the convening of the court, however, the troops fired on the mob in King Street. Now instead of two defendants whose lives were imperiled by popular thirst for immediate vengeance there were fifteen, nine of whom were British soldiers. Although the judges "chose to postpone the Trials until there might be some Chance of Justice being uninterrupted," "the people being very uneasy that the criminal tryals were not brought on, the Court found it necessary in order to keep them a little quiet to arraign Richardson." "Had a trial been refused," Judge Oliver said later, "it was rather more than an equal chance that the Prisoners [Preston and the soldiers, too] would have been murdered by the Rabble; and the Judges been exposed to Assassinations."[24]

According to the anonymous reporter whose narrative is in the Bernard Papers:

> Richardson was arraign'd on a Monday and directed to prepare for his tryal on the Friday following. Accordingly on the Friday he was brought to the Bar and ask'd by the Court if he was then ready. He observ'd to the Court that he had made application to almost every Lawyer in town to undertake his cause, which no one would do, that the Constables had refused summoning his Witnesses, that the Jailer, had used him in so cruel a manner that he was even frequently debarred the Liberty of conversing with his friends, that every Newspaper was crouded with the most infamous and false libels against him in order to prejudice the minds of his jury; that without Counsel, without the privilege of calling upon his Witnesses to support his innocence he was now to be tried for his life. The Judges moved with compassion at this representation put off

> the trial to a further day. The Court then made application to the several Lawyers present to appear as his Counsel but this one and all of them declined. The court finding that a requisition had no effect asserted their Authority and order'd Mr. Fitch the advocate General to appear on his behalf on his trial. Fitch made use of a variety of arguments in order to excuse himself which the Court did not judge sufficient. He concluded with saying that since the Court had peremptorily ordered him, he would undertake it, but not otherways.

Fitch, however, reported sick twice when the case was called for trial, the last time being April 17. The Court promptly appointed Josiah Quincy to represent Richardson and Wilmot, and three days later, Friday, April 20, the trial began, before "a vast concourse of Rabble."[25]

Contemporary and eye witness accounts tell the rest of the story.

> Richardson's Trial continued till late on Friday night. After the witnesses were examined and the lawyers had done pleading the Judges gave their charge to the Jury. They said it appeared by the Evidence that the prisoner was attacked in his own house by a number of tumultuous people. That what he had done was in his own defence. That self-defence was a right inherent in every man. That the persons who had encouraged putting up these *hands* were guilty of the murder and not the prisoner and they were convinced the jury could find him guilty of nothing more than manslaughter.[26]

> The Court upon summing up the Evidence to the Jury were all of opinion that if what the witnesses on both sides had sworn was believed the fact could amount to no more than Manslaughter. Mr. Just. Oliver doubted whether it could amount to that and with great spirit charged the death of the Boy upon the Promoters of the Effigies and the Exhibitions which had drawn the people together and caused unlawful and tumultuous assemblies and he did not excuse such as had neglected suppressing these Assemblies as the Civil Magistrate had done.[27]

> [W]hilst one of the Judges was delivering his Charge to the Jury, and declaring his Opinion, that the Case was *justifiable Homicide*, one of the Rabble broke out, 'D--n that Judge, if I was nigh him, I would give it to him'; but this was not a Time, to attempt to preserve Decorum; Perservation of Life was as much as a Judge dared to aim at. After the Judges had done speaking the mob became very outrageous, called out that they hoped no Jury dare acquit him. 'Remember jury you are upon Oath.' 'Blood requires blood.' [The mob] designed to have hanged the Prisoner as he came out of the Court House, to be returned to Prison until the Jurors Verdict was settled; and they provided an Halter, ready at the Door of the Court Room, for

> the Purpose; but the Court had ordered the Sheriff, with the Peace Officers, to lock him into the Court Room until the Mob had dispersed. The judges found it necessary to remain in Court for upwards of an hour, and also to detain the prisoner until the mob were in some measure dispersed least they should destroy him in his way from the Court house to the Jail. It is said they had a rope in Court ready to hang him. The judges were hissed and abused in a most shameful manner in passing from the bench to their carriages.[28]

The jury deliberated from eleven that night until nine the next morning, bringing in a verdict which acquitted Wilmot and convicted Richardson of murder. "An universal clap ensued," and "the Court Room resounded with Expressions of Pleasure." Faced with a verdict which appeared to them "directly against law," and unable "in the state of the town to order the jury out a second time, or to refuse or delay sentence after the verdict was received," the judges merely received the verdict, and then adjourned court without passing sentence. The heart of the dilemma, it should be realized, was the inability of the eighteenth-century law to cope with a jury's rendering a patently wrong verdict. This interesting legal problem need not concern us, for it is a mere detail in the overall picture; if the trial had been fair from the start, the legal issue would never have arisen.

In an effort to solve the deadlock, the court called in all the jurors and examined each of them. This unusual procedure only intensified the court's difficulty, for it revealed that the eleven jurors who favored conviction had won over the single holdout by convincing him that "if the verdict was not agreeable to law the Court would not receive it." The court ultimately did nothing more. It left Richardson in jail, while the official wheels slowly ground out a royal pardon. On March 10, 1772, the inhabitants of Boston being at town meeting, Richardson was brought into court, asked if he knew any reason why sentence of death should not be passed upon him, and, upon his producing the pardon, released. "The Rabble heard of it, and pursued him to execute their own Law upon him, but he happily escaped." Even as late as 1774, however, the mere rumor of Richardson's presence in Boston was enough to raise a mob.[29]

The peculiar incident which convenience and ignorance have

dubbed the Boston Massacre in some ways marked the nadir of law, authority, and justice in the period under consideration. It is to Boston's credit that none of the soldiers or their officers died for the event, but that credit was not easily earned. Indeed, it is abundantly clear from the contemporary sources that the radicals did everything possible to bring on the trials immediately, even to the extent of physically intimidating the judges.

The town brought its own weight into court as well, retaining special counsel, Robert Treat Paine, to stimulate and assist the prosecution. It should also be remembered that four civilians were indicted, on testimony later proved to be perjured, for firing out of the custom house window. Even though at their trial the evidence against them was so thin that the jury returned an acquittal without going from the box, the fact remains that the lives of these civilians were in jeopardy for a time, and their prosecution was allowed to continue even after the military men had all been freed.[30]

The Massacre trials abound with paradoxes. The lineup of counsel, for example, found the two radicals, Josiah Quincy and John Adams, defending the military men, while loyalist Samuel Quincy (Josiah's older brother) led the prosecution. John Adams and Josiah justified their participation by reference to a lawyer's obligation to ensure that any accused person should receive competent counsel. Others, however, have suggested that Josiah Quincy, and, more particularly, Adams, were there not simply to present the defense but to make certain that Boston itself was not put on trial, and that the activities leading up to the shooting did not obtain too thorough an airing. If this was one of the goals of Adams and Josiah Quincy, it was not wholly unjustified. The available documents suggest strongly that the loyalists, and particularly the military, hoped to use the trials as showcases demonstrating the hostility the troops had encountered at the hands of the townspeople since their arrival in 1768. The radicals, of course, were eager to show that the soldiery had been persistently and deliberately provocative. Thus each side hoped to use the trials for propaganda purposes.[31]

There was also a serious problem of conflicting defenses.

To a certain extent, it was to the joint interest of Preston and his men to justify the shootings, and to establish that the mob was threatening the lives of all. But beyond that point, it was to Preston's advantage to argue that the men fired without orders; and it was to the men's advantage to argue that they had only followed their captain's orders. As the case developed, however, this problem did not arise; the motive of self-defense soon became clearly paramount. Prior to Preston's trial, however, the idea of presenting just such a defense was very much in the minds of some of the soldiers. Several of them even petitioned the court to be tried with Preston, insisting that they had fired on his orders.[33]

The unreality of the trials is heightened by the knowledge that Lieutenant Governor Hutchinson had been instructed, no matter what the outcome, to respite the prisoners; that is, to delay sentencing until a pardon could come over from England. True, there was an interim risk of lynching, but that was a problem that had been present from the beginning, and the possibility seemed to become more remote as the loyalist efforts to delay the trials were successful.

When the first trial, that of Preston, finally commenced the jury as selected included the following talesmen: William Hill, the baker who supplied the Fourteenth Regiment; Philip Dumaresque, who "had repeatedly declared in presence of divers witnesses that he believed Captain Preston to be as innocent as the Child unborn, and that if he happened to be upon the Jury he would never convict him if he sat to all eternity;" Joseph Barrick and William Wait Wallis, who were later loyalist exiles; and Gilbert Deblois, who had gotten Preston "several valuable evidences [witnesses], and gave him the character of many of the persons return'd for Jurors, by which means he was enabled to set aside most of those return'd by the Town, who were men of violent principles, and pick out some of the moderate ones sent up from the Country." Upon exhausting the venire, Deblois, according to Preston's own later testimony, "got himself put on the Panel, where during the tryal which lasted a week, he was confin'd in the Jail along with the other Jurors, to the great neglect of his business . . . By his strict attention and close examination he detected some of the evidences of perjury; And . . . by his personal influence on the rest of the Jurors he was a great means of said Preston's being aquitted."[33]

All this makes the significance of the trials hard to assess. We can all agree with John Adams that "As the Evidence was, the Verdict of the Jury [that is, juries] was exactly right."[34] But that does not really illuminate the contradictions of the cases. Nor does it explain why, if the result was so just and obvious, it was necessary to go to such extraordinary non-legal lengths to ensure it. One can only conclude that in cases involving political subjects, the Massachusetts judicial system of 1769-1771 was under such powerful pressure from both sides, that a fair trial was, without extralegal assistance, unlikely, if not impossible. As Sir William Holdsworth has written, "The existence of a state of public opinion which prevents a fair trial is a danger to which the jury system is always open; and it is a danger against which there is no remedy except the existence of an impartial, a humane, a courageous and a learned bench." Even this safeguard is useless without a civil authority strong enough to keep the peace. Thus it was in Boston, where neither sheriff nor justices of the peace could or would attempt to suppress the physical violence which so often erupted.[35] No trial in the shadow of a mob can possibly be fair.

The apparent exceptions serve only to emphasize the rule. The *Corbet* decision, for example, was certainly just and legally right; yet the winning counsel himself could not credit the acquittal to the law and the evidence. It was the corruptness of Hutchinson, John Adams always insisted, which accounted for the verdict. As for the Massacre trials, it is hard to conceive of a more satisfactorily packed jury than the one which decided Preston's fate; and it should be remembered that four civilians were indicted and allowed to be tried on evidence so thin, so manufactured, that the Crown's star witness was forthwith convicted of perjury. It will not excuse the spirit of the times to say that the civilians were freed; the point is that they should never have been tried at all.

In assessing the state of justice in Massachusetts during this period, it is important to realize that the time of bench and bar was not spent solely, or even in major portion, on such historically notable cases as those considered here. Throughout these years, the lawyers and the courts found themselves confronted with quantities of ordinary litigation between man and man, litigation which the surviving records, files, and papers suggest continued to be disposed of in a normal, almost routine manner. But it is not in its treatment of the ordinary affairs of *meum* and *teum* that a judicial system receives its ultimate test. Even the most arbitrary government arranges to have private disputes decided routinely. The true litmus of liberty is the availability of unfettered justice to every litigant or accused criminal, including men who may be unpopular or even demonstrably dangerous to the social structure. It is a test which no society ever passes; there are only degrees of failure. The evidence suggests that in pre-Revolutionary Massachusetts the failure was complete.

LAW AND AUTHORITY

FOOTNOTES

1. *Boston Gazette*, May 10, 1773; *Boston Gazette*, March 10, 1772.
2. Thomas Hutchinson to John Sullivan, March 29, 1771, Massachusetts Archives, State House, Boston, XXVII, 136; hereinafter cited as Mass. Arch.
3. Vice Admiralty Minute Book, Files, Office of the Clerk, Supreme Judicial Court for Suffolk County, Boston; hereinafter referred to as Suffolk Files.
4. See Rex v. Corbet, No. 56, in L. Kinvin Wroth and Hiller B. Zobel, eds., *Legal Papers of John Adams* (Cambridge, Mass. in press); hereinafter cited as *Legal Papers of John Adams*.
5. John Adams, *Works*, 10 vols. (Boston, 1850-1856), II, 224; hereinafter cited as Adams, *Works*.
6. See editorial note, "Admiralty - Criminal Jurisdiction" in *Legal Papers of John Adams*.
7. 6 Anne c. 37 (1707). "A Journal of the Times," May 5, 1769, cited in Oliver M. Dickerson, *Boston Under Military Rule* (Boston, 1936), 95; hereinafter cited as Dickerson, *Boston Under Military Rule*.
8. Adams, *Works*, X, 209-210. Thomas Hutchinson, *The History of the Colony and Province of Massachusetts-Bay*, ed. Lawrence Shaw Mayo, 3 vols. (Cambridge, Mass., 1936), III, 167; hereinafter cited as Hutchinson, *History*.
9. Adams, *Works*, II, 225, and III, 503-504.
10. See Rex v. Ross, No. 60, in *Legal Papers of John Adams*. "Alexander Ross," *Dictionary of National Biography*. Suffolk Files 89147.
11. Massachusetts *House Journal* 1769, 83 (session of July 15, 1769). Depositions were taken July 24, 1769; *Boston-Evening Post*, October, 2, 1769. "A Journal of the Times," July 25-30, 1769, Dickerson, *Boston Under Military Rule*, 119-123. Worthington C. Ford, "John Wilkes and Boston," Massachusetts Historical Society, *Proceedings*, XLVII (1913-1914), 205-206.
12. Suffolk Files 101575. Superior Court of Judicature, *Records* 1769, fol. 253, 1770, fol. 22, Suffolk Files.
13. See Gill. v. Mein, No. 5, and Longman v. Mein, and Wright & Gill v. Mein, No. 12, in *Legal Papers of John Adams*. Mein's affidavit, February 22, 1770, Massachusetts Historical Society, Hancock Papers. John E. Alden, "John Mein: Scourge of Patriots," Colonial Society of Massachusetts, *Publications*, XXXIV (1942), 571. Letter to Editors, *Legal Papers of John Adams*, April 30, 1963.
14. Herbert H. Edes, "A Memoir of Dr. Thomas Young," Colonial Society of Massachusetts, *Publications*, XI (1906), 36. George Mason to Joseph Harrison, October 20, 1769, Bernard (New England) Papers, Houghton Library, Harvard University, III, 53; hereinafter cited as Bernard Papers. Alden, work cited note 13.
15. Thomas Hutchinson to Lord Hillsborough, November 11, 1769, Bernard Papers, III, 53. Thomas Hutchinson to Thomas Pownall, May 28, 1770, Mass. Arch., XXVI, 484. Thomas Hutchinson to ————,

no date, Mass. Arch., XXVII, 280, 281.

16. The full account of the proceedings appears in *Legal Papers of John Adams*. James Murray to Elizabeth Smith, March 12, 1770; Nina Moore Tiffany and Susan I. Lesley, eds., *Letters of James Murray, Loyalist* (Boston, 1901), 169-170. Suffolk Files 89248 and 101964.
17. *Letters and Diary of John Rowe . . .*, ed. Anne Rowe Cunningham (Boston, 1903), 192; hereinafter cited as Rowe, *Letters and Diary*.
18. John L. Sibley and Clifford K. Shipton, *Biographical Sketches of Graduates of Harvard . . .* (Cambridge and Boston, 1873-), XI, 277-280. Suffolk Files 89228 and 102135.
19. John Adams, *Diary and Autobiography*, ed. Lyman H. Butterfield, 4 vols. (Cambridge, Mass., 1961), I, 348-349; hereinafter cited as Adams, *Diary and Autobiography;* Superior Court of Judicature, *Records* 1772, fol. 109, Suffolk Files. Hutchinson to ———————, no date, Mass. Arch., XXV, 437, 438.
20. *Massachusetts Gazette*, January 11, 1770.
21. See Rex v. Richardson, No. 59, in *Legal Papers of John Adams*.
22. Thomas Hutchinson to Thomas Gage, February 25, 1770, Mass. Arch., XXVI, 448. Bernard Papers, III, 70. *Boston Evening-Post*, February 26, 1770.
23. Rowe, *Letters and Diary*, 197. *Boston Gazette*, March 5, 1770.
24. Peter Oliver, *Origin and Progress of the American Rebellion*, ed. Douglass Adair and John Schutz (San Marino, California, 1961); hereinafter cited as Oliver, *Origin and Progress of the American Rebellion*. Bernard Papers, III, 76.
25. Bernard Papers, III, 76. Oliver, *Origin and Progress of the American Rebellion*, note 24, above.
26. Bernard Papers, III, 76.
27. Thomas Hutchinson to Lord —————————, April 21, 1770, Mass. Arch., XXVI, 463.
28. Oliver, *Origin and Progress of the American Rebellion*, note 24 above. Bernard Papers, III, 76.
29. Bernard Papers, III, 76. Hutchinson, *History*, III, 206. Rex v. Richardson in Massachusetts Historical Society: Robert Treat Paine Papers. Oliver, *Origin and Progress of the American Rebellion*, 87. Frank W. C. Hersey, "Tar and Feathers: The Adventures of Captain John Malcom," Colonial Society of Massachusetts, *Publications*, XXXIV (1941), 449.
30. See Rex v. Preston, No. 63, and Rex v. Wemms, No. 64, in *Legal Papers of John Adams*.
31. Thomas Gage to Dalrymple, June 17, 1770, in Randolph Adams, *New Light on the Boston Massacre* (Worcester, 1938), 54-55. Albert Matthews, "Captain Thomas Preston and the Boston Massacre," Colonial Society of Massachusetts, *Publications*, VII (1900), 4.
32. The petition is in the Boston Public Library. See Colonial Society of Massachusetts, *Publications*, V (1897), 66.
33. George M. Elsey, "John Wilkes and William Palfrey," Colonial Society of Massachusetts, *Publications*, XXIV (1941), 425. E. Alfred Jones,

The Loyalists of Massachusetts (London, 1930), 25, 116. Lorenzo Sabine, *Biographical Sketches of Loyalists of the American Revolution*, with an Historical Essay, 2 vols. (Boston, 1864), I, 592. Public Record Office, London, A. O. 13/44:159.

34. Adams, *Diary and Autobiography*, III, 79.
35. William S. Holdsworth, *History of English Law*, 13 vols. (London, 1922-1952), IX, 231-232. Thomas Hutchinson to Thomas Gage, February 25, 1770, Mass. Arch., XXVI, 445. Thomas Hutchinson to Thomas Bernard, October 20, 1770, Mass. Arch., XXVII, 26, 30.